SOUTH SIDE HITMEN

THE STORY OF THE 1977 CHICAGO WHITE SOX

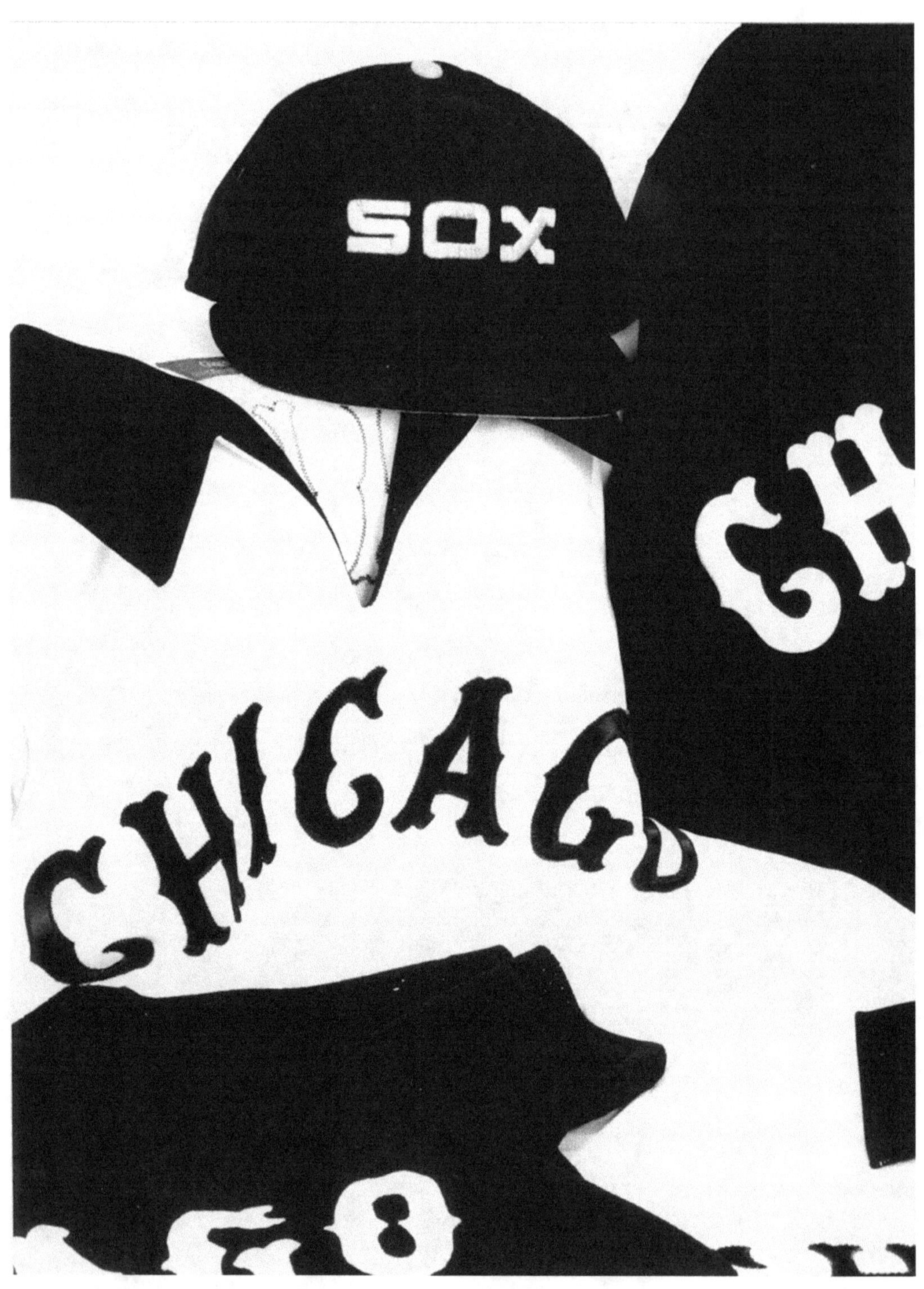

This collage of 1977 South Side Hitmen uniforms, ball, and hat comes from the Gerry Bilek memorabilia collection. (Photo by Mark Flectcher.)

SOUTH SIDE HITMEN

THE STORY OF THE 1977 CHICAGO WHITE SOX

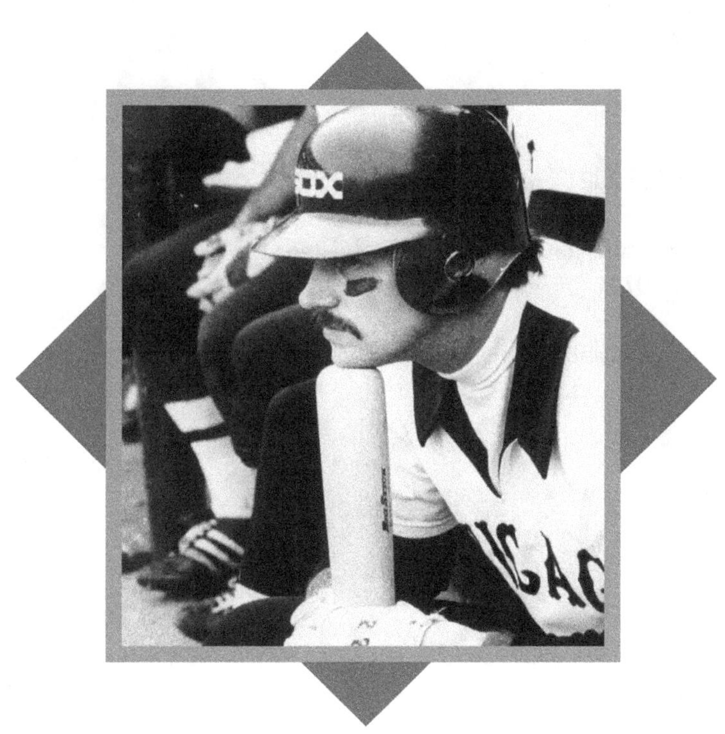

Dan Helpingstine,
with photographs from Leo Bauby

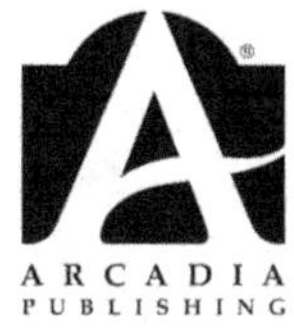

ISBN 978-1-5316-2384-5

Published by Arcadia Publishing
Charleston, South Carolina

Library of Congress Catalog Card Number: 2005931665

For all general information contact Arcadia Publishing at:
Telephone 843-853-2070
Fax 843-853-0044
E-mail sales@arcadiapublishing.com
For customer service and orders:
Toll-Free 1-888-313-2665

Visit us on the Internet at www.arcadiapublishing.com

This book is dedicated to Nancy Puhr-Morris.

Thanks for the friendship and professionalism.

One day I will pay you back fully.

CONTENTS

Acknowledgments 6

Introduction 7

1. 1967: End of the No-Hit Era 9

2. 1976: Barely Hanging On 23

3. April to May: Proving them Wrong 41

4. June: The Non-Swoon 59

5. July: A Fast, Furious Ride to the Top 73

6. August to September: Winding Down 91

7. 1977 Hitmen Remembered 103

8. The South Side Hitmen—Aftermath 115

How the South Side Hitmen Were Dismantled 128

ACKNOWLEDGMENTS

The first thing I would like to do is thank three individuals who helped me with this book and who also assisted on my first book published by Arcadia, *The Chicago White Sox: 1959 and Beyond*. These three gentlemen provided the book's photographs, and they also provided technical expertise, memories, and historical perspective.

The overwhelming majority of the photographs in this book come from the Leo Bauby collection. Bauby's collection spans most of the 20th century and neatly captures the storied history of the White Sox. The pictures can be viewed at http://www.chicago-baseball-photos.com, a collection that brings back powerful memories in images. His collection of White Sox photos is staggering.

Gerry Bilek's basement recreation room looks like a small White Sox museum. He has a turnstile from old Comiskey and other relics that would take a Sox fan down a true nostalgic trip to the past. His recollections and photograph contributions are an essential part of this book.

Mark Fletcher is a photographer as well as a collector. His expert photography has helped restore past feelings about the White Sox. He took photographs of some of Bilek's memorabilia to bring back the flavor of 1977.

I would also like to thank Vivian Jones of the Chicago White Sox Media Relations office for helping me secure the interviews with former White Sox.

I am also appreciative to White Sox fan and historian Mark Liptak. Liptak still follows the team religiously from his home in Idaho, where he claims to be one of the few Sox fans in that part of the country. (He is probably right.) I am more than grateful for all his ongoing help.

Keith Scherer was gracious enough to allow me to use an online ESPN article of his in which he gave a great analysis of what derailed the White Sox in August 1977. Scherer's well-written article appeared in 2003 and illustrated the staying power the South Side Hitmen.

The author used his own memories, newspaper accounts from the *Chicago Sun-Times*, and *Chicago Tribune*, and interviews with the people listed in the following introduction. One of the handiest resources was *The White Sox Encyclopedia* by Rich Lindberg with photographic history from Mark Fletcher.

I would like to thank Arcadia editor Jeff Ruetsche for his ongoing confidence in me. Ruetsche allowed me the creative freedom to put my spin on this little slice of Chicago White Sox history.

The year 1977 was very special for me personally, as I got married that September. My wife Delia has been very supportive of me in my writing throughout all these years and that is something I do not take for granted. She also helped with the editing of this book, cleaning up my sometimes awkward phrasing.

INTRODUCTION

Baseball was still young in 1977. Yes, the sport had its problems—as it always has—but the seven-day-a-week, 24-hour-a-day hype wasn't over-exposing the industry. If a fan wanted to know what was happening with his team and couldn't watch or listen to the game, he picked up the paper in the morning. There is something simple and gratifying about reading about it in the newspaper. Today's glut of cable TV and radio talk shows is simply too loud. I am happy to include some of the memories of sportswriters who covered the South Side Hitmen.

Long time columnist Bill Gleason, now retired, has often been considered the city's number one White Sox fan. When he lived in Chicago, the last four digits of his home phone were 1959. During the second half of the 20th century, he covered Bill Veeck, the Allyns, and Jerry Reinsdorf. Gleason helped form the panel on the radio show, the Sportswriters, which aired Sundays from 4:00 to 6:00 p.m. on WGN-AM, 720. Former boxing promoter Ben Bentley, *Chicago Tribune* sports editor George Langford, and *Chicago Tribune* sports reporter Bill Jauss discussed with him the state of Chicago and national sports. The Sportswriters did not take calls from listeners. However, Gleason and other panelists often read listener letters and actually treated listener opinions with respect. I learned a great deal about the White Sox from Gleason and I am pleased to have several of his observations in this book.

Bill Jauss covered two key series in the 1977 South Side Hitmen season. He was at rollicking Comiskey for both the July 4 holiday weekend four-game set against Minnesota and the four-game series against Kansas City that ended the month. A few of his keen observations are also quoted in the book. Jauss has always been a fan advocate, and it was great talking to him about the 1977 season.

One of the hardest things for any reporter to do is to write some tough things about people he knows and associates with on a daily basis. I am grateful to former *Chicago Sun-Times* reporter Joe Goddard for recalling a story he did on Sox manager Paul Richards in 1976. It was still somewhat painful for Goddard to remember his story about a man who otherwise had a great baseball career. Maybe Goddard should write a book about the White Sox someday. He knows a great deal about the team and has an excellent memory for detail.

Gary Peters is profiled in chapter 1. Peters was one of the toughest left-handers in the American League during the mid-1960s. I am grateful for the time he gave me recalling his White Sox career. This included memories of the 1967 White Sox, a team that came very close to a World Series, but has been almost forgotten in the fog of baseball history.

Eric Soderholm also gave his time. His comeback season in 1977 had a profound impact on him. His return, his career year, and his bonding with Sox fans have been a great story. Soderholm was somewhat surprised that a book about the 1977 Sox was being written. He shouldn't have been surprised; 1977 was a historic season for the team in many ways.

Steve Stone is now a large part of Chicago baseball history. He has won over many Cub fans for his candor in the broadcast booth. As a student of the game, I enjoyed my conversation with him. I never would mind Steve Stone disagreeing with me. I would gain from the experience of listening to someone who knows the game. His comments to me about 1977 were as honest as anything that has been said on the air.

Rich "Goose" Gossage was a large part of the 1977 White Sox since he was packaged in the trade that brought Richie Zisk to Chicago. But no fan with vivid memories of the 1970s will forget Gossage's windmill motion and a fast ball most hitters couldn't see. His recollections about Bill Veeck and the 1976 season help put a perspective on the state of the franchise during the mid-1970s.

I remember sitting at a bar enjoying a beer and watching Oscar Gamble golf one deep into the right field upper deck for a three-run homer. Gamble made Sox history in 1977 even though he had expected to play for the Yankees that year. I appreciated the time Gamble gave me as he recalled the "offensive balance" of the 1977 team and dreamed of what would have been if the team had been kept together until more pitching arrived.

Nancy Faust will be forever connected to the South Side Hitmen. Picking up on the frenzy and emotion of the most exciting days of the summer of 1977, musician Faust played a song that remains a rallying cry for the team. Faust understands that entertaining fans largely comes from spontaneity. Are you listening, Major League Baseball?

History doesn't occur in a vacuum. This book is not just a recollection of an emotional and memorable season. The author has attempted to put the team in its proper place in Chicago White Sox history. To say that 1977 was a breakthrough season is an understatement. It is also safe to say that the South Side Hitmen helped keep the team in Chicago. It is hard to imagine the future of the White Sox had they gone through another 90-loss season in 1977. Instead, the team had its best attendance since 1960, the year after it went to its last World Series of the 20th century. More importantly, it gave fans their greatest memories of the 1970s that have lasted into the 21st century.

1

1967
End of the No-Hit Era

The seeds of the exciting, 1977 slugging South Side Hit Men were actually sown exactly 10 years earlier by a White Sox team that couldn't hit a beach ball into Lake Michigan while standing on the sand. In one of the last years of one divisional play, the 1967 team was not eliminated from the pennant chase until the 160th game of the season. Although it competed gamely in a race with the Twins, Red Sox, and Tigers, where there was a strong possibility of a four-way tie for first, the 1967 White Sox are rarely talked about in the same breath as other great Sox teams. They put together a 10-game winning streak in early May and were in first place from June 10 until August 13. Yet, the contending White Sox had to fight off criticism that they were a boring team that relied too much on pitching while lulling their fans to sleep with a small-ball offense. Even Manager Eddie Stanky, a staunch defender of his club, thought they were boring, calling them the "dullest ball club I have ever seen."

Getting anywhere near the World Series was not expected when the 1967 season began. The consensus of experts predicted a fourth place finish. From 1951 through 1967, the Sox had sported winning records, one of the most successful such runs by any Major League Baseball franchise. There was the pennant year of 1959 and six 90-win seasons. They had three straight second place finishes in the then one ten-team division from 1963 to 1965, winning 94, 98, and 95 games, respectively. But in 1966, their record slipped to 83-79, and they needed a strong finish to again land on the sunny side of .500.

Starting with the second game of a doubleheader against Cleveland on April 30, the Pale Hose went on their 10-game winning streak. Except for a 13-1 blowout of Baltimore, the wins were low scoring affairs which included two 1-0 triumphs, one of which was in 10 innings. The streak ended when Chicago was shut out 1-0 by Minnesota's Dean Chance. The White Sox were perched in first place at the All-Star break, but they were not running away with anything. They led second place Detroit by two, and third place Minnesota by two and a half games. To shore up their low scoring attack, Chicago picked up two aging sluggers in late July: Ken Boyer from the Mets and Rocky Colavito from the Indians.

Boyer and Colavito made only occasional contributions and may have disrupted team chemistry. As the season progressed, cynics were ready to bury the White Sox any time they lost, especially when their weak offense failed to support their excellent pitching. Manager Eddie Stanky lashed out at the naysayers on September 9, when his club blew a 3-0 ninth inning lead and lost to co-contender Detroit 7-3 in a nationally televised game.

"They discount the guts of this club," Stanky said, defending his often maligned but winning team. "All year long this team had guts."

The Sox somewhat vindicated Stanky the next day with a doubleheader sweep by shutting out the heavy hitting Tigers in both games. In game one, righty and Cy Young Award candidate Joe Horlen delivered a brilliant performance when he pitched a no-hitter, beating Detroit 6-0 for one of his 19 wins that year.

By the end of September, the White Sox were in excellent shape and ready to prove their detractors wrong once and for all. With five games remaining in the season, the second place Sox were but one game behind first place Minnesota. The remaining Sox schedule looked easy as they faced the last place Kansas City Athletics twice in Kansas City, and the seventh place Washington Senators three times to close out the year at Comiskey Park.

A rain out in Kansas City forced a Wednesday night doubleheader. That September 27, 1967, became known as "Black Wednesday" as Chicago sent out their ace pitchers Gary Peters and Joe Horlen and still lost 5-2 and 4-0. They barely avoided a double shut out by scoring two in the ninth in game one. The South Siders went from being on the verge of the World Series to getting eliminated unless they swept the lowlife Senators.

Tommy John started the Friday night game at Comiskey and gave up an unearned run in the first. So desperate for any kind of offense, the Sox lifted John for a pinch hitter in the fifth even though they trailed only 1-0. There was no designated hitter back then, and the Sox could have used one.

Phil Ortega, on the mound for the Senators, hadn't won a game in nearly two months. After giving up two singles in the first, Ortega surrendered only two more hits for the remainder of a complete game performance. Facing the virtual end of their season in the ninth when they trailed 1-0, the Hitless Wonders couldn't put the ball into fair territory. Ken Boyer struck out, Ron Hansen fouled out to the catcher, and J. C. Martin struck out. Ortega pitched one of the best games of his 46-62 career, and the banjo hitting White Sox proved their critics right by getting shut out in a must-win game. Elimination came on that 160th game of the season even though a great pitching staff had thrown eight shut outs during the stretch month of September. And after losing the last two games of the season, the White Sox actually finished in fourth, three games behind pennant winning Boston.

In many ways, Gary Peters—a 1960s Chicago White Sox icon—symbolized the South Side ball club during that decade. From 1963 to 1967, he was one of the toughest left-handed pitchers in the American League. Though 1967 wasn't his winningest year, in many ways it was a career year for Peters and his last great season with the White Sox. He made his only All-Star appearance in Anaheim, pitching three perfect innings. In the process he fanned Willie Mays, Orlando Cepeda, Dick Allen, and Roberto Clemente. Peters finished the year with 215 strikeouts, and, with Tom Bradley and Ed Walsh, was one of three White Sox pitchers to record 200 or more strikeouts in two or more seasons. Yet Peters was not concerned with piling up strikeouts or pitch counts.

"I didn't consider myself a power pitcher," Peters told the author in 2005. "I threw my fast ball high and inside. I never left it out over the plate. I had a sinker and slider and in one complete game I only threw 70 pitches."

In the middle of that wild pennant race in 1967, Peters was involved in a somewhat typical and yet amazing type hitless-wonder win.

On September 13, the White Sox beat the Cleveland Indians 1-0 in a 17-inning night game. Peters started the game and walked 10 batters in 11 innings. He gave up a second inning triple to catcher Joe Azcue and nothing more. Peters ended up throwing nine and two-thirds innings of hitless ball only to get a no-decision. Reliever Don McMahon picked up the win by pitching a scoreless 17th inning. The Sox finally won with the help of a passed ball.

"We had guys who knew how to pitch," Peters recalled. "We didn't have many seven run leads. We couldn't just let them hit it. We could never afford that mentality."

As a result, Peters said, this philosophy (of not giving in to hitters) was reflected in the staff's low earned run average of 2.45 in 1967. But the shortage of offense finally caught up with the White Sox during the September 27 doubleheader against Kansas City. Peters, however, doesn't hold any grudges against his offense. He takes the responsibility for one of the most significant losses for the White Sox during the 1960s.

"Kansas City was in a good position where they could play the spoiler," Peters remembered, "but I didn't pitch that well. I gave up too many runs. That's just the way I look at it."

Peters also thinks the 1967 White Sox should be remembered as a good team, and that their boring persona was overblown.

"I came up in the fall of 1959," Peters said. (Peters made two appearances and pitched one inning.) "Everybody thought that team was exciting. It [the 1967 team] was the same kind of club but in '59 we had more guys who could steal. I never heard that we weren't exciting. We weren't playing to be exciting. We were playing to win."

The collapse during the final week of the 1967 season actually helped set the stage for the fan euphoria of 1977. After seeing their team average a little over three runs a game in 1967 and sleep walking through decades of low scoring games, White Sox fans were ready to leave the legacy of the Go-Go White Sox behind them. The 1-0 wins and the 3-2 losses had grown old and stale. How about a team that could just hit the cover off the ball? Bill Melton won the American League home run championship on the last day of 1971, and Dick Allen had his MVP year in 1972. The Sox even led the American League in homers in 1974. But the first truly exciting offensive club to come along to thrill fans didn't appear on the scene until a decade after a great World Series opportunity was lost due to an anemic offense that had a hard time getting the ball out of the infield.

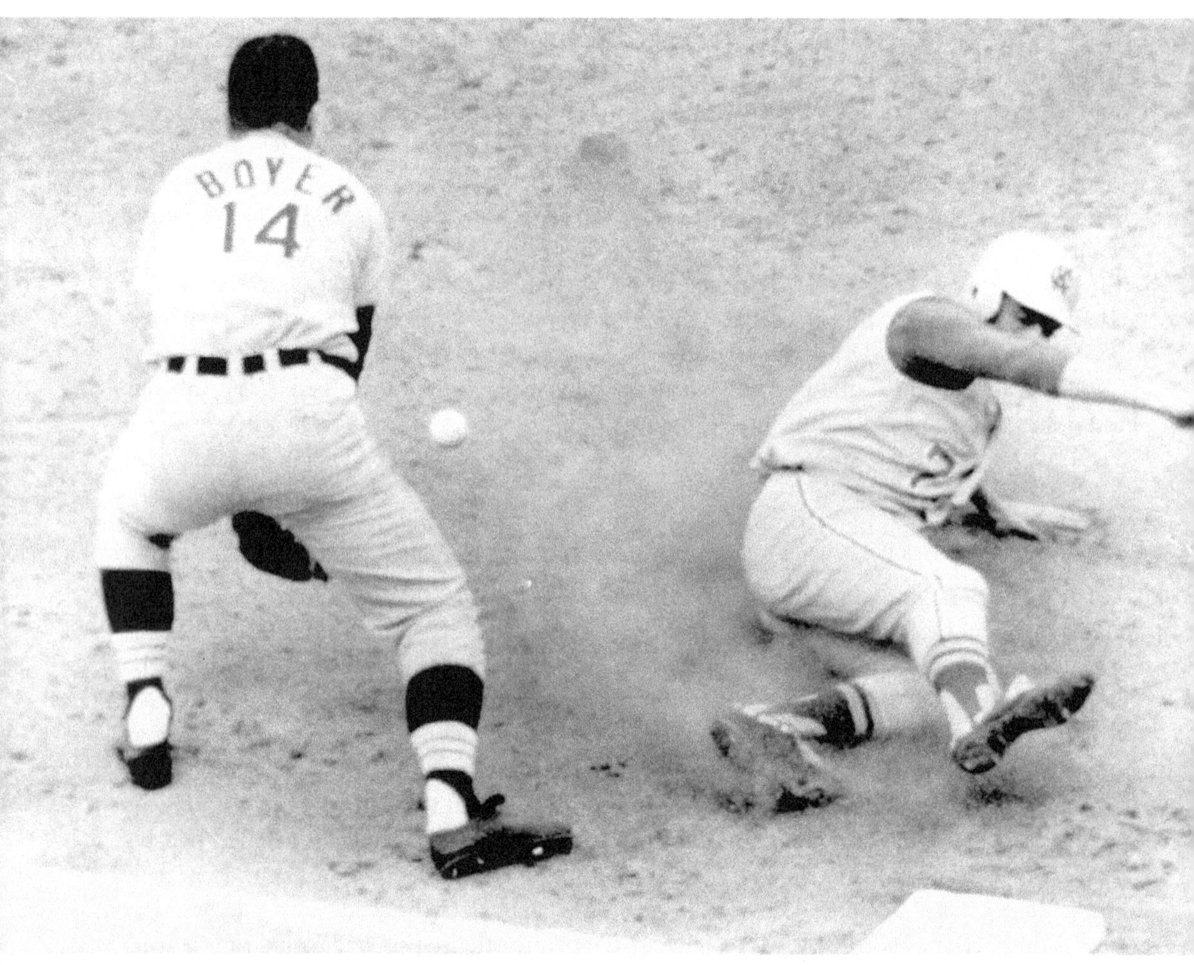

Boyer and Bando were two great third baseman. Sal Bando slides into third while Ken Boyer appears to have a sinking, helpless feeling. Boyer won the National League Most Valuable Player Award in 1964 while leading St. Louis to a World Championship. Bando played on the World Champion A's of 1972–1974. This play occurred on Black Wednesday, September 27, 1967, when Kansas City swept the Sox in a mid-week doubleheader and virtually ended Chicago's season. (Leo Bauby collection.)

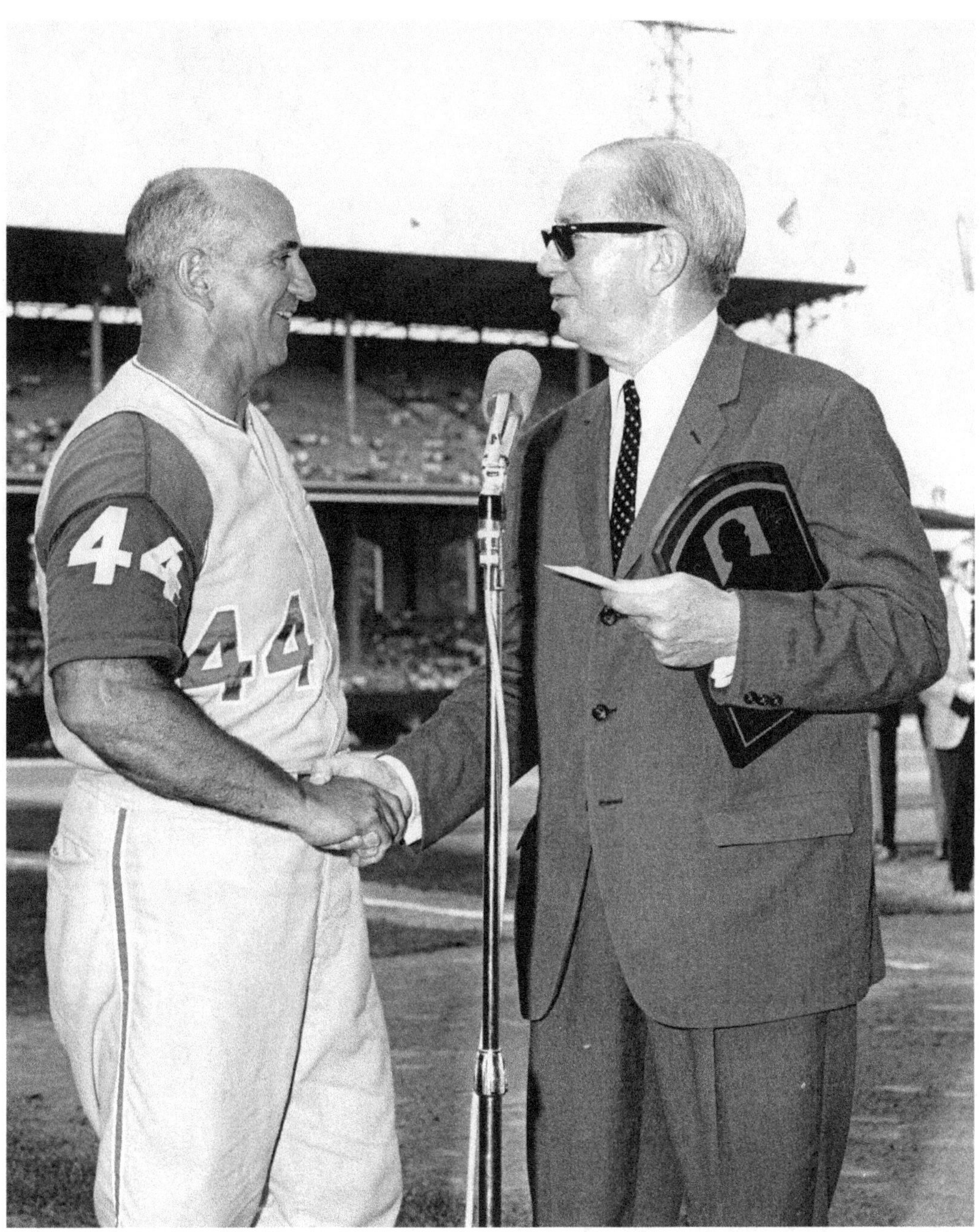

Ex-White Sox great Luke Appling takes part in pre-game ceremony with long-time Sox radio play-by-play announcer Bob Elson. Ironically, Appling was the interim manager of the Kansas City A's on Black Wednesday. Appling finished his career with 2,749 career hits, a .310 lifetime batting average, and he set the single season record for batting average for the White Sox with a .388 mark in 1936. (Gerry Bilek collection.)

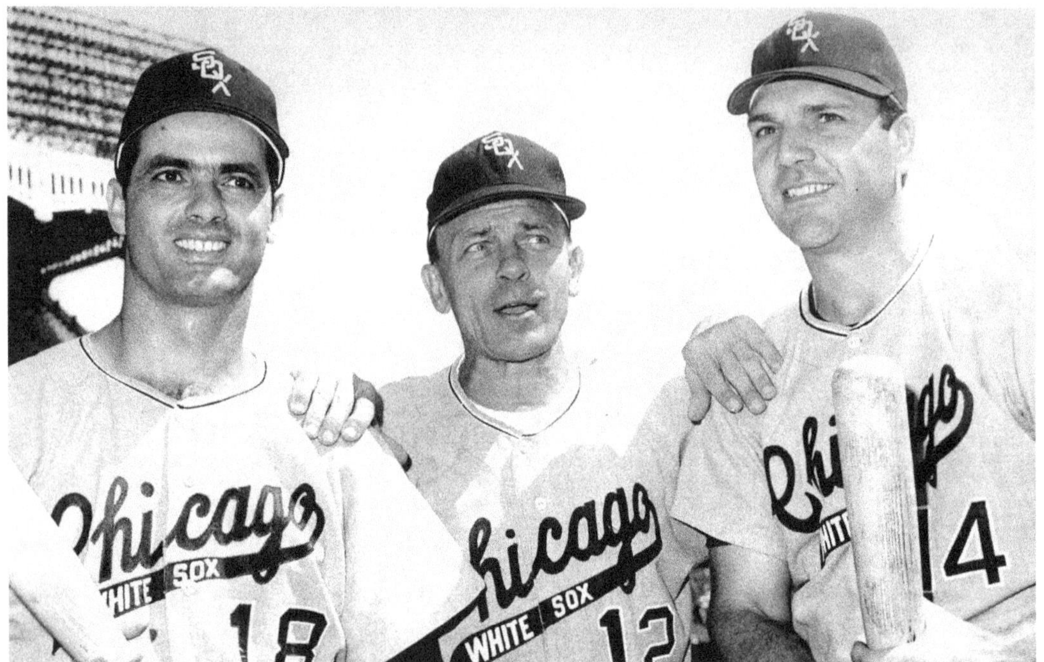

Manager Eddie Stanky stands in between sluggers Rocky Colavito (left) and Ken Boyer. The two hit a combined 656 home runs in their careers and a total of seven in the last half of 1967 after they were acquired in mid-season trades. It would have been great if the Sox had picked them up in 1964 when each was still in his prime.

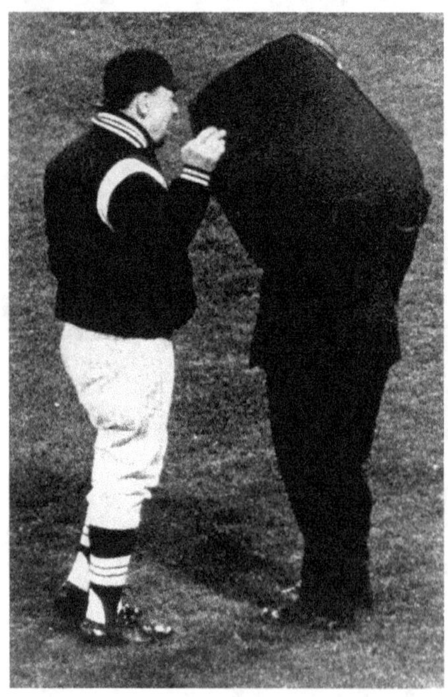

In this picture, it appears that the umpire is hiding from Eddie Stanky. Stanky was not shy about arguing with umpires—or anyone else. Even though he admitted his 1967 team was as dull as it could be, Stanky took high offense at anyone who suggested the same. Richard Nixon had a better relationship with the media. (Gerry Bilek collection.)

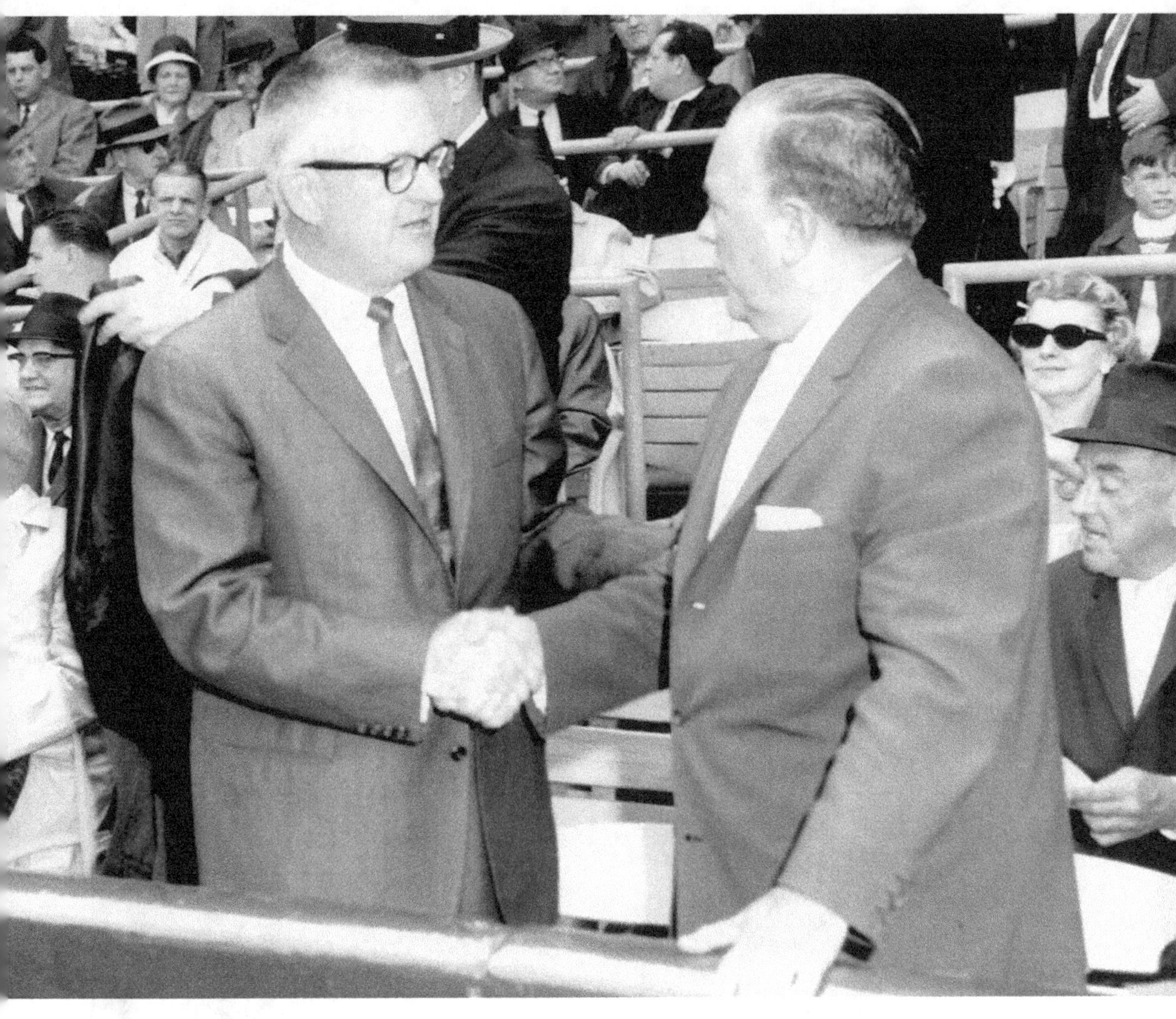

Arthur Allyn and Richard J. Daley were the two biggest White Sox fans during the 1960s. Allyn owned the Sox from June 1961 until September 1969. Daley was "His Honor," the mayor of Chicago, a position he held from 1955 through his death in December 1976. (Gerry Bilek collection.)

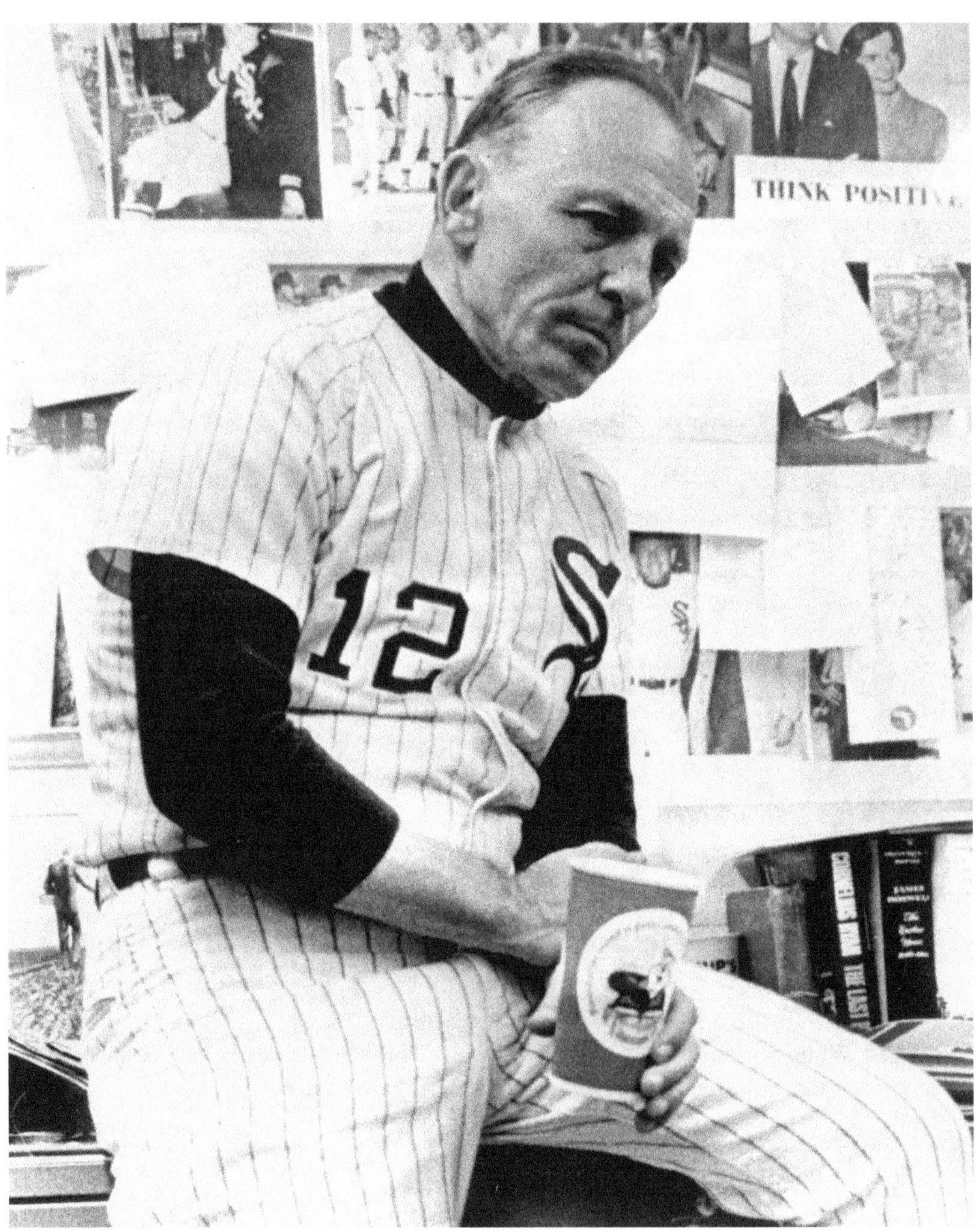

Eddie Stanky is seen here after the White Sox were officially eliminated from the 1967 pennant race by the Washington Senators. Washington shut out the Sox 1-0. The crusty manager, who defended his team time and again during the grueling last month of the race, ended up leaving the room in tears. White Sox fans cried right along with him. (Leo Bauby collection.)

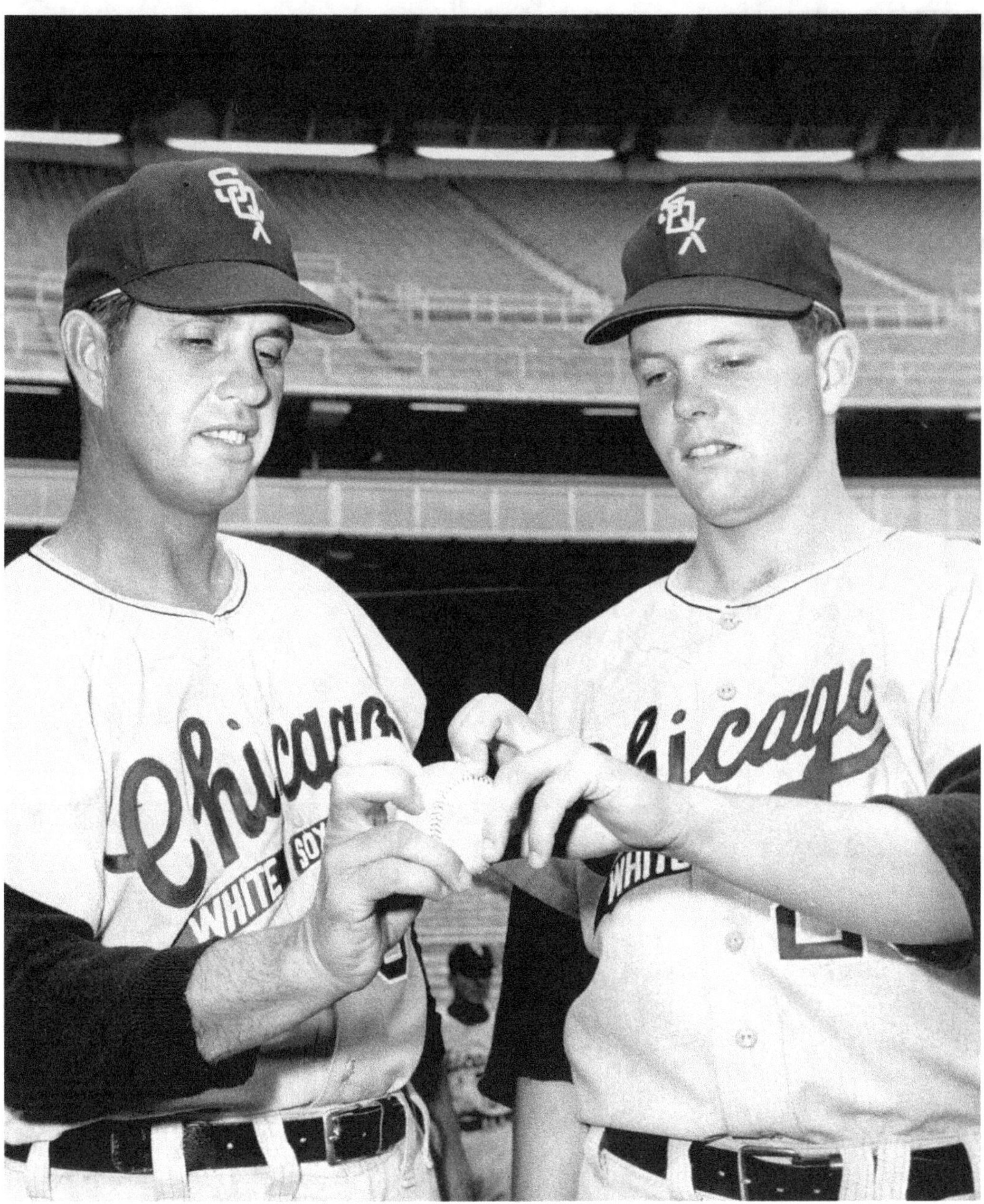

Wilbur Wood and Hoyt Wilhelm were the lefty-righty knuckle ball combination coming out of the bullpen for the Sox. According to Roland Hemond, Wood was not crazy about the shift to a role as a starting pitcher in 1971, as Wood thought he had found himself as a reliever. In his career, Wilhelm appeared in 1,070 games. The two men were a combined 12-5 in the tragic year of 1967. (Leo Bauby collection.)

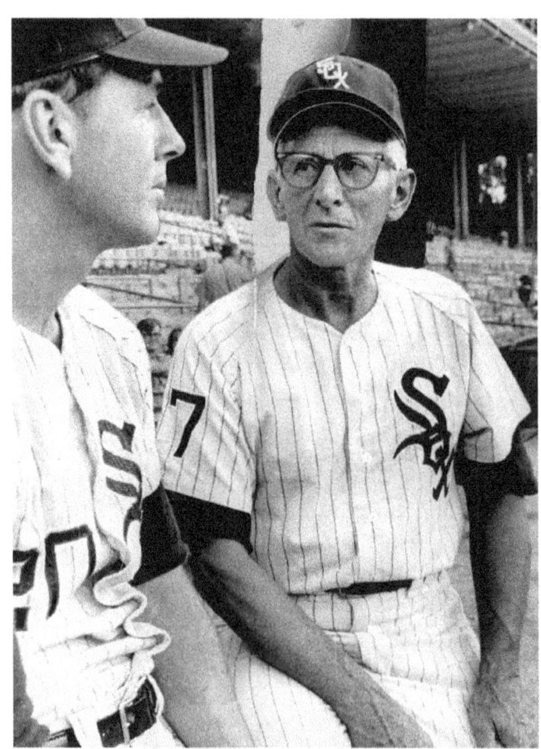

Nineteen-game winner Joe Horlen is pictured with mentor and pitching coach, Ray Berres, in 1968. It is funny how there so few sore arms on the Sox staff when Berres was coach. (Leo Bauby collection.)

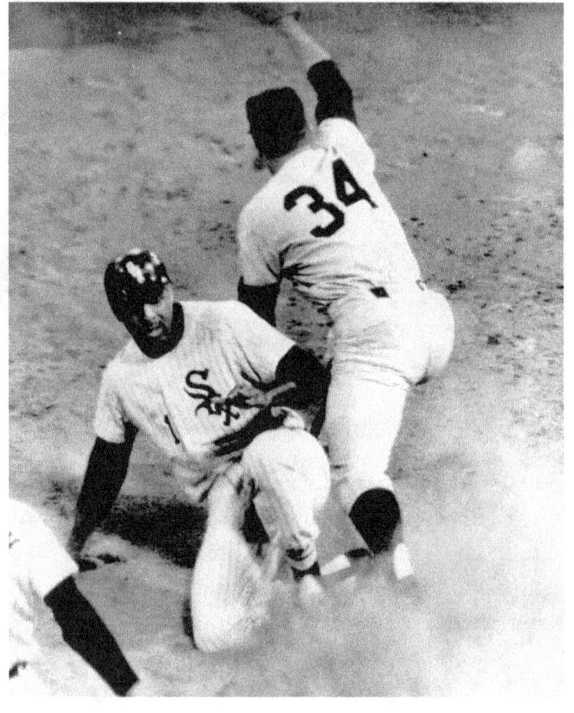

Center fielder Tommie Agee disappointed Sox fans when his averaged dipped to .234. He was traded to the Mets after the season and starred in the 1969 World Series. No White Sox player played in a World Series until 2005, unless they did it for other teams. (Gerry Bilek collection.)

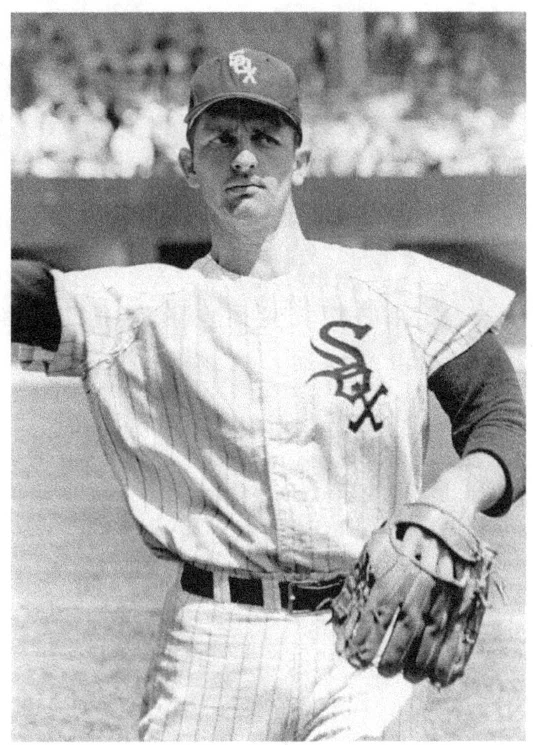

Considered a great clutch hitter, shortstop Ron Hansen grounded out to third to end a White Sox rally (at least by 1967 standards) and finish off the first game of the doubleheader against the Kansas City A's on Black Wednesday. The bases were loaded at the time, and a grand slam would have put the Sox ahead by one. He is shown here in 1964, a year in which he hit 20 homers. (Leo Bauby collection.)

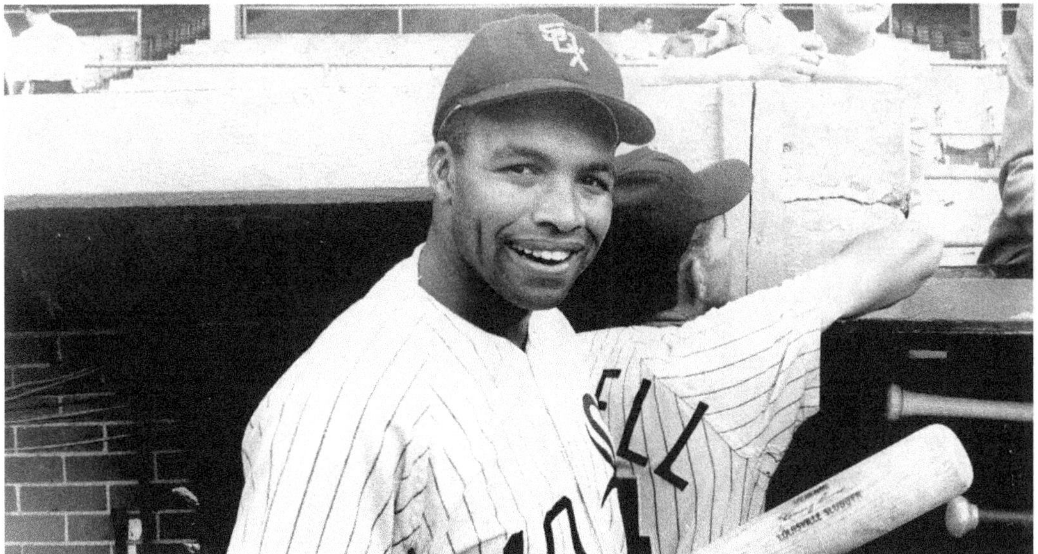

Tommy Davis looks awfully happy here, but looks are truly deceiving. Acquired in an after-season trade between the 1967 and 1968 campaigns, the two-time National League batting champion was looked as the offensive savior for the White Sox in 1968. He was nothing of the kind. His batting average dropped 34 points and he had 50 lonely RBIs. (Gerry Bilek collection.)

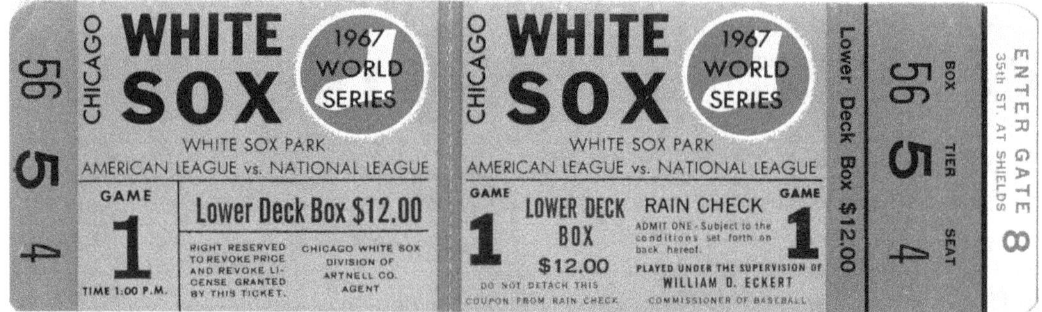

This 1967 World Series ticket was never used. The 1967 season was over-achieving and ended in a nightmare. The 1977 South Side Hitmen, who never really came close to winning anything, overshadow this club in many ways. Regardless, it would have been an interesting had the hitless 1967 wonders played in the World Series against the Cardinals. (Leo Bauby collection.)

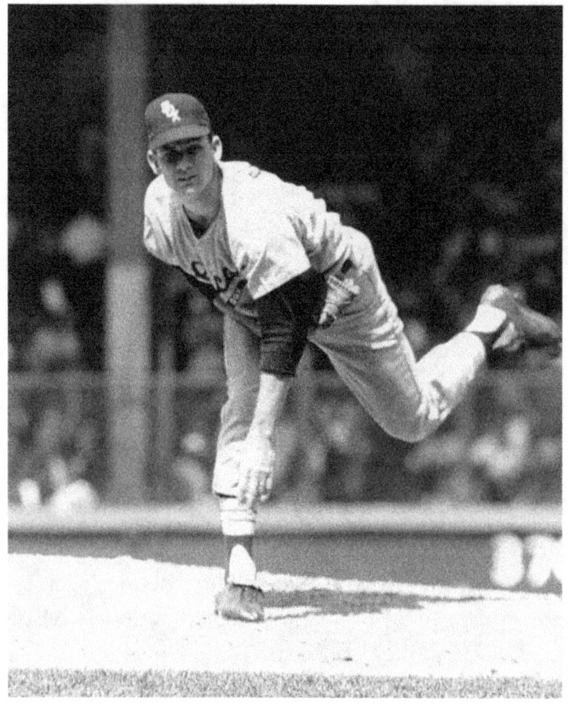

Gary Peters shows the form that made him one of the great left-handed pitchers in the American League during the mid-1960s. He won 16 in 1967. He would have won more with a better hitting team, which is a real understatement. (Leo Bauby collection.)

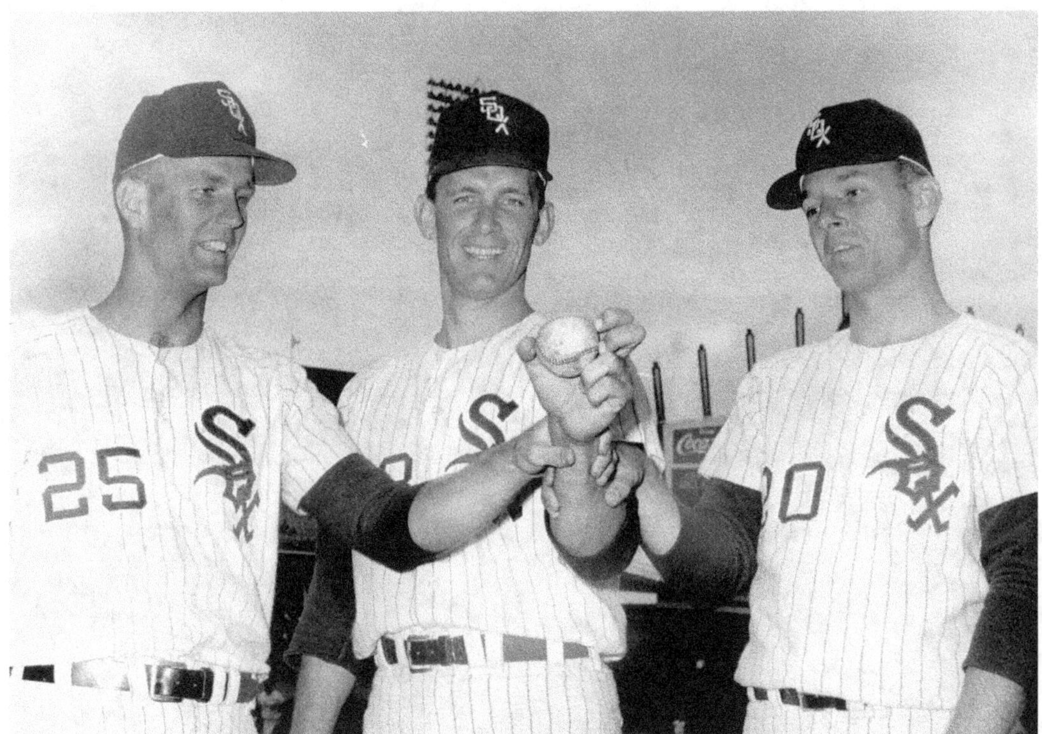

Tommy John (left), Gary Peters (middle), and Joe Horlen were the top three pitchers for the White Sox in 1967. The three threw a combined 15 shutouts that year. (Leo Bauby collection.)

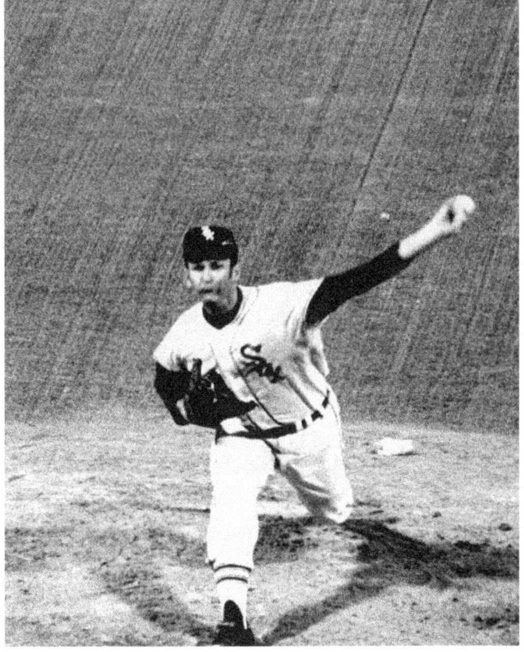

Tommy John is shown here during the disastrous 106-loss 1970 season. John started and lost the pennant-race eliminating game against the Washington Senators in 1967, even though he gave up only one unearned run in five innings. The run was scored in part because Senator Fred Valentine got new life when his foul ball landed in a camera well set up for a hoped for World Series. There was no World Series. You can't win when you can't score. (Leo Bauby collection.)

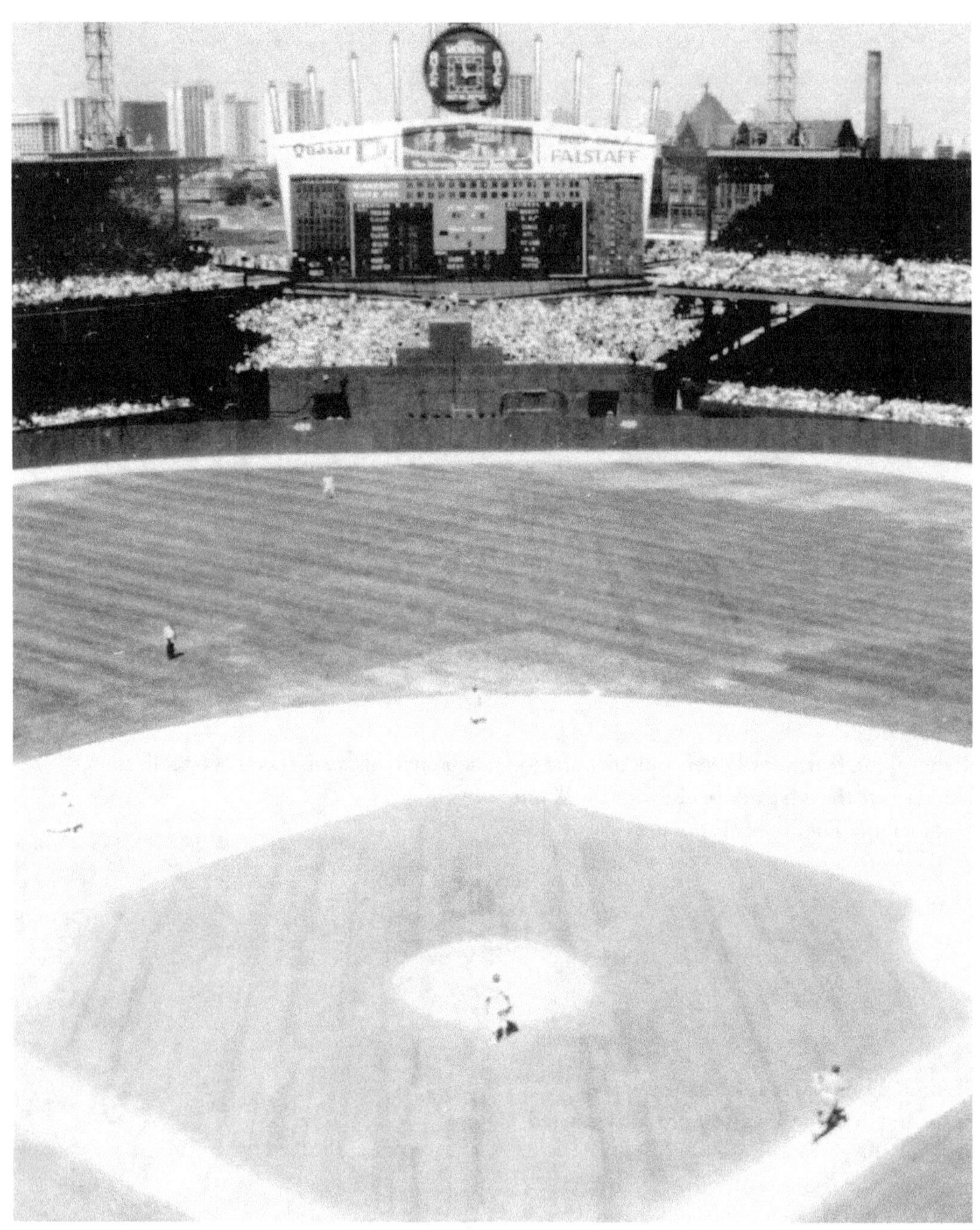

In 1969, much to the dismay of the pitching staff, the White Sox installed Astroturf in the infield to help their ground balls sneak out to the outfield. According to Gary Peters, the turf helped the opposition more because the Sox staff was full of low-ball, sinker throwing pitchers. Additionally, it made the infield look like a pool table and ruined the natural beauty of Comiskey Park. (Leo Bauby collection.)

2

1976

Barely Hanging On

At the start of the 1976 season, the Chicago White Sox were still a franchise at a crossroads. In late 1975, it appeared that the charter member of the American League was on its way out of Chicago. Financially strapped owner John Allyn had just seen his team draw barely over 770,000, a drop of almost a quarter of a million from 1974. One-time budding stars Bill Melton and Carlos May neared the end of their careers. After putting together four straight 20-win seasons, Wilbur Wood slumped to 16-20 with an ERA of over four for the first time in his career. No one from the Sox farm system showed any real promise of reviving the team. And after winning only 75 games and finishing 22 ½ games out of first place, the club had little talent to offer in the way of trades.

As the winter meetings approached in late 1975, Seattle loomed as the new home for the White Sox. The Sox had been losing money every year since 1970. By the end of 1975, the franchise had lost $8 million. That was a lot of money in those days.

"Poor John Allyn is broke," one American League owner said of the Sox boss. "If he doesn't get rid of the club soon, he won't have a dime left."

Finally, Bill Veeck, the last owner to take a White Sox team to a World Series, at that time, stepped in with an investment group to purchase the club when no other local businessman or entities were interested in risking money on the sagging franchise.

Bill Veeck was not your stereotypical owner. After wrestling control of the White Sox from the Comiskey family, he constructed "the Monster" in center field at Comiskey Park. "The Monster" was the huge fireworks-erupting scoreboard that celebrated rare White Sox home runs, delighting Chicago fans and infuriating opponents and the baseball establishment. He was the first owner to put names on the backs of uniforms, a move that drew intense criticism. Veeck took the Sox to the World Series in 1959, but some fans thought he sold the future of the team away by trading young promising players for veterans in an attempt to repeat the next year. Fans also felt deserted and betrayed when Veeck sold the team to Arthur Allyn in June 1961.

No matter how his baseball legacy would be judged, the American League wasn't impressed with Veeck's offer to purchase the White Sox in 1975. (A majority of owners must approve the sale of any franchise.) In addition to some owners not wanting the renegade Veeck back in major league baseball, the powers that be didn't think Veeck had enough financial backing and resources to make the purchase. So they gave him a chance to restructure his deal. If he failed to deliver, however, the franchise's 75-year old connection to Chicago and the Midwest would end.

Fans, with the prompting of WBBM/Channel 2 TV sportscaster, Johnny Morris, offered to send in donations to keep the team in the city. However, Illinois State law prevented Veeck from having more than 50 investors in his group. Legally, Veeck could not form a partnership with the fans to keep the White Sox in Chicago.

"There are people who say they have only a couple of bucks, but they're pulling for me," Veeck said, touched by fan sentiment. "Those are the ones who get to you."

On December 10, 1975, Veeck presented his new financial package to the owners. Whether they wanted him in their exclusive little group or not, the American League owners approved the sale by a 10-2 vote. The White Sox stayed in Chicago.

In a move to revive memories of the "Go-Go" Sox of the 1950s, Veeck brought back 67-year-old Paul Richards to manage the club. During his first tenure as Sox manager, Richards had averaged 88 wins from 1951 to 1954 with a 154-game schedule, even though Richards left the club on September 10, 1954, due to a salary dispute.

A new optimism greeted the Sox in the Bicentennial year of 1976. The media was behind Veeck, even praising the new paint job Comiskey Park had received. An hour or two before the home opener, Veeck made his way through the stands and was greeted by fans grateful for his keeping the Sox in the city. A crowd engulfed him, patting him on the back and shaking his hand as he walked through the lower deck on the third base side. Along with this newborn optimism, the sweet smell of marijuana was in the air. The 40,318 fans, hopefully more high on the occasion, attended the successful season home opener in which Wilbur Wood threw a 4-0 whitewashing of the Kansas City Royals. Nothing could spoil the day, not even the scoreboard firing a dud after a Jim Spencer two-run homer to right.

Later in the season, Veeck dressed his team up in shorts to get publicity and have fun. The Sox won one game largely because a Texas outfielder couldn't find a fly ball in the early June fog. Attendance climbed back over the 900,000 mark—not great but quite an improvement after the apathetic 1975 campaign nearly drove the team out of the city.

The year 1976, however, was not good for the White Sox. On May 9, Wood took a line drive on the knee off the bat of Tiger outfielder Ron LeFlore in Detroit. Wood was only 4-3 at the time but had an ERA of 2.25. His absence for the remainder of the season didn't help an already thin pitching staff. The short pants stunt drew derision as well as laughter. By the end of August, the *Chicago Sun-Times* depicted manager Paul Richards as a lonely man who had taken a job that wasn't right for him at that time in his life. More than one player complained to reporter Joe Goddard about Richards.

"He'd fall asleep during games," Goddard recalled in 2005. "He was late for games, not that he would be late for the actual start, but he would show only a half hour before. One time he gave a lineup card to third baseman Bill Stein to run out to the umpires. Stein noticed there were four outfielders but no third baseman. When Stein went back, Richards asked Stein where he usually batted. Stein said third and Richards said, 'put yourself down for third.'"

"His heart just wasn't in it," Goddard concluded.

According to Goddard, almost everybody connected with the White Sox organization didn't appreciate the story. Bill Veeck told Goddard that he "should have let the team be sold to Seattle." Veeck's son, Mike, angrily told Goddard that it "took a lot of guts" for Goddard to show up the day after the story ran. Harry Caray lit into Goddard claiming that Richards had taken the managerial job for one year as a favor to Veeck, an arrangement that Goddard said he knew nothing about. Goddard said he actually felt bad writing a story about an otherwise good baseball man.

Meanwhile—as Richards dismissed the article and showed enough class to co-exist with Goddard—Jim Spencer and Jorge Orta went on to lead the team in the home run department with 14 each, a puny number, hardly enough to entertain fans. In the last half of September, the team mailed their season in, failing in their last 15 of 16 games. The squad, labeled as quitters, finished with a last place record of 64-97, their second worst season in 25 years.

"It was a three ring circus, and we were the third act." This Rich Gossage quote easily described the 1976 Chicago White Sox season. Equipped with little pitching, defense, or hitting, the team's biggest accomplishment was staying in Chicago after the near move to Seattle at the end of 1975. However, Gossage wasn't referring to the team's performance where they barely missed losing 100 games.

Throughout his career, Bill Veeck was criticized for denigrating the sport by doing just about anything to draw attention and fans. Pinch hitting little people, martians landing in the middle of the Comiskey Park, and the exploding scoreboard offended many. Gossage holds Veeck in high regard, but he had little use for the many similar Veeckian brainstorms in 1976.

For almost his entire career, Gossage was a relief pitcher. The nickname of "Goose" was in reference to the number of zeros he placed on the scoreboard. He had a Hall of Fame type career notching 310 saves. But in 1976, he was slotted into the starting rotation for the pitching-poor White Sox. His changed routine of warming up before games, instead of in the middle as a reliever, was constantly interrupted by some eye-catching promotion.

"There were cattle, elephants, and dancing girls," Gossage said in 2005, still not amused. "Many times I didn't get a chance to warm up. It's hard to pitch the first inning when you haven't thrown. But the umpires wouldn't delay the game."

"He was a great promoter," Gossage said of Veeck. "But it got old."

Gossage also had few fond memories of the 1976 Sox, the team Veeck worked so hard to promote. He remembered leaving games with leads that weren't protected and a team defense that did little to reassure a pitcher.

"Bart Johnson [Sox right-hander] was on the mound and Paul Richards went out to talk to him," Gossage recalled. "He told Johnson to pitch around the next hitter. Johnson pointed to the Sox outfield and asked, 'How do I pitch around them?' Richards said, 'Young man, you have a point.'"

Needless to say, Johnson didn't pitch around the next hitter.

A little more than two months after the 1976 season mercifully ended, Gossage was traded to the Pirates along with Terry Forster in exchange for Richie Zisk and pitcher Silvio Martinez. Despite spending his formative major league years with the White Sox, Gossage said he was "happy to get out of that situation," not only because he was departing from a bad team, but because he was able to rejoin former Sox manager, Chuck Tanner, who was now managing Pittsburgh.

"It was a good trade for both teams," said Gossage, who wasn't surprised by the success of the South Side Hitmen. "Getting Zisk was good for the White Sox. They really needed the hitting."

Free agency was in its infancy in 1977. Other teams, even those that would be considered small market teams today, began signing star players to expensive, long-term contracts. Bill Veeck, the one-time players' advocate, had little means to seriously compete in this market. Yet, to improve attendance he couldn't field a team as boring as the 1976 edition. He might have been looked upon as a savior in late 1975, but White Sox fans had had enough of losing teams contending for last place.

So what did the White Sox do? They began by trading two of their hardest throwing pitchers—Rich Gossage and Terry Forster—to the Pirates for right fielder Richie Zisk. They also signed free-agent third baseman Eric Soderholm. Soderholm had injured his knee in a freakish, off the field accident in September 1975 and spent 1976 rehabbing. Finally, two days before the season was to begin, the White Sox sent shortstop Bucky Dent to the New York Yankees for pitchers LaMarr Hoyt and Bob Polinksy, and outfielder Oscar Gamble.

Zisk, Gamble, and Soderholm would end up leading the Sox to an incredible year. White Sox fans, so used to watching dull teams scratch for runs and then lose, fell in love with a club that could just plain hit. Huge Comiskey Park rocked with large crowds singing good-bye songs to vanquished opponents and demanding players come out of the dugout to acknowledge curtain calls after dramatic home runs. Many of the players, once considered outcasts, fed off the energy and emotion to have career years. Baseball was not merely revived on the South Side of Chicago; the enthusiasm from a once dormant fan base attracted national attention.

The 1977 White Sox became known as the South Side Hitmen, a name they more than lived up to. They didn't win the World Series or even a division championship, but they posted their best record in 12 years and set a White Sox attendance record. Their 192 home runs set another team record. They thrilled home crowds with long homers, come-from behind victories, and an offensive barrage that left opponents dazed and defeated. Two years earlier, many were ready to see the team leave for the great Northwest. Now they bonded with their favorite baseball club in a way that hasn't been matched since.

The 1977 South Side Hitmen. Just the name stirs memories of excitement and hope that had abandoned Chicago during the late 1970s. They are arguably one of the most loved teams in franchise history. Too bad they didn't have more pitching. Or more defense. Or the luck that always seemed to elude Chicago baseball teams. But in 1977, when baseball was still young, the South Side Hit Men were what the sport should be all about.

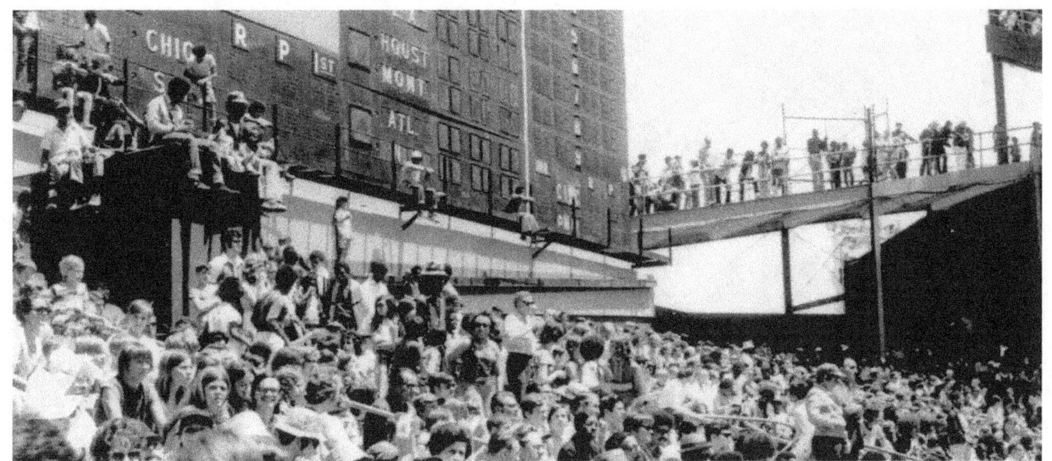

The White Sox had their problems with attendance during the late 1960s and mid-1970s. This was not the case on May 20, 1973. In those days, there was a great deal of general admission seating at Comiskey. Many fans ended up not seeing the game because there was no place for them to stand or sit. (They received refunds for the tickets.) Many sat in the aisles or, as in this photograph, stood on the scoreboard catwalk. The emotion at the ballpark was at near 1977 levels when Bill Melton and Carlos May homered in the first game, which the Sox won 9-3. (Leo Bauby collection.)

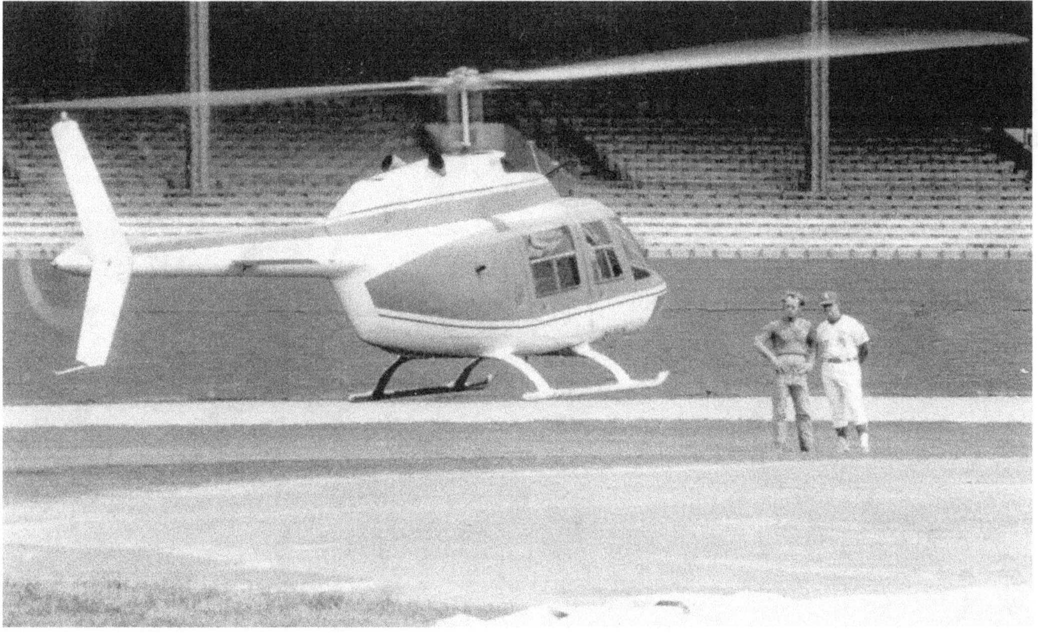

No, this was not some Bill Veeck–type stunt like bringing martians to Comiskey. Early Chicago springs are often cold and wet putting a damper on everything. In 1973, a helicopter was brought into Comiskey to dry the wet turf. (Leo Bauby collection.)

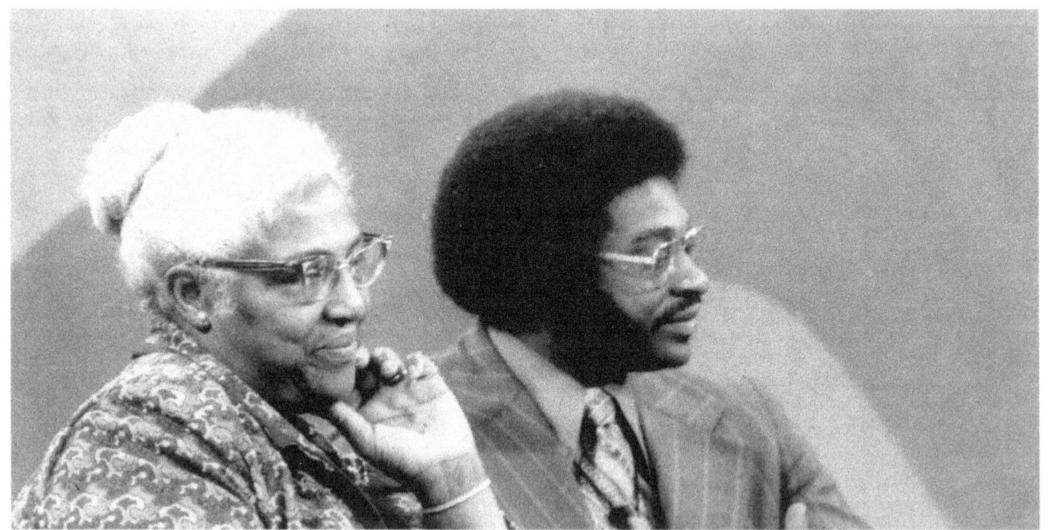

Dick Allen was the rage when he had his MVP season in 1972. Here he is shown with his mother on his TV show. Allen "retired" in the early part of September 1974 and then returned to play for his once hated Phillies. The White Sox tinkered with the idea of bringing him back in 1977 but thought better of it. It turned out to be a very wise decision. (Leo Bauby collection.)

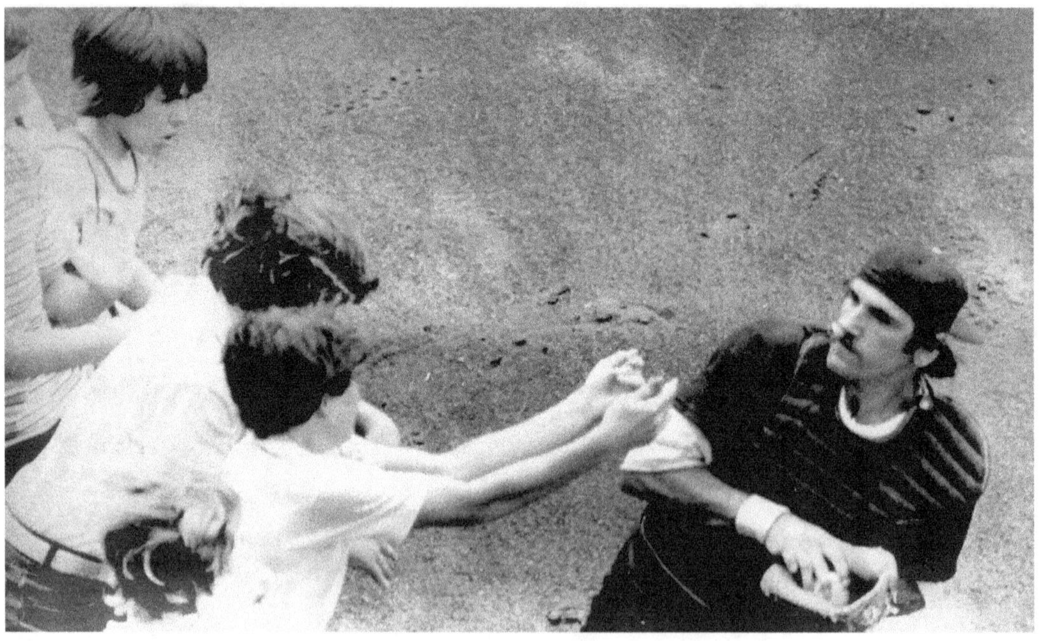

Jim Essian fights with a fan for foul ball in 1976. Essian ended up being the main compensation to the Sox when they traded Dick Allen after the disappointing 1974 season and would have a nice year for the 1977 South Side Hitmen. (Leo Bauby collection.)

Flame-throwing Terry Forster mows them down and looks great while doing it. It was short pants day at Comiskey on August 8, 1976. It was actually a kind of brisk day for August, never getting out of the 1970s. Yet the Sox were dressed for a day at the beach. They won the game but never were that fashionable again. (Leo Bauby collection.)

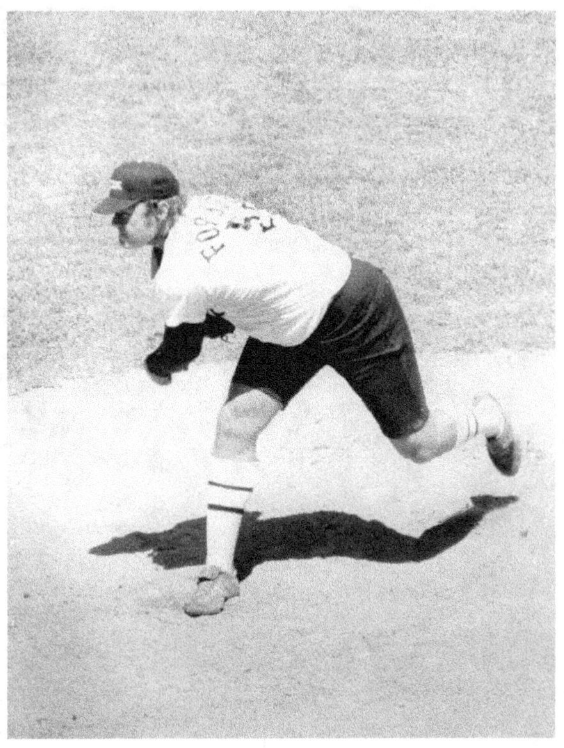

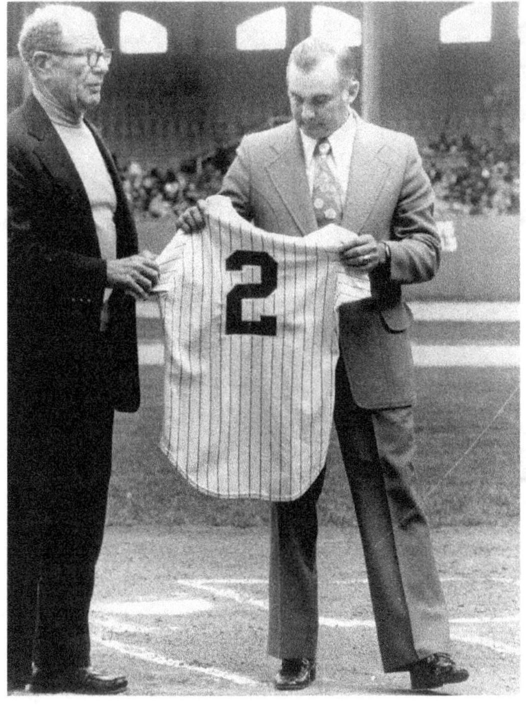

The number of Nelson Fox is retired. The second baseman was one the most memorable players from the Go-Go era, and won the American League Most Valuable Player Award in the 1959 pennant-winning season. Fox was a throwback player, never worrying about getting hit by a pitch, and more than willing to use his body to block a ground ball. He was also an excellent bunter. Fox died on December 1, 1975, and a well-organized campaign helped get him elected to the Hall of Fame in 1997. His uniform was retired during this 1976 ceremony. (Leo Bauby collection.)

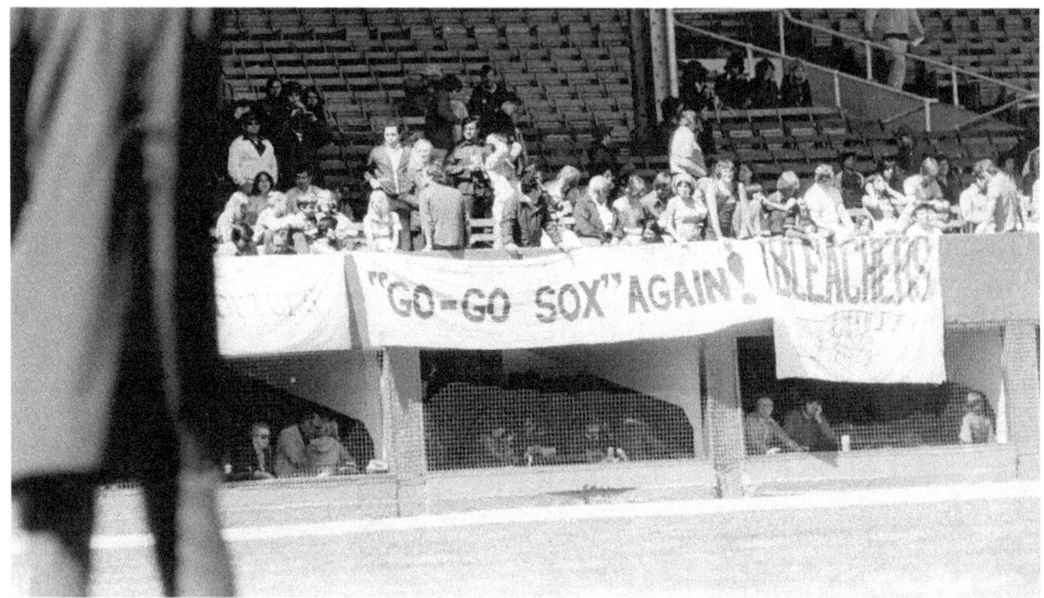

Banners in the left field seats celebrate what some fans thought was the reincarnation of the winning teams of the 1950s. Not quite in 1976, although the Sox did show some speed running after the ball after they missed it. (Leo Bauby collection.)

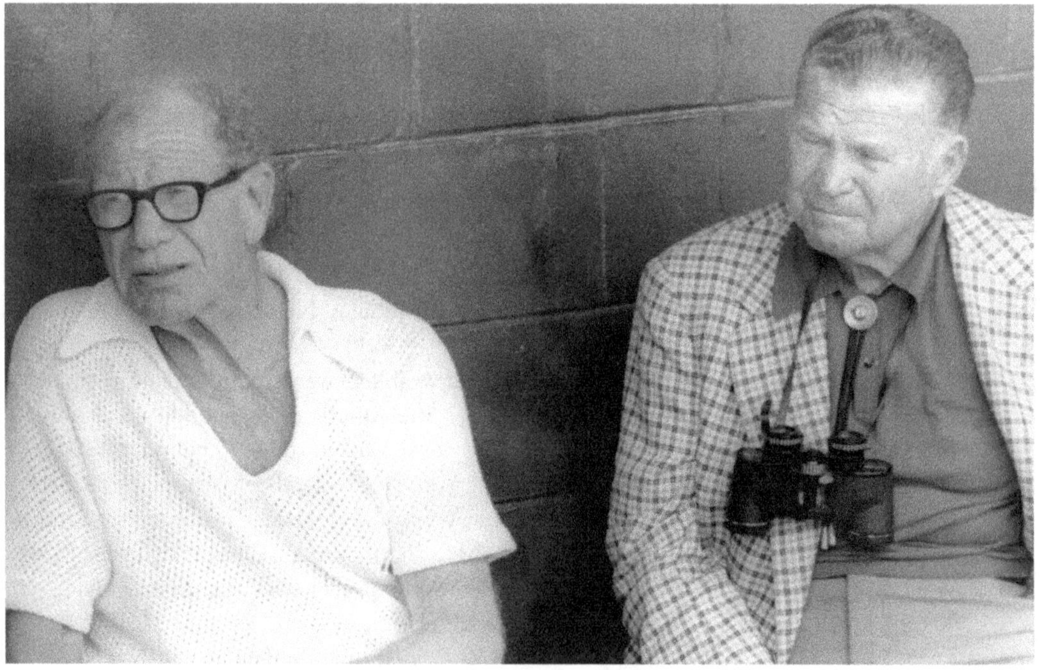

Another blast from the Go-Go past—Bill Veeck poses with former GM Frank Lane. (Leo Bauby collection.)

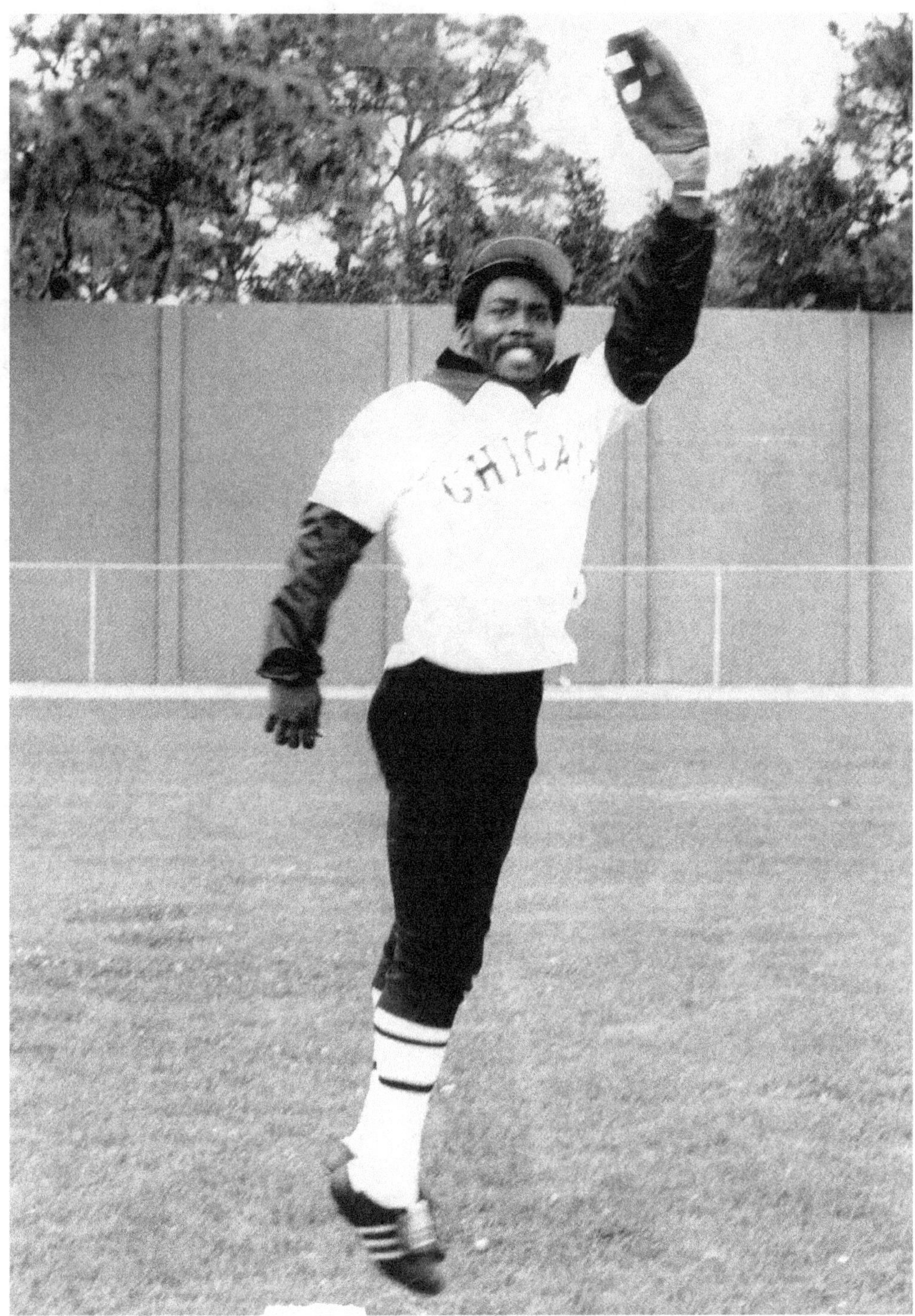

Chet Lemon is pictured just before he started his first full season with the White Sox in 1976. The ball club was a little uncertain where it wanted to play him—third base or center field. Lemon ended up in center, which turned out to be a good choice. (Leo Bauby collection.)

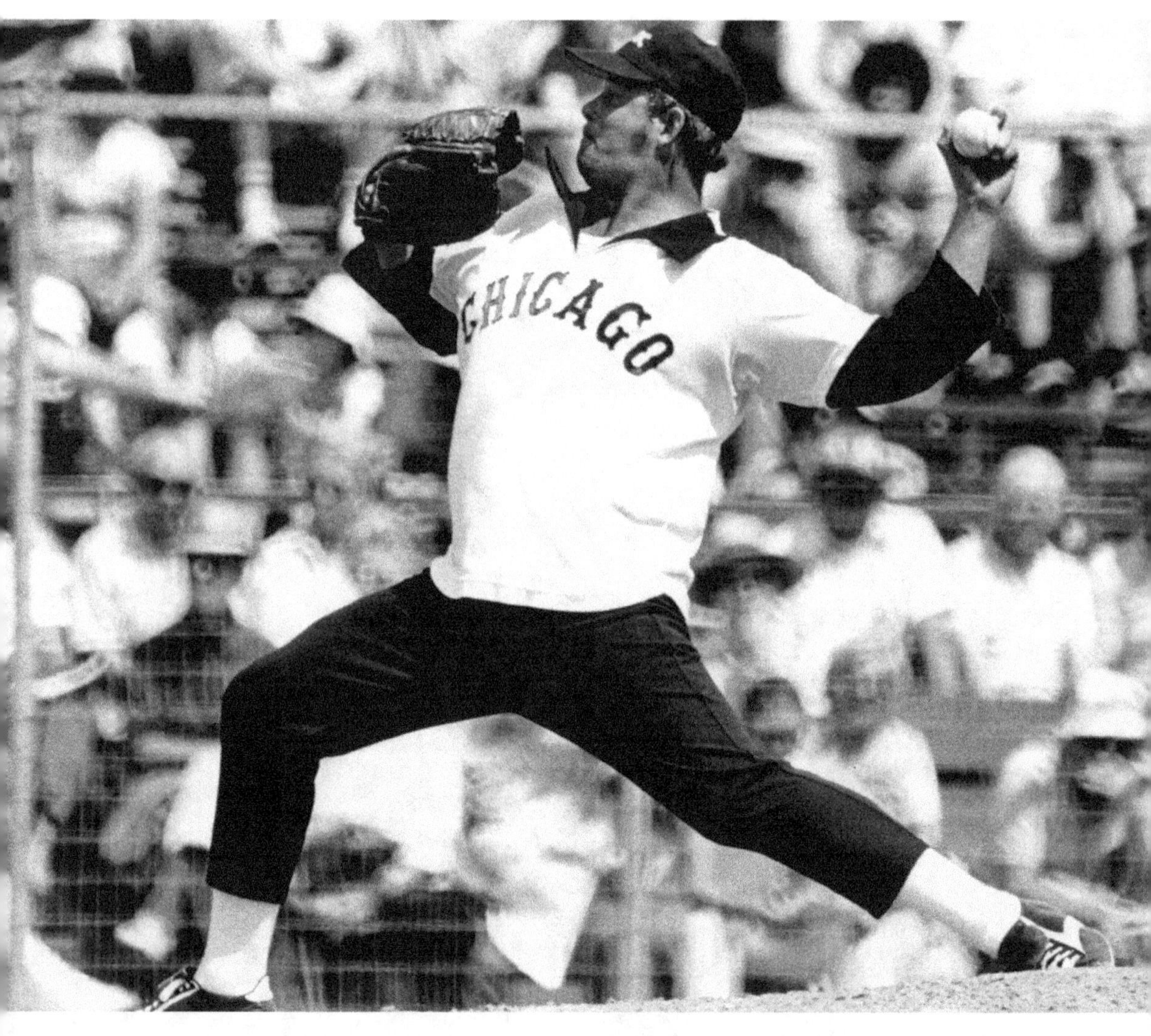

Wilbur Wood gets in tune during spring training, 1976. Despite losing 20 games in 1975, Wood was still considered the number one pitcher on the staff as the White Sox headed into the 1976 season. Even with the 20-loss season, Wood was one of the amazing stories in baseball during the first half of the 1970s. (Leo Bauby collection.)

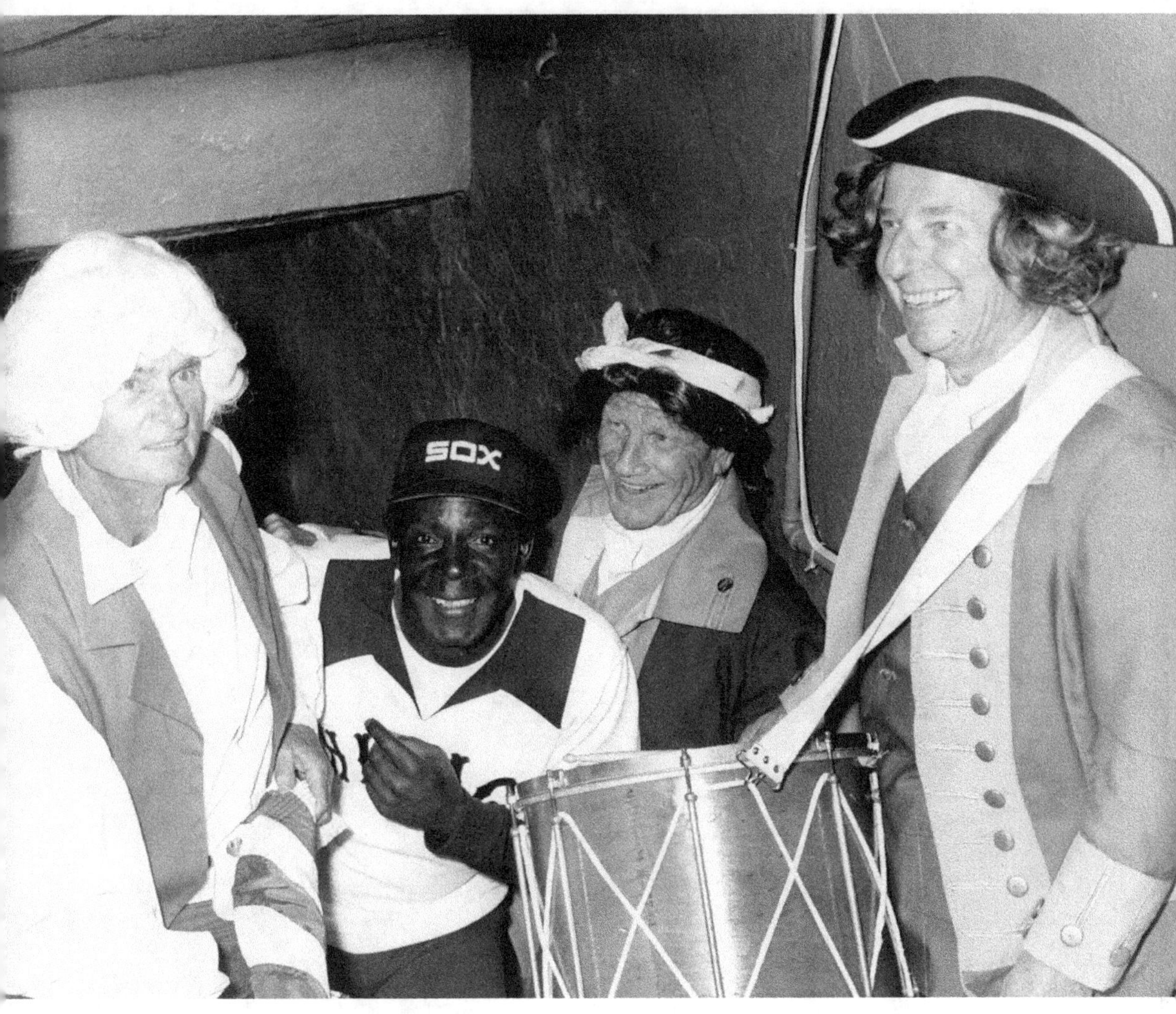

If nothing else, Bill Veeck was a great showman. On Opening Day at Comiskey during the bicentennial year, Veeck and company marched out on the field in 1776 wear. Veeck looked like a natural with his peg leg. It was a great day for the White Sox as fans were grateful that the team had been saved from a move to Seattle. The Sox won 4-0 on a sunny day that was basked in a new optimism. (Leo Bauby collection.)

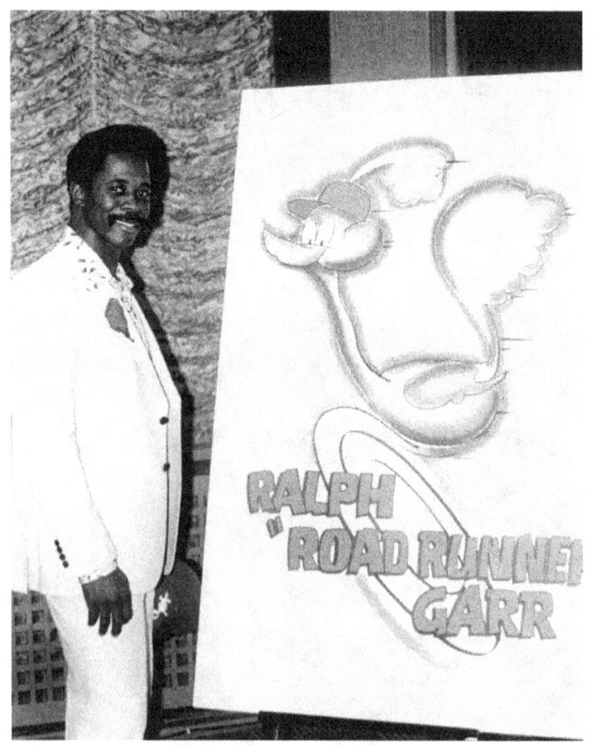

The spirit of 1976 was also wedded to the spirit of the Go-Go 1950s. Ralph Garr was obtained from Atlanta in an effort to put speed on the basepaths. Here Garr is shown beaming next to a poster of the roadrunner. Garr led the White Sox in hitting with an even-steven .300 average. (Leo Bauby collection.)

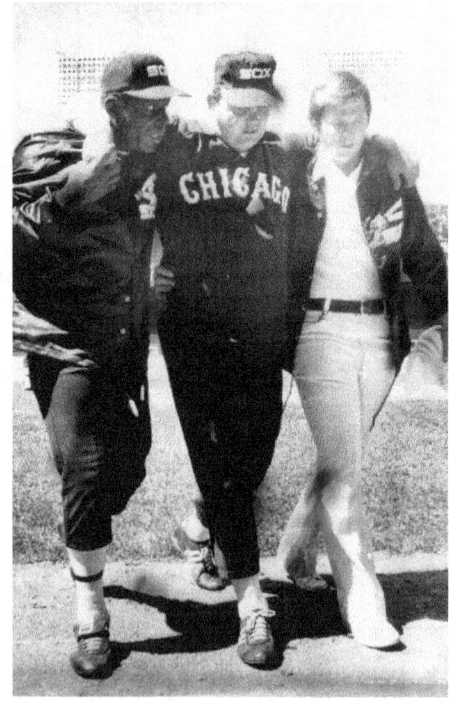

The end of the 1976 season came on May 9. Here, Wilbur Wood is being helped off the field after a line drive hit by Detroit's Ron LeFlore ripped into his knee. There was no way the Sox could recover from this bad break. They had no one else on the staff that could start between 40 and 50 games and log in well over 300 innings. Wood tried to make a comeback in 1977 and 1978, but the knuckleballer was never the same again. (Leo Bauby collection.)

Wilbur Wood recovers in the hospital after his injury. Doesn't look good, does it? In this case, looks were not deceiving. (Leo Bauby collection.)

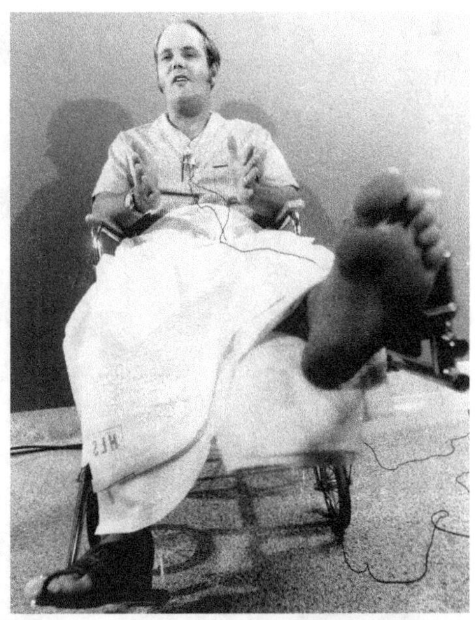

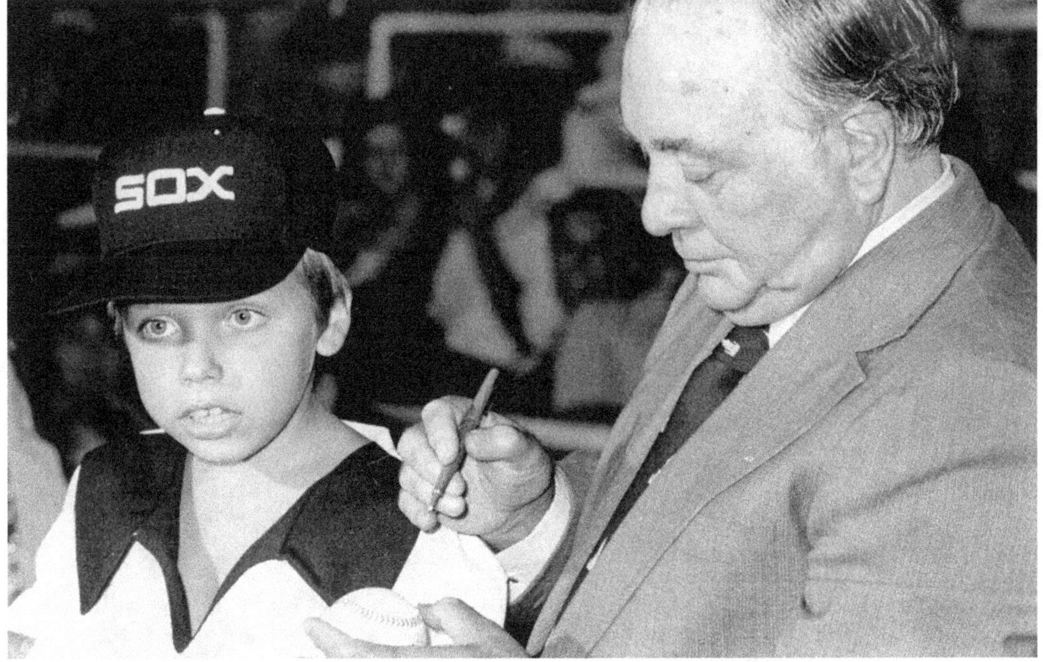

Mayor Richard Daley is seen in the last year of his life. Almost living in the shadows of Comiskey Park, Daley loved his White Sox. He was one Chicago mayor who could say that the White Sox played in a World Series during his lifetime. He set off the city fire sirens the night the Sox clinched in 1959, and people feared many things, including an attack from the Soviet Union. Unfortunately, the White Sox still hadn't been to a World Series by the time the Cold War was over and the Soviet Union had dissolved in 1989. (Leo Bauby collection.)

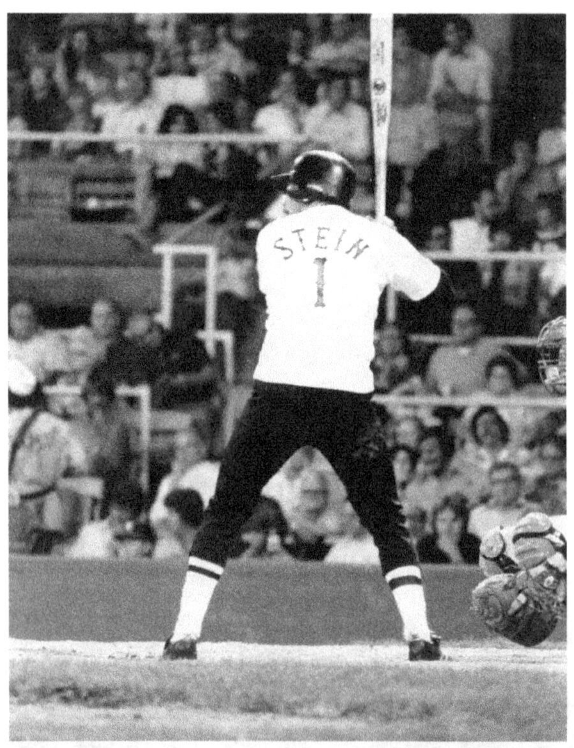

Third baseman Bill Stein looks foreboding at the plate in 1976. According to former *Chicago Sun-Times* reporter Joe Goddard, Stein was a lineup messenger for manager for manager Paul Richards. On one occasion, Stein examined the lineup card and saw that Richards had penciled in four outfielders. (Leo Bauby collection.)

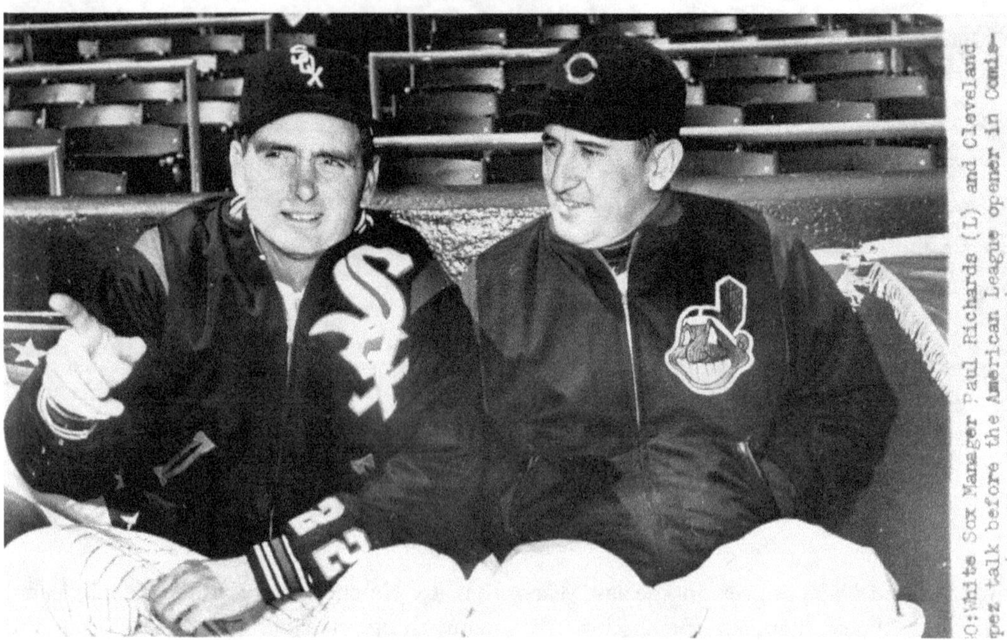

Paul Richards is shown here in happier with Indians manager Al Lopez in 1952. That year the Sox finished 81-73, 14 games out of first. Winning 81 games would have been a accomplishment for the 1976 team—even with the 162-game schedule. (Leo Bauby collection.)

A real rare occurrence in 1976 was a runner barreling for home plate. The runner in this case was Jorge Orta. From a certain angle, it appears that Orta will be tripping over a discarded bat. That would be just the type of the luck the Sox were running into during the mid-1970s. Although, it must be said that bad luck alone was the reason the Sox dropped 97 games in 1976. (Leo Bauby collection.)

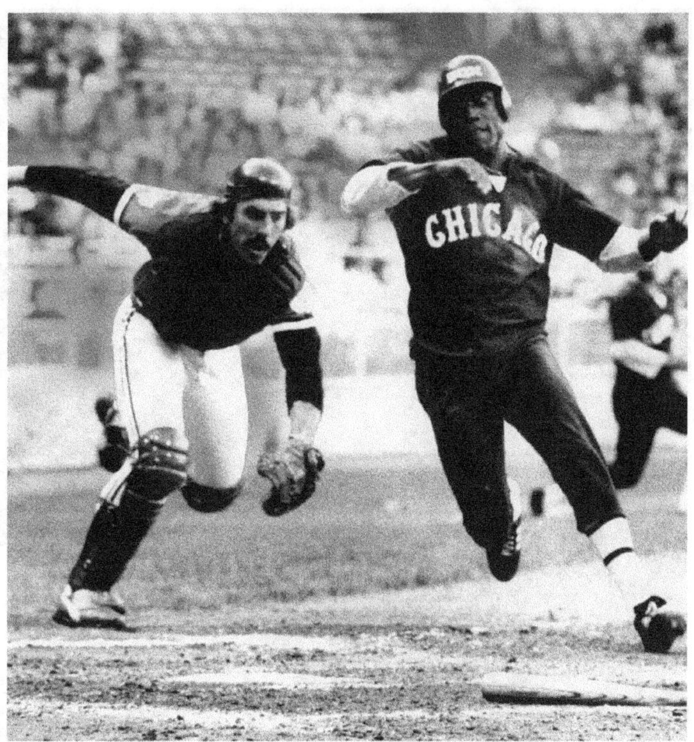

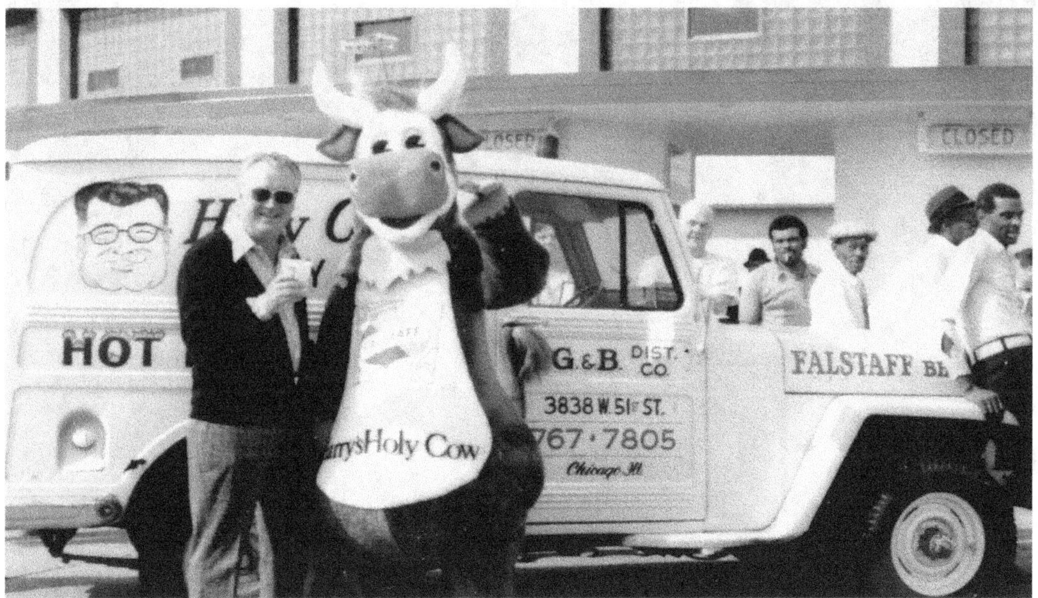

Before he was a Bud man, Harry Caray was a Falstaff man. Here Caray poses with the Falstaff mascot right outside Comiskey Park. Fans drank plenty of Falstaff during the early to mid-1970s. They had to. They needed something to kill the pain after seeing the White Sox playoff hopes dashed year after year. (Leo Bauby collection.)

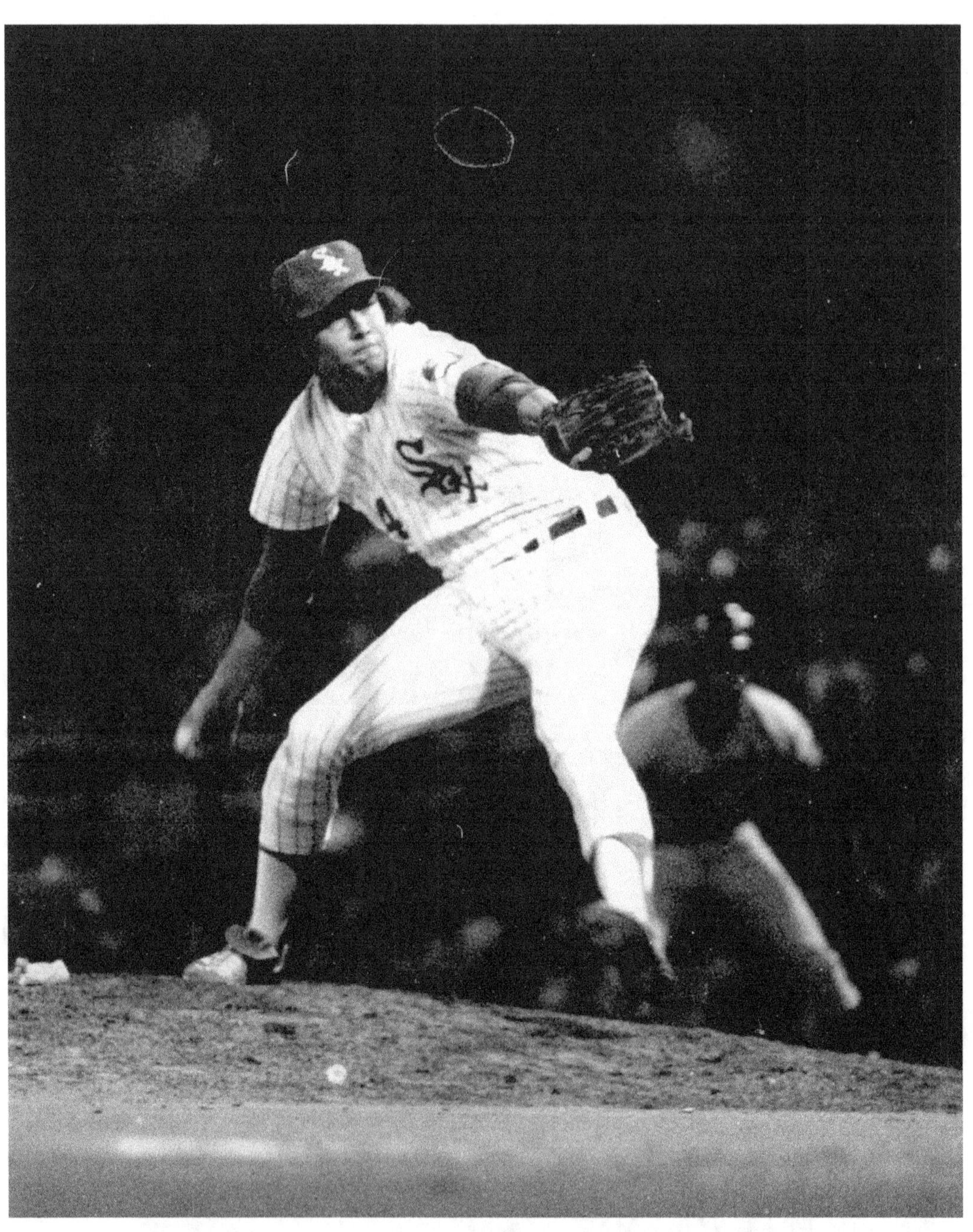

Rich Gossage is seen here in 1975 when he won American League Fireman of the Year Honors. He was a big man with a big windup. Gossage, unlike many of today's relievers, didn't wait until the last inning to enter game. Many times Gossage was there in the eighth or even the seventh. Can you imagine what a modern day pitcher would think if he knew he didn't have to get past the seventh before turning the ball over to Rich Gossage? (Leo Bauby collection.)

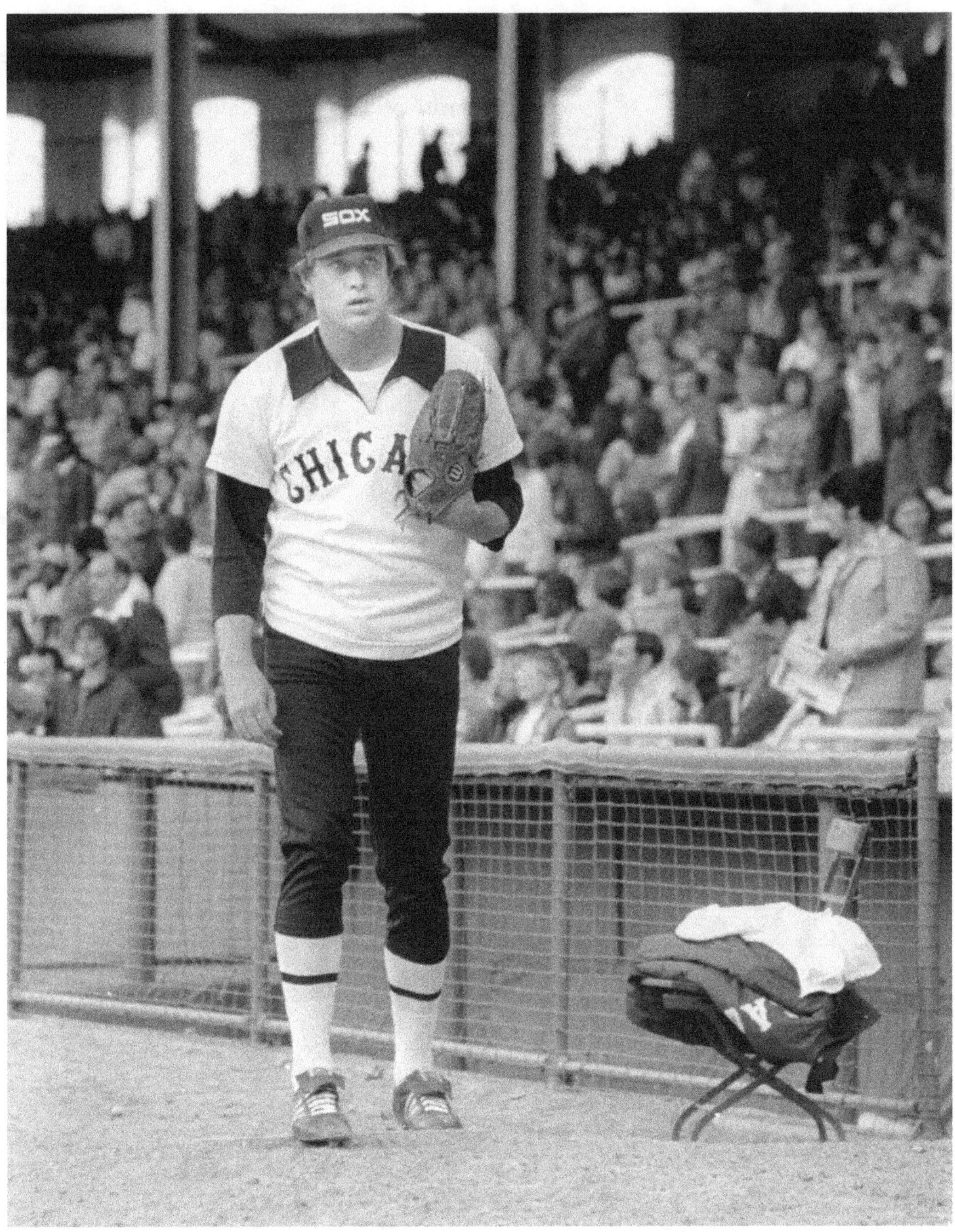

Rich Gossage tries to warm up in 1976. According to the Goose, warming up before game time in 1976 was next to impossible with the pre-game distractions caused by Bill Veeck promotions. When Gossage lashed out after being traded in December 1976, Veeck responded by saying Gossage was a very nice, young man. The nice young man had some great years for some other teams. (Leo Bauby collection.)

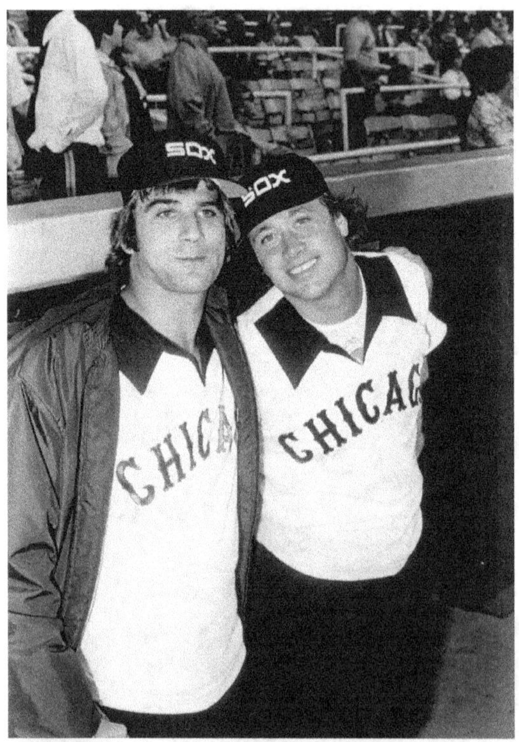

Two young pitchers that got away—Pete Vuckovich (left), who had some great years with Milwaukee, including a Cy Young year in 1982, and "Goose" Gossage. (Leo Bauby collection.)

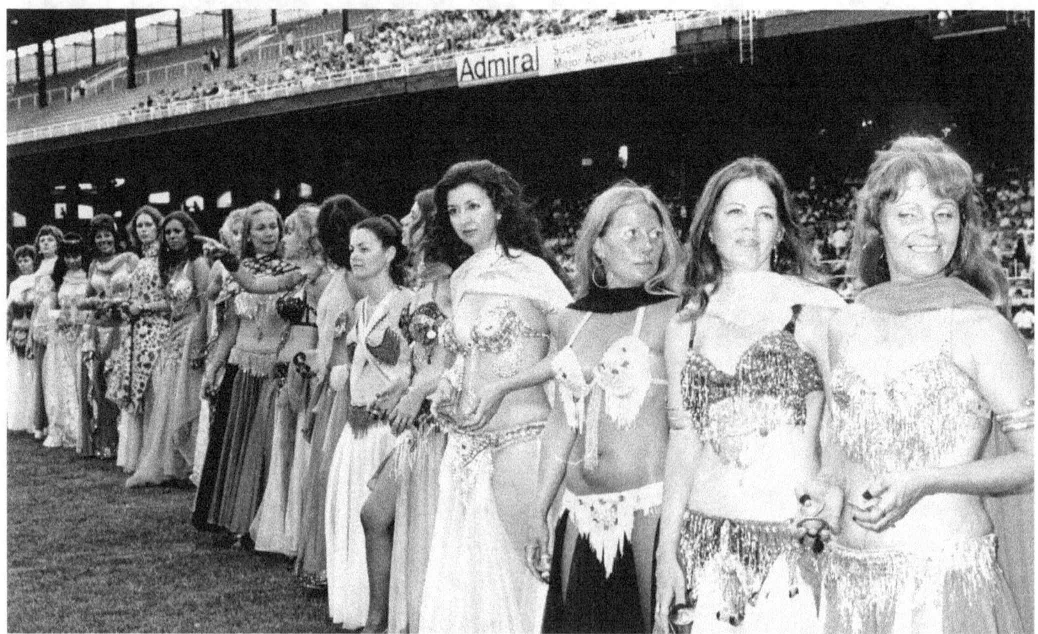

Are these the dancing girls Rich Gossage was talking about? What would have happened if one of them stepped in the box to face the Goose? Would she get a ball in the ear? (Leo Bauby collection.)

3

April to May

Proving Them Wrong

Very few White Sox fans had high expectations when the 1977 season began. It had been 10 years since the 1967 team had blown an excellent chance at the World Series by dropping the last five games of the season in the middle of a crazy four-team pennant race. In the next decade, the South Siders only contended in a serious manner once, in 1972. Even then they had a nearly impossible task of overcoming one of the best teams of the 1970s, the Oakland A's. Free agency had begun and big name players were going every direction but Chicago. White Sox fans—more accustomed to agony of defeat than the thrill of victory—expected 90 losses rather than 90 wins.

Very few in the media had any expectations for this team, either. Of the seven *Chicago Tribune* sportswriters making baseball predictions, no one picked the Sox higher than fourth. Rick Talley and Robert Markus even placed the Sox last, below the expansion Seattle Mariners. That wasn't much of a stretch considering that the 1969 White Sox actually ended one rung below the first year Kansas City Royals.

"Unhappy ballplayers, unsigned ballplayers, not enough ballplayers," Bob Verdi wrote, joining to chorus of Talley and Markus. "This will be a depressing summer for the White Sox."

Verdi picked the Sox to land in sixth, writing that the best thing the club had going for them was the first year Mariners. Even Verdi had some doubts Chicago could finish ahead of a team that had yet to play one major league game.

Across the street, longtime *Chicago Sun-Times* sportswriter, Sox fan, and Veeck admirer Bill Gleason wrote a desperate column about what he considered a desperate team. Gleason quoted a depressed Sox fan who had a fistful of opening day tickets, but didn't want to go. The discouraged fan was tempted to eat the money and stay home, atypical for a baseball fan in the hope-filled spring. Gleason almost pleaded with Bill Veeck to do something. It didn't matter what that something was, just do it.

When asked in 2005 about this column, Gleason naturally didn't remember specifics. But the feeling of desperation was nothing new for the veteran sportswriter, and Gleason replied, "Why should I have felt any different in 1977 than in any other year?" Gleason's pre-season prediction had the Sox in fifth.

Peter Gammons, in his preview of the American League West in Sports Illustrated, wrote that Veeck was a great innovator and salesman. But Gammons also thought Veeck would need more than a new paint job of Comiskey Park and gimmicky promotions to have any success in 1977.

Basically, the honeymoon was over for Bill Veeck. He had succeeded in keeping the team in Chicago, but was now faced with a group of championship-starved and cynical fans. And from the fans' mood and the media's Armageddon type predictions, the expectations for a championship were surpassed by the dread of another forgettable, losing season.

Fans didn't need the media or a sense of history to despair about the prospects of the 1977 White Sox. At third base, they had a guy with a bad knee that hadn't played in a year. At shortstop—well, after trading Bucky Dent for Oscar Gamble, they had no one. The Sox had little idea who was going to fill that giant hole, and then decided on Alan Bannister, a guy with an injured arm. And to complete the left side of the field was Ralph Garr. Known as the "Roadrunner," the speedy Garr often kicked up infield dirt behind him as he tore around the bases. Garr had won the National League batting title with a .353 mark in 1974 but saw his 1975 average drop over 70 points. He got back to exactly .300 during his first season with the Sox in 1976, but still hadn't met a cutoff man he liked.

The starting pitching staff was okay in spots with still-developing Steve Stone and a young Francisco Barrios. Yet was anyone predicting a Cy Young Award coming to the South Side of Chicago? They weren't, unless they wore a straight jacket.

Then there was the unhappy Oscar Gamble. Having come up in the Cubs system, Gamble understandably looked forward to playing with the Yankees in 1977. New York had gone to the World Series in 1976 and looked like they would be making a return trip in 1977. But Gamble now found himself traded to the White Sox right before the season started, a team that hadn't been to a World Series in 18 years. The outfielder began making salary demands before he played one inning for his new ball club, threatening retirement if his pay didn't increase from $75,000 to $100,000. In 2005, Gamble explained that he wasn't as angry as he was caught off guard. He said he fully expected to be with the Yankees in 1977, and Chicago was now un-familiar territory to him. He took solace in the fact that good friend Ralph Garr was with the White Sox.

There was a host of other players in contract limbo or battling with the White Sox for more money. Speculation about a championship didn't seem to fit in the mix; it centered around the type of string and baling wire Veeck would use to keep the team together.

The White Sox were chosen to provide the first competition for the expansion Toronto Blue Jays. Fans who thought playing a first year team, from a hockey town no less, was an easy way to start the year with a victory, but were sadly mistaken.

In a game where snow blurred the TV screen (Joe Goddard recalled Sox players squaring off for a touch football game and second baseman Jack Brohamer turning a pair of shin guards into make shift skis) the Sox left two runners on in the first, two in the second, three in the third, two in the fourth, two in the fifth, three in the sixth, two in the seventh, two in the eighth, and one in the ninth. The 19 stranded demonstrated a lack of clutch and opportunistic hitting and set a record for RBI futility for a single game. Chicago lost 9-5 despite—or maybe because—they had put 24 men on base. Of course it would have helped if they hadn't given up nine runs and 16 hits themselves.

The teams split the next two games, giving the Blue Jays their first ever series win.

With this dubious start and generous play to Toronto, the White Sox returned to Chicago for their home opener on April 12.

Bob Lemon took charge as manager in 1977 after working as pitching coach for the Yankees in 1976. Winner of 207 games as a pitcher for the Cleveland Indians, Lemon actually hit 37 career homers and had a career pinch-hitting average of .284 in an era long before the designated hitter. He won 20 games or more seven times and pitched a no-hitter against the Tigers on

June 30, 1948. His career ERA stood at 3.23, a mark many pitchers have a hard time achieving in a single season today. Lemon was elected to the Hall of Fame in 1976.

He looked more like the guy down the street than a big league skipper. With a portly body and an over sized nose, the middle aged Lemon could have easily passed for Sox fan on a barstool.

Bob Lemon's philosophy was simple: "The two most important things in life are good friends and a strong bullpen." With the departure of Gossage and Forster, it was doubtful that the Sox had a strong bullpen. Whether he made friends of Sox fans depended on the team record. Another 90-plus loss season would have the Sox fans calling for Barrabas.

"Bob had been a great player who didn't take himself seriously," according to Bill Gleason. "He enjoyed a drink, and enjoyed the give and take with the media. He was a free spirit which was one reason he appealed to Veeck."

His sense of humor was another good trait which Gleason felt Lemon would need "considering the team Veeck had given him."

"We were on a roll most of the year," third baseman Eric Soderholm later recalled. "Bob didn't have to do much. He just filled out the lineup card and let us play. And that's not a bad thing. Sometimes that's what you need."

Though optimism wasn't in full bloom with some fans threatening to eat their tickets, attendance exceeded 34,000 for the April 12 home opener against the Boston Red Sox. The White Sox prevailed 5-2 on the strength of a single, double, triple, and two RBIs from Jorge Orta. Chicago had scored one in the first and four in the second while pitchers Ken Brett and Dave Hamilton held off a potent Boston offense.

Although the White Sox home opening win had not quite dispelled the cloud that hung over the club, the team had one thing going for them: Richie Zisk.

Zisk, a Brooklyn native, came up through the Pirates organization. He had been developing into a power hitter from 1971 through 1976. His free agency status after the 1977 season had to be one factor in trading him to Chicago.

Zisk homered in his first at bat for the Sox with a 430 foot blast to straight away center and added three more hits in the otherwise forgettable game against Toronto. Two weeks later he clubbed two off Oakland A's left hander Vida Blue and drove in four in an 8-2 Sox win. Amazingly, the Sox were in first place at this point. Zisk became only the second hitter to hit two homers in a game off the flame throwing Blue.

Zisk hit a solo shot in Detroit four days later in a game in which the Sox overcame a 6-1 deficit and eventually won 10-7 in 14 innings. The right fielder finished the month of April with seven homers, and the Sox record was a decent 10-8.

"Chicago, like many of the great American cities," recalls Sox fan Gerry Bilek, "has its roots with great immigrations of the 1890s through the 1920s. Eventually, Chicago contained the second largest Polish population, second only to Warsaw. Being of Polish heritage, I certainly felt a connection to the slugging outfielder whose hard-nosed approach to the game appealed to the working class ethnic population of Chicago."

Ethnic pride and respect for hard work may have endeared Zisk to Sox fans. Unlike Oscar Gamble who didn't appear happy to leave New York, Zisk was content to be in Chicago and was willing to sign a new contract. But the Sox were cold to the idea, apparently almost resigned to the fact that Zisk would be leaving once he became a free agent at the end of the season.

Chicago Tribune reporter Bill Jauss was with the team on its initial visit to play the first year Seattle Mariners. The Kingdome, a matchbox of a domed stadium, was the new home to the expansion American League franchise. Jauss remembers Zisk being mesmerized by the hitters' ballpark.

"Wow," Jauss remembers Zisk saying as he gazed about the indoor park, "this is Wrigley Field with a dome on it."

Joe Goddard remembers Zisk striking out to end a game and just standing at the plate for a long time while everyone else left the field. The *Chicago Sun-Times* reporter later asked Zisk over drinks why he had stayed so long in the batter's box.

"He, [umpire Jerry Neudecker] didn't say 'strike three,'" Zisk told Goddard. "He didn't say 'you're out.' He told me to take a f—— hike."

So upset by what he considered unprofessional behavior by Neudecker, Zisk wanted to register a complaint about the umpire to the American League office. Goddard helped him craft his complaint, and Zisk was ready to mail the document to the American League main office. But before doing so, Zisk showed the letter to Bob Lemon and the White Sox manager emphatically told Zisk not to make any waves.

"Don't mail that," Lemon reportedly said. "Jesus Christ, if you do that every umpire is going to tell you to take a f—— hike." (Maybe it was a good thing there was no e-mail in those days.)

Goddard also recalls Zisk as a very thoughtful and intelligent man who may have been a little paranoid. In the late 1970s, a Soviet space satellite fell out of orbit and was on its way down to earth for a crash landing. Goddard said that Zisk feared the satellite would fall on his head.

"It landed somewhere in Australia," Goddard says. "When I called him to kid him about it, he said, 'that's not funny, that's not funny.'"

As Zisk became accustomed to American League stadiums or ceased fighting with umpires and recovered from his fear of falling objects from outer space, the right fielder began to enjoy playing in the American League. The White Sox traveled to Cleveland for a three game series on the weekend of May 6, 7, and 8. After winning the first game of the series 7-5, the Sox were set to face Wayne Garland, the Indians ace in the Saturday afternoon game.

Garland had a great year in 1976, going 15-3 for Baltimore with a 2.67 ERA. But the right-hander, having signed a then-astounding $2.3 million 10-year contract—felt the sting of a bitter fan backlash after getting off to an 0-3 start. During his last appearance, he was treated to an ovation of boos. A good start against the White Sox would help Garland regain his old confidence and at least get Indian fans off his back.

Garland actually was pitching fairly well as the game was tied at 2 in the eighth. Alan Bannister had led off with a single. The Sox were pretty much a station-to-station team in 1977, but this was a tough game against a tough pitcher. Zisk was up next and manager Bob Lemon called for a hit and run, a Sox rarity in 1977. Just trying to make contact, Zisk took a cut at a high fast ball that he normally would have taken for a ball. His drive went to straight away center. Indian outfielder Rick Manning drifted back but stopped just short of the wall and watched as Zisk's long fly cleared the center field fence by plenty, giving the Sox a 4-2 lead and an eventual 5-2 victory. The bargain basement Sox had beaten the millionaire pitcher Garland who saw his record fall to 0-4.

"It wasn't even a strike," Zisk said about the home run pitch. "You're not supposed to hit a pitch like that. I just muscled it. What can I say?"

Sox fans warmed up to Zisk, and the love affair between fans and player had begun. By the end of May, Zisk had 14 home runs, equaling the output of 1976 team home run leaders Orta and Spencer. The right fielder was overwhelmed by the enthusiasm of the White Sox faithful. Although he had some good years in Pittsburgh, he felt that he had really just come into his own in 1977, especially with the long ball.

Expectations rose during the next two months in ways that few could ever have imagined. June and July 1977 have to go down as the most exciting time of the decade for the franchise. Those two giddy months also defined the legacy of the South Side Hit Men, and produced some of the most intense emotions ever experienced in team history.

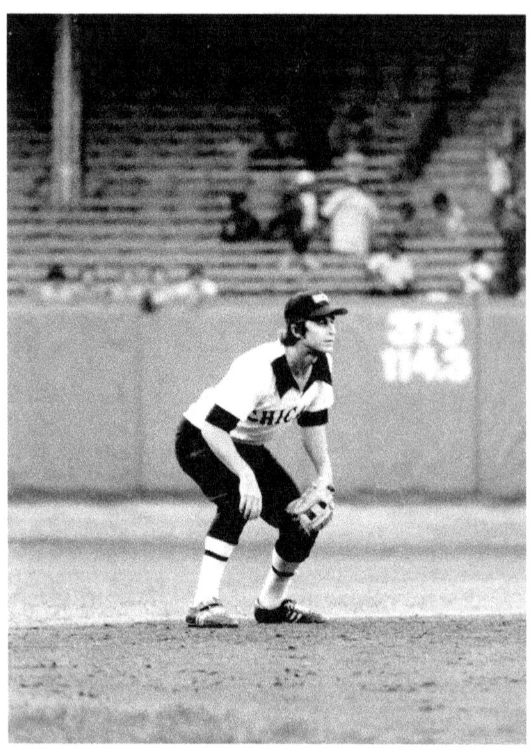

Alan Bannister is in at shortstop. Bannister was thrust into this role when the Sox traded Bucky Dent. He is often maligned for the defensive year he had in 1977. Who knows what he would have done if he had a decent arm? No doubt he would have committed less than 40 errors. (Leo Bauby collection.)

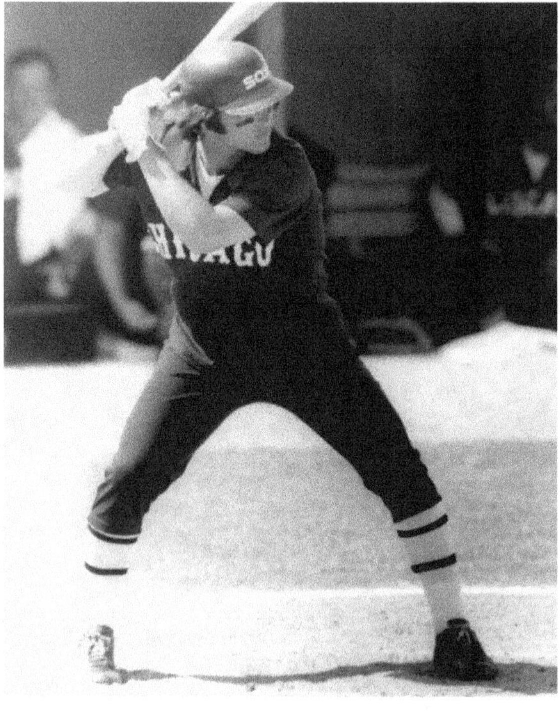

Bucky Dent stands at the plate during Spring Training in 1977. Rumors had surrounded Dent all during the pre-season. Trading him to the Yankees helped put the final touches on the formation the South Side Hitmen. The hole at shortstop would never really be filled until the arrival of Ozzie Guillen in 1985. (Leo Bauby collection.)

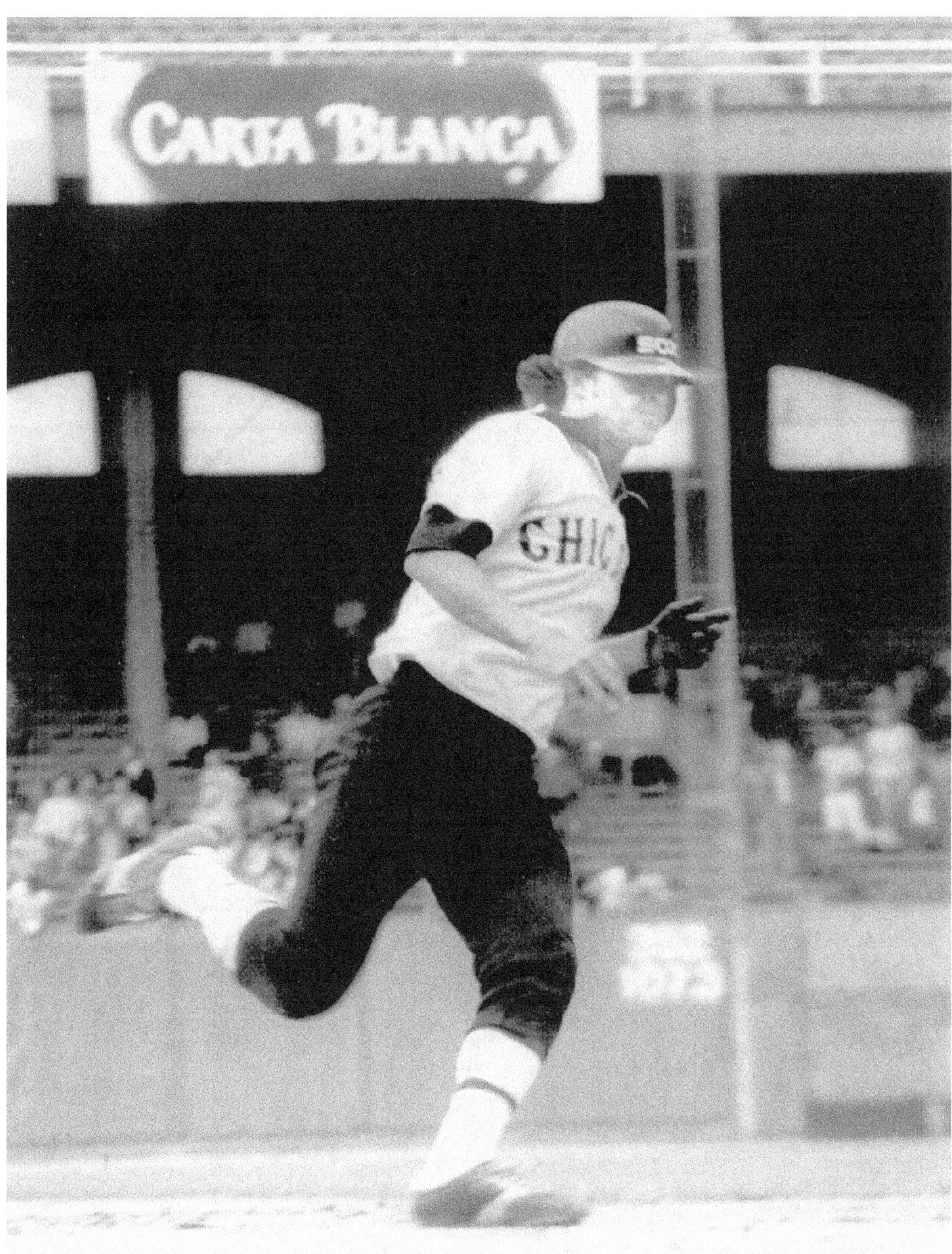

Alan Bannister rounds third. Defense was not Bannister's forte, but offense was. He scored 87 runs in 1977, providing a solid presence at the top of the lineup. He also hit a key homer against the Twins in a big July series. (Leo Bauby collection.)

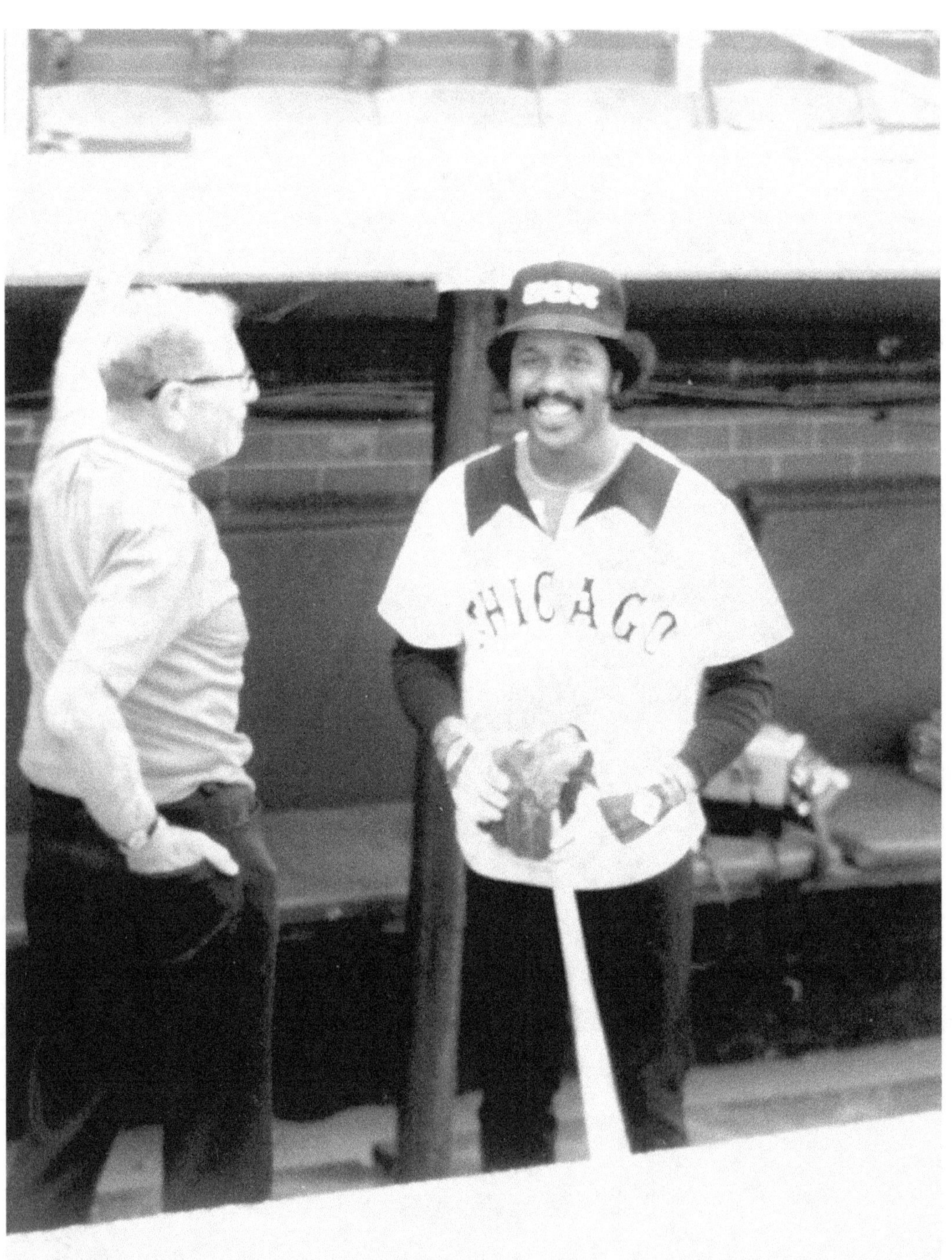

Bill Veeck (left) and Oscar Gamble—everything is all rosy. Veeck took a gamble on Gamble, at least for one season, and it was a short-term success. It is hard to imagine the South Side Hitmen without Gamble, who thought he was going the play the 1977 season with the New York Yankees. (Leo Bauby collection.)

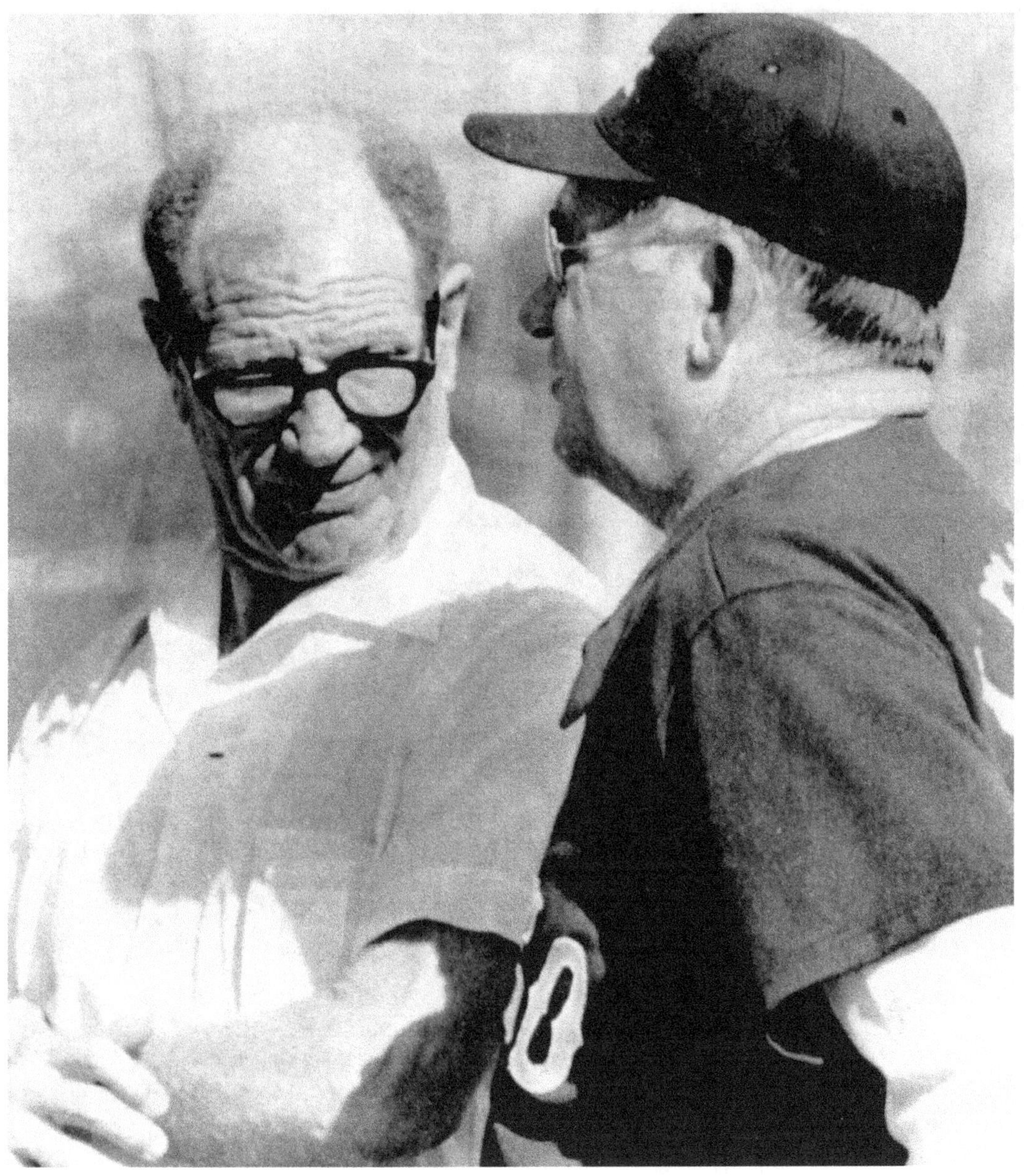

Pictured here is the brain trust of Bill Veeck and Bob Lemon. They were two free spirits who naturally attracted to each other. Lemon was probably just the right choice for the job. So many things worked in 1977. (Leo Bauby collection.)

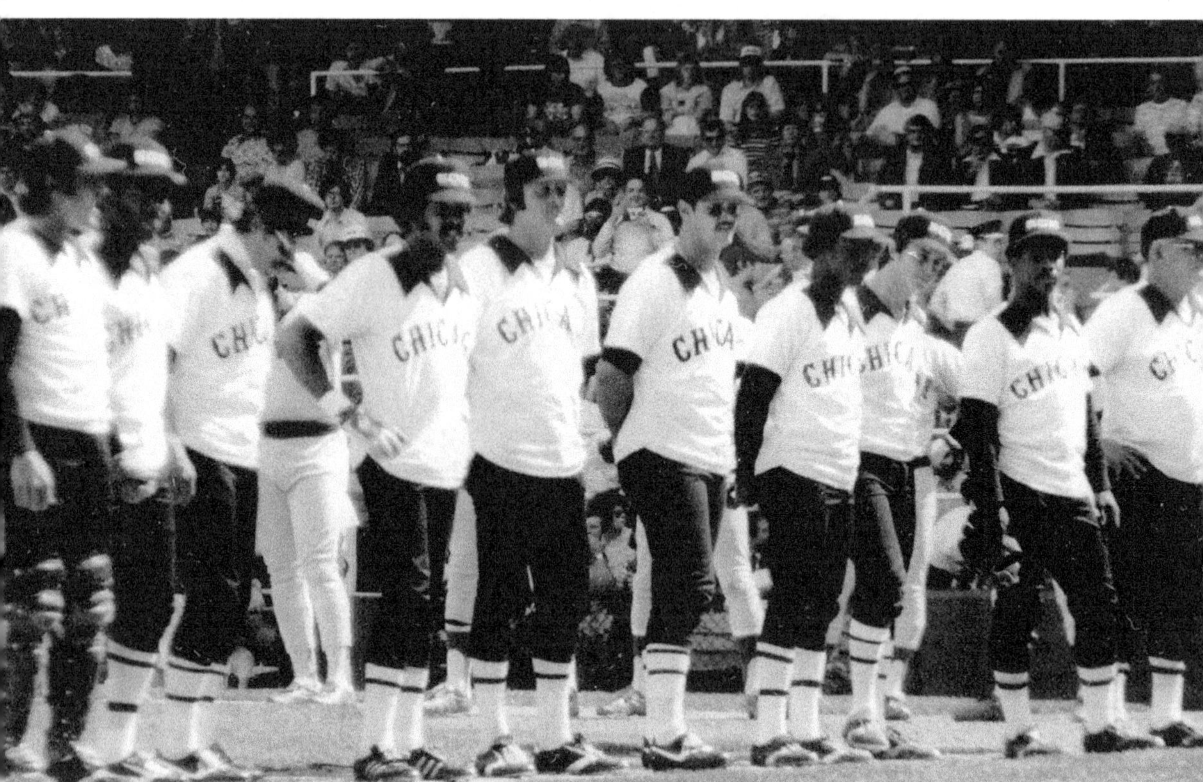

The Hitmen line up for opening day ceremonies at Comiskey Park. Did you ever see a more motley crew? The outcasts gave their fans a great and memorable season. What would have happened to the White Sox if they didn't have the lovable 1977 all-hit, no-field team? (Leo Bauby collection.)

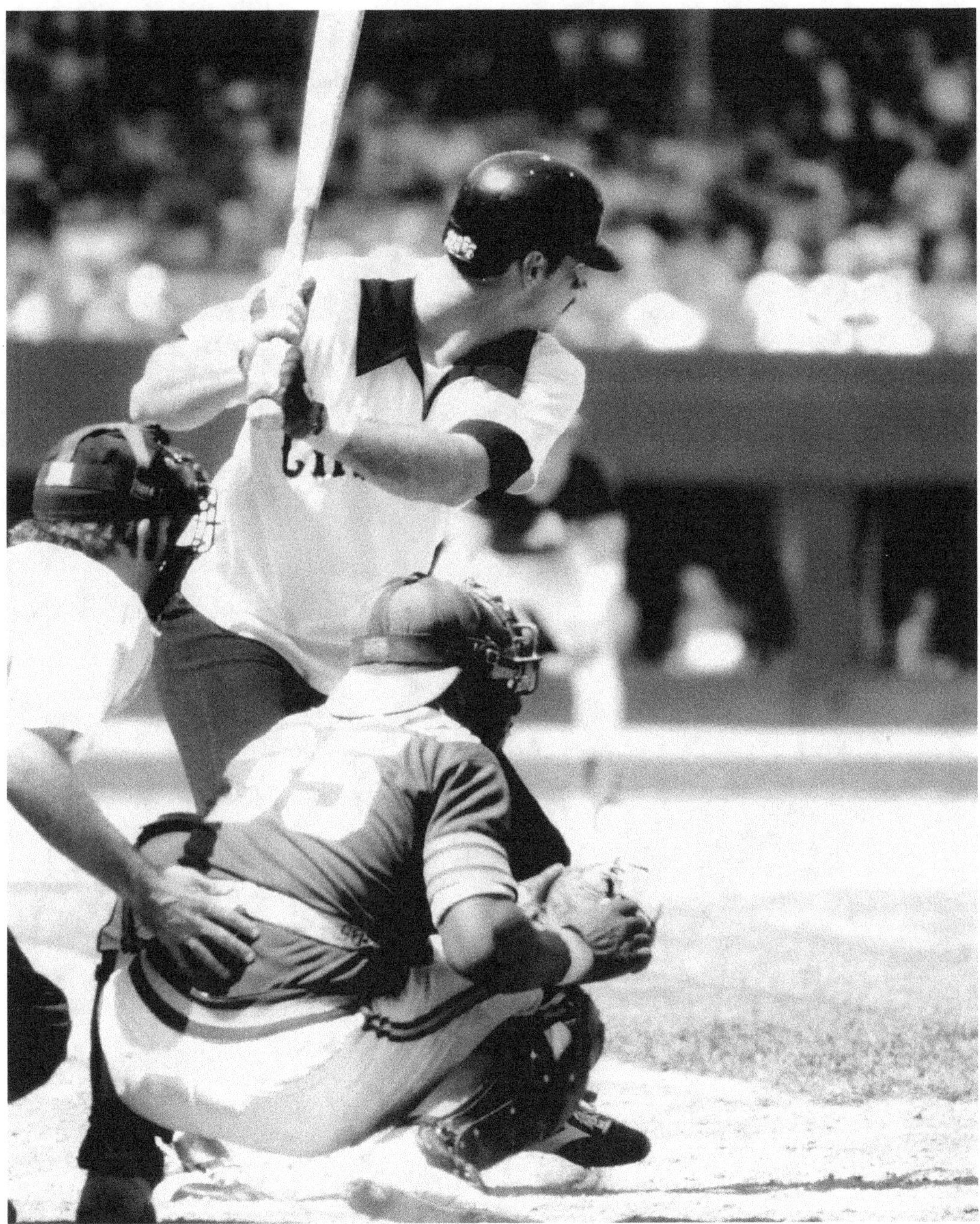

The early season hero was Richie Zisk. By the end of May he already had 14 homers and was bonding with Sox fans. He then picked up a roof shot after knocking a homer into the center field bleachers. Eventually fans held banners that read "Pitch at Risk to Rich Zisk." (Leo Bauby collection.)

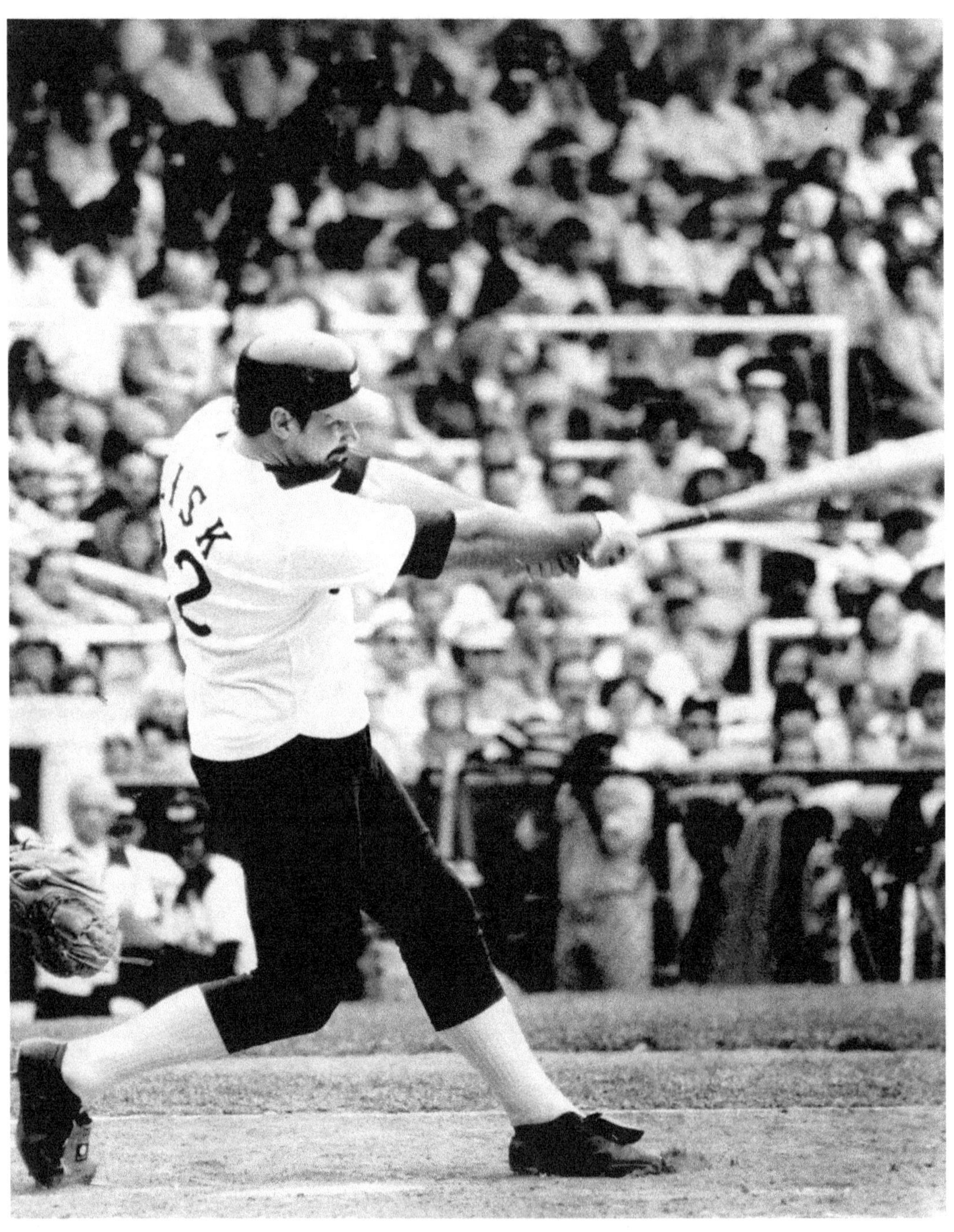

Richie Zisk follows through. His swing looks picture perfect, doesn't it? (Leo Bauby collection.)

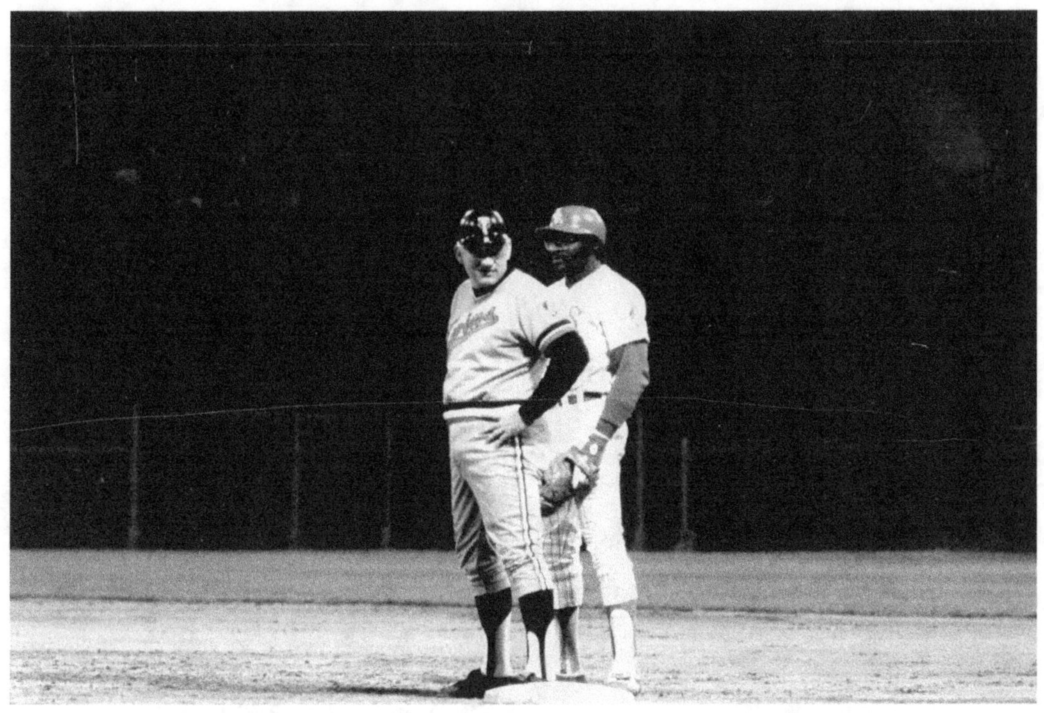

Dick Allen (right) poses with another feared, slugging first baseman, Harmon Killebrew. Killebrew was near the end of a career where he amassed 573 homers. Killebrew's compact swing had been something to watch. (Leo Bauby collection.)

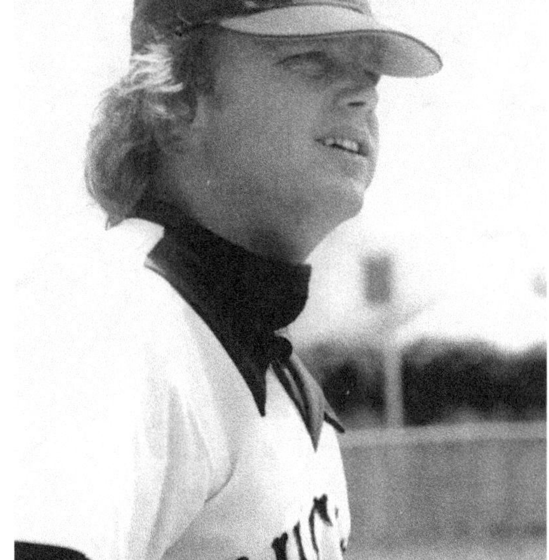

Dave Duncan is pictured during spring training 1977. Duncan would not make the club, but he would return as pitching coach during the early 1980s, which included the Winning Ugly year of 1983. (Leo Bauby collection.)

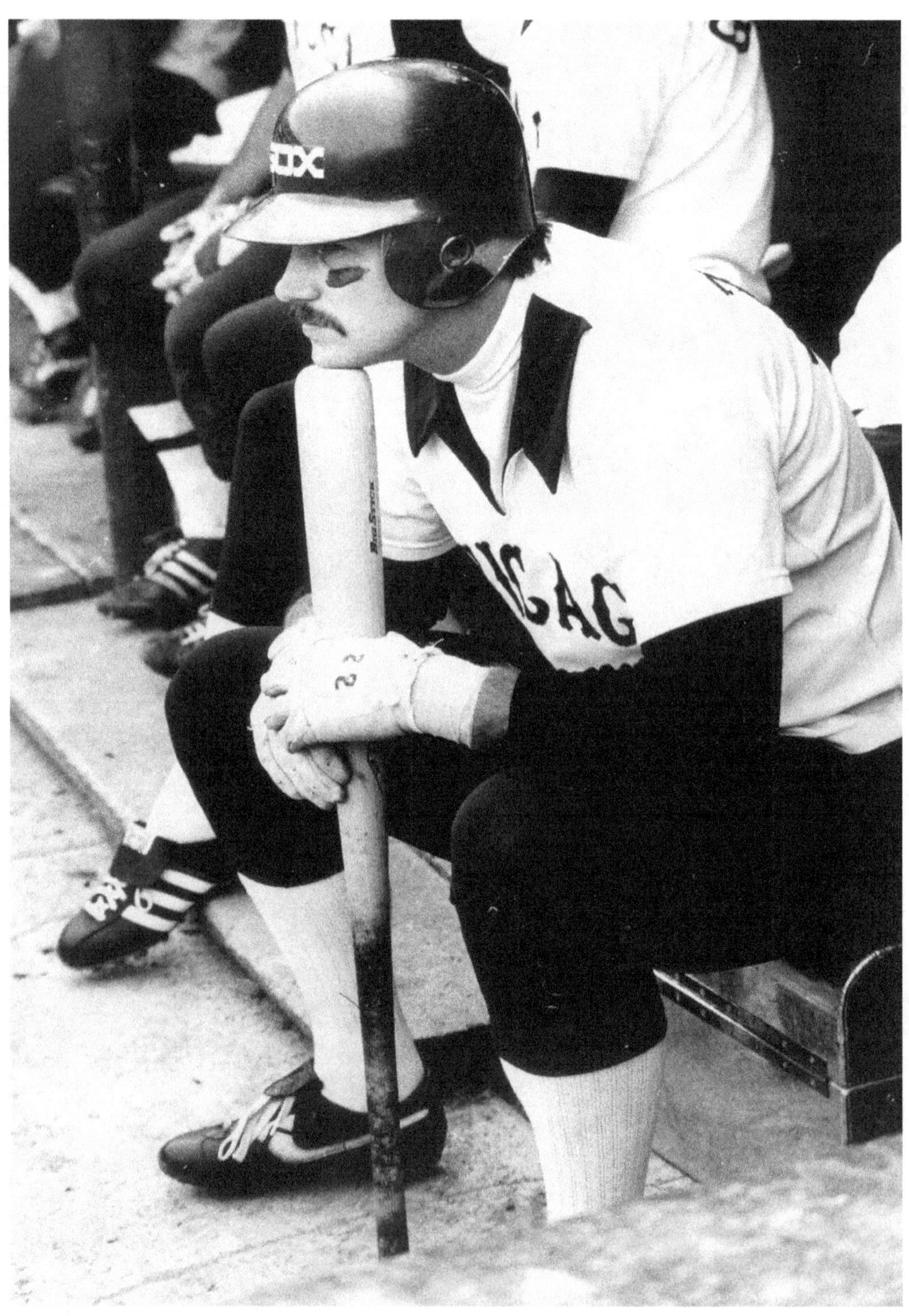

Richie Zisk is pictured in a pensive mood. Maybe he was thinking of another roof shot. (Leo Bauby collection.)

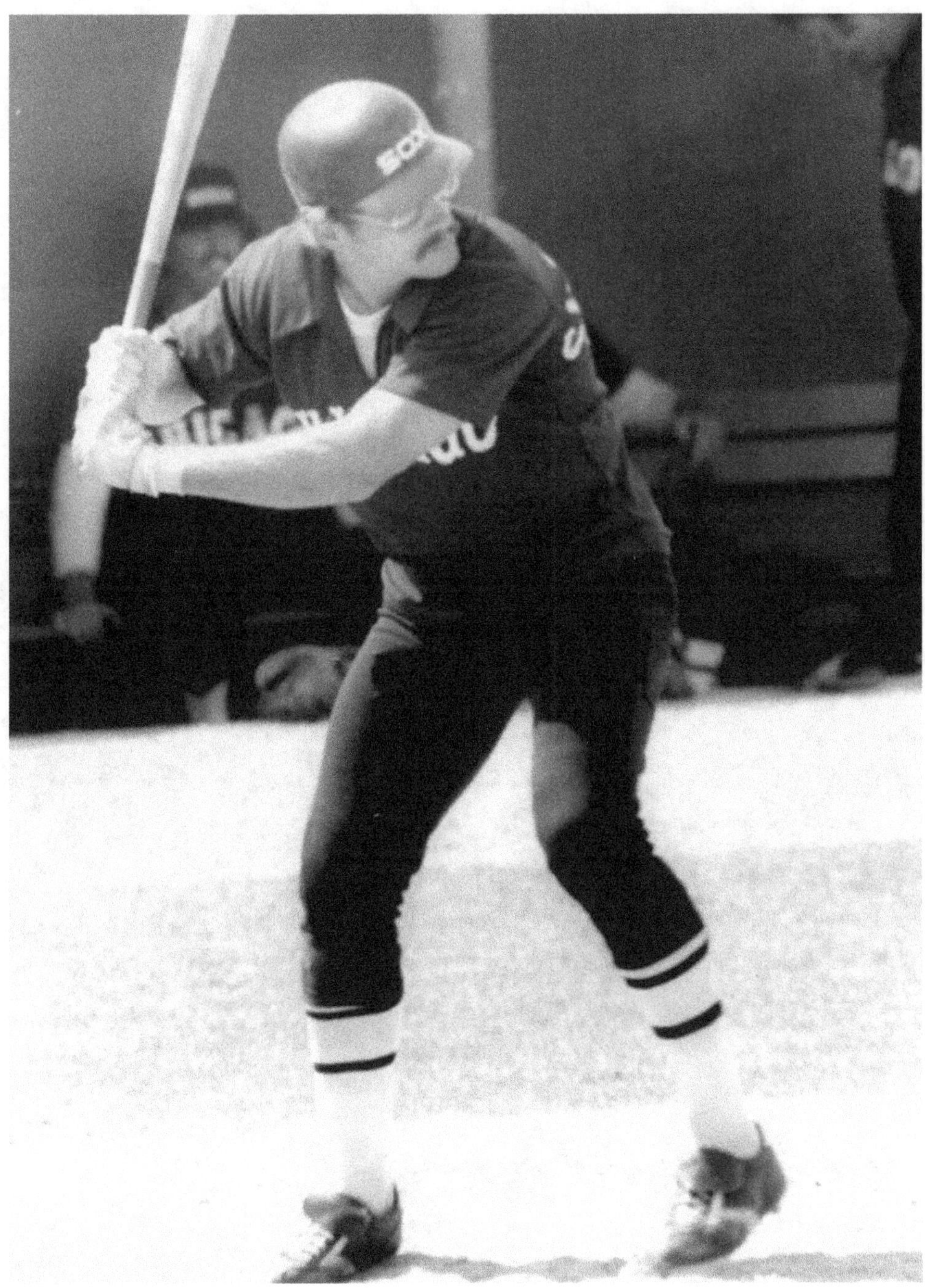

Eric Soderholm gets in shape during spring training. Soderholm was coming off a yearlong rehab stint for an injured knee. He felt he had a real chance to come back when he grounded deep in the hole at short and was thrown out at short. Making an out wasn't a great sign; running at full speed to first and slamming his foot down at the bag without getting hurt was the good sign. (Leo Bauby collection.)

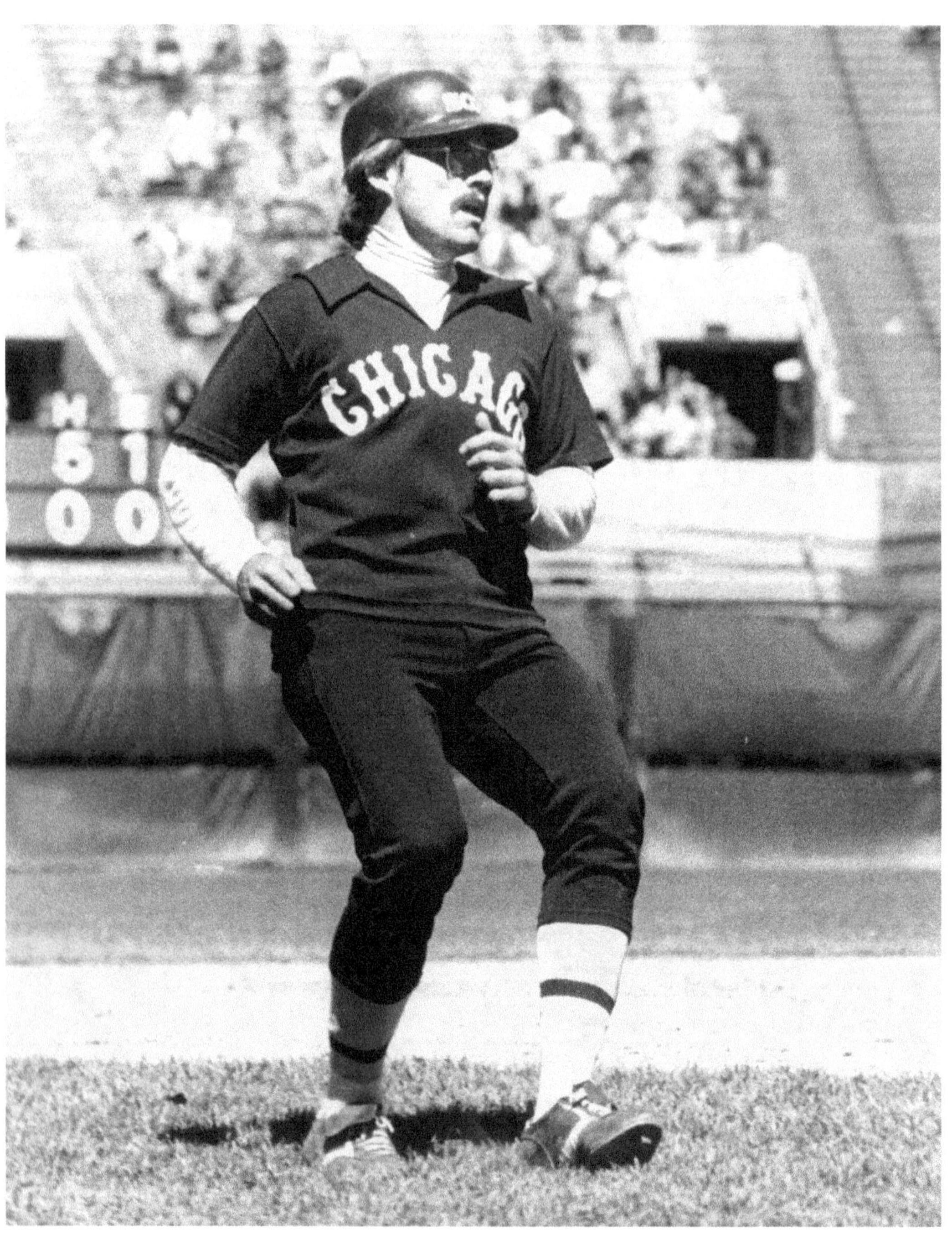

Soderholm is pictured during an early May series with the Cleveland Indians. The White Sox won two of three from the Tribe and slowly began to make believers out of their fans. (Leo Bauby collection.)

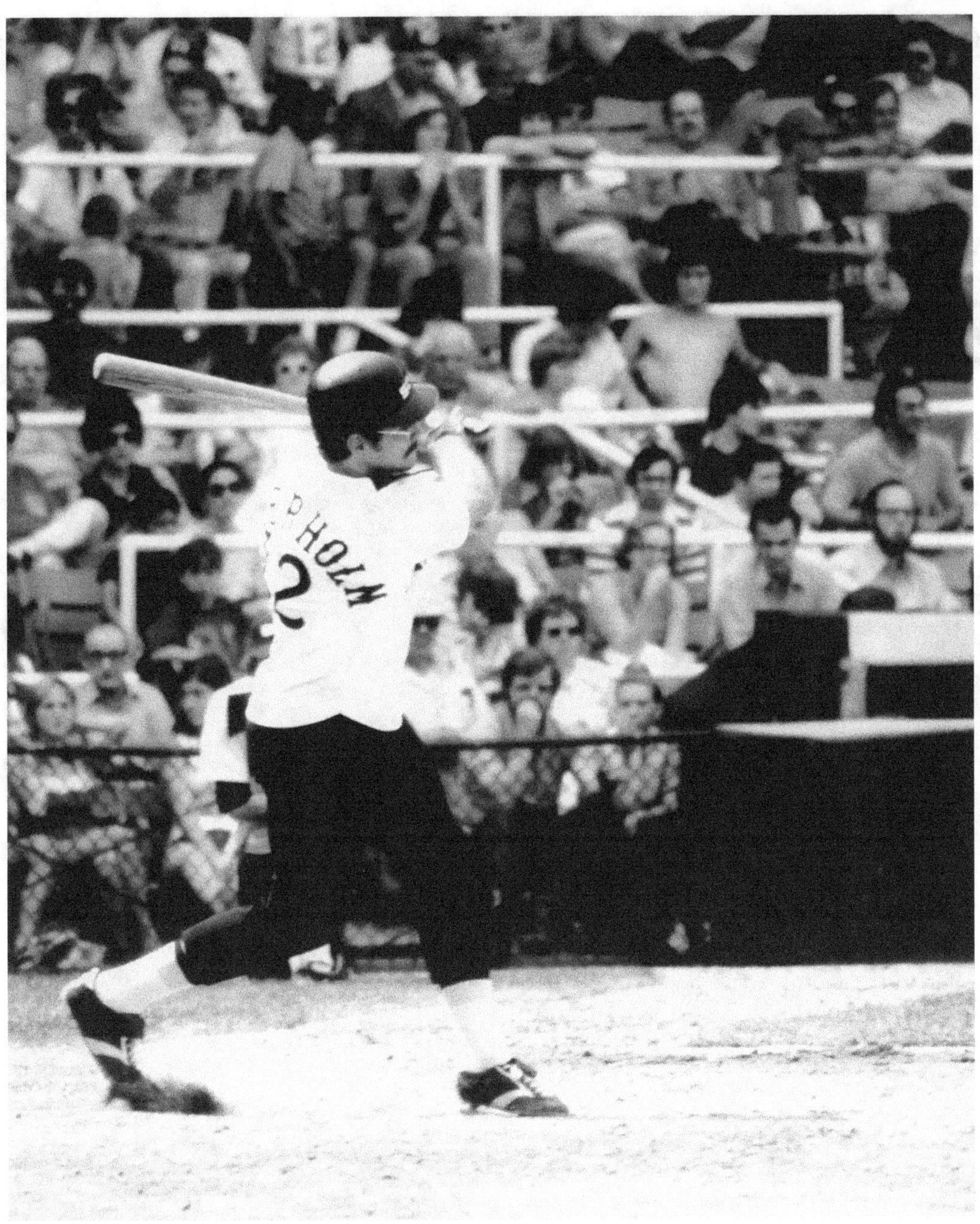

Soderholm takes a powerful swing for the fence. He hit 25 round trippers in 1977. (Leo Bauby collection.)

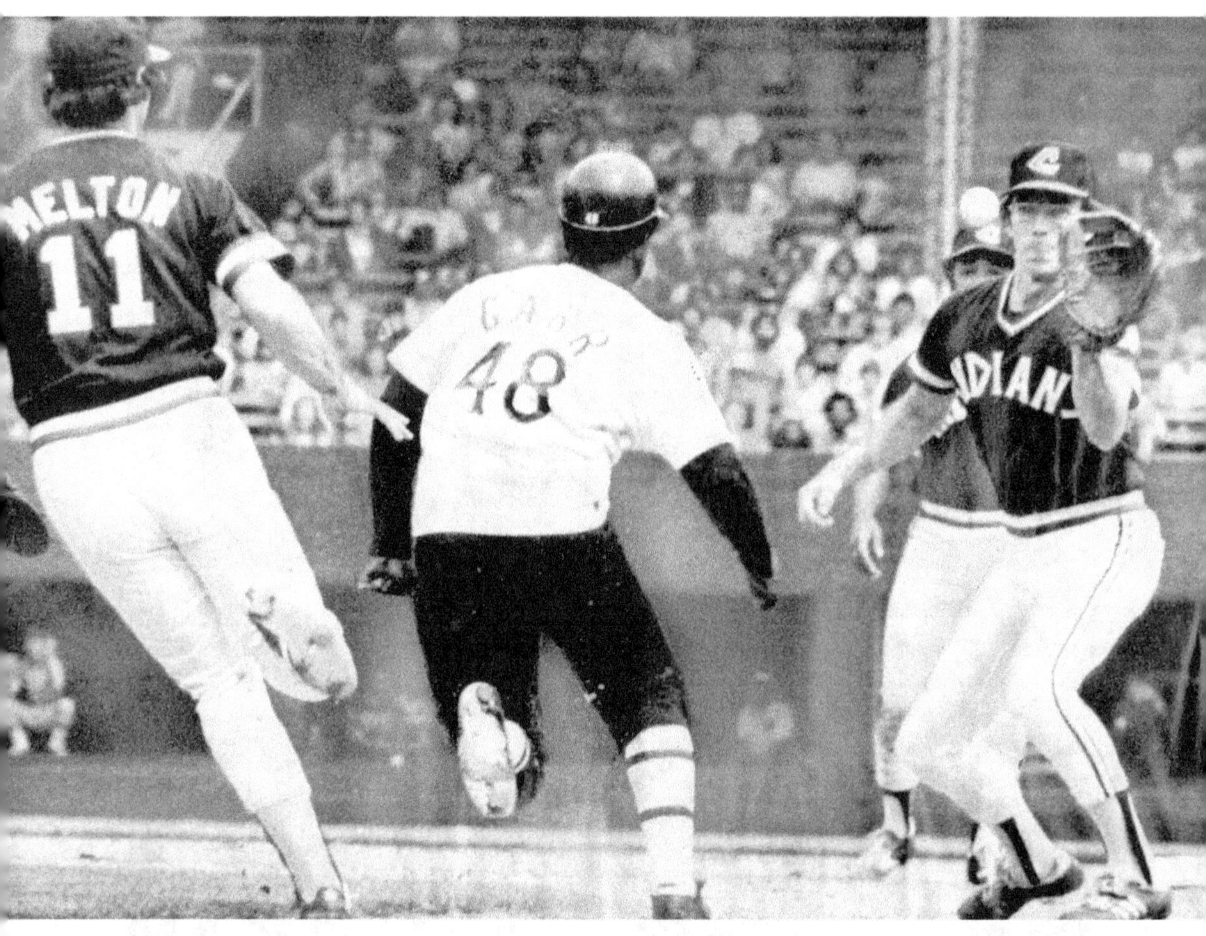

Ralph Garr is caught in a crowd of Indians. This was another Veeck brainstorm. Play a game in the morning and hopefully get done in time for brunch. The guy who was done in time for brunch was Jim Spencer who knocked in eight runs and had the day off after three at bats. The game was played on May 18, and had an 11:00 a.m. starting time. The White Sox won in a walk, 18-2. (Leo Bauby collection.)

4

The June Non-Swoon

The June Swoon. This Chicago baseball tradition breaks the hearts of both White Sox and Cub fans by derailing any chance of their favorite team playing into the later stages of October. Even though White Sox fans were pleasantly surprised by their team's decent start in April and May, attendance figures revealed they weren't believers quite yet. The fans had recent and painful memories reminding them not to fall in love with a .500 team masquerading as a contender. Both the 1973 and 1974 seasons had started off strong only to end in frustration.

The White Sox faced a good swoon test at home at the start of June 1977. They faced the Baltimore Orioles who had been to two World Series and had won two other division titles up to that point in the 1970s in a two game series. That was followed by a three game set against the Yankees, the defending American League champions.

The White Sox began by beating the usually unbeatable Jim Palmer. Taking advantage of the few scoring opportunities they had, the Sox scored two in the second and two in the seventh. They won 4-2 behind the complete game pitching of lefty Ken Brett. It was the last White Sox win for the lefty, as Brett was traded to California two weeks later.

Game two was more like the MO of the South Side Hitmen. The Sox scored one in the first, two in the second, and four in the third to run out to a 7-0 lead. Baltimore scored three in the seventh and one in the eighth to make it interesting, but the O's went down meekly in the ninth and the Sox had another win.

Although some fans began to believe in the Sox at this point, there were still plenty of doubters. For the two games against a good draw like Baltimore, only 18,125 showed.

After their defeat in the 1964 World Series to St. Louis, the Yankees lost their luster. But with their appearance in the 1976 series, they had returned to their old championship tradition. The era of Mantle, Maris, and Berra had transitioned to the late 1970s tradition of Jackson, Munson, and Randolph. Though each team was in second place in their division at the start of this three game series, the White Sox surprisingly had a slightly better record at 27-19 compared to the Yankees' 27-22.

The White Sox took game one 9-5. The difference was the seven runs they piled on in the fourth inning when they sent 12 men to the plate. New Yorker skipper Billy Martin was so flustered by the Sox onslaught that he was tossed out of the game as he came in to make a much-needed pitching change in the fourth inning.

After losing the next two games, the White Sox didn't appear to have made any statements in the series by losing two of three at home. However, in addition to drawing nearly 90,000 for the three games, they began to show that no team could relax against them even with a big lead.

The Yankees had a seven run inning of their own in the second inning and ran out to a 7-0 lead in game two. With tough lefty Don Gullet on the mound, Yankee fans probably thought the game was a walk through the park.

As it turned out, it was a like a walk through crazy Central Park. The Sox clubbed three homers including Zisk's shot that went bouncing around on the Comiskey Park roof. By the ninth, the 7-0 Yankee advantage had dwindled to 8-6. Sparky Lyle, who later won that year's American League Cy Young Award, was on the mound to mop things up, and, for a moment, it looked routine. Jim Essian struck out and Brian Downing flied out. One more out and the Yankees had their win.

But it wasn't routine. Alan Bannister and Jorge Orta singled and suddenly the winning run was at the plate in the form of Richie Zisk. It was the same Richie Zisk who had a roof shot in the second inning. Zisk flied out to left and Yankees had to be relieved that the Hitmen hadn't clobbered them to death.

In the series finale, New York again scored early by getting one in the first, two in the second, and three in the third. Again, the Sox wouldn't let the Yankees run away with anything. When the Sox plated a run in the seventh, the Yankee advantage was down to 7-6. A Bucky Dent homer in the ninth gave New York some insurance. Lyle again had to come in the ninth in nail down another 8-6 victory. Yankee fans breathed a little easier with this ending even though Chet Lemon represented the tying run when he tapped back to the mound for the final out.

Yes, they lost two of three, but the Sox scored 21 and pounded out 36 hits in the series against a team that once again was a contender. The series was lost, but it was just the beginning of a hit-barraged summer.

Dreams of first place; June is way too early to begin fantasizing about the playoffs, especially if you are a Chicago baseball fan. But almost right smack dab in the middle of June, the White Sox had their fans fantasizing of the near impossible after recent seasons of disappointments and finishes nowhere near first place.

In a mid-month weekend series against the once powerful and now 90-pound weakling Oakland A's, the White Sox more resembled the mild mannered offense of 1967 than the South Side Hitmen. They actually handled the A's with solid starting pitching allowing them to win three low scoring games in the four game set.

The White Sox began their winning by scratching out runs in the second and sixth during a Saturday afternoon game on June 18. In the second, two of the team's best home run hitters helped manufacture a run. Richie Zisk walked and went to third on an opposite field single by Eric Soderholm. Zisk then came in on a sacrifice fly by shortstop Kevin Bell.

In the sixth, Ralph Garr led off with a single. The Roadrunner would have been picked off by A's lefty Vida Blue, but Blue threw the ball away. Garr advanced to second, and, one out later, scored on a Jorge Orta single to center. The Sox led 2-0.

The Sox still led 2-0 going into the eighth inning. Lefty Ken Kravec had shut down Oakland on two hits and started the inning by getting Jim Tyrone to strike out looking. Then the A's threatened as they picked up singles from Rodney Scott and Manny Sanguillen, with Scott going to third. Kravec needed a strike out to keep Scott at third and got one when he set Mitchell Page down.

Dick Allen represented the go-ahead run with two out, and Bob Lemon summoned closer Lerrin LaGrow. Sox fans no doubt feared that Allen could clout one of his trademark Comiskey Park homers, but the former Sox slugger grounded out to short. For all their bluster, the A's came up with nothing.

LaGrow set the A's down quietly in the ninth, striking out the last two. The White Sox had one of their rare 1977 shutouts (they had three that year) and the young Kravec had earned his second win of the season.

The old man of the staff, Wilbur Wood, was slated to start game one of the next day's doubleheader. From 1971 to 1975, Wood was more than just the ace of the Sox staff. Often pitching with two days rest, the left handed knuckleballer logged in 1,681 innings during those five seasons, had 99 complete games, and won 106. But his May 9 injury ruined his 1976 season, and he was still rehabbing when the 1977 season started. The Sox rotation included the inexperience of Kravec, Chris Knapp, and Francisco Barrios. The more seasoned Steve Stone was coming off an injury himself although he felt he was completely healed when the season began. If the White Sox were actually going to contend, they needed iron man Wilbur Wood who had held up the staff during early and mid-1970s.

Wood looked like his old dominating self against the A's. In an eight-inning plus stint, he gave up one run on seven hits. He got a break in the fifth when Oakland's Earl Williams apparently had scored on a sacrifice fly by Rob Piccolo. But the Sox appealed, with Soderholm saying that Williams had left too soon. The third base umpire agreed, and instead of going ahead, Oakland saw its rally stifled when the embarrassed Williams was called out.

Very much unlike themselves, the Sox did next to nothing offensively. Except for Lamar Johnson, no one in the Sox lineup picked up a hit. Johnson, a multi-talented guy who sang the national anthem before the doubleheader, slammed two homers and a double. When closer LaGrow again set the A's down in the ninth after Wood walked the leadoff hitter, Chicago won another 1967 type nail-biter, 2-1.

"If Johnson sings the national anthem Monday night [the next date for the two teams], we're going to pitch around him," A's manager Bobby Winkles said.

Fan Mark Liptak had attended a Comiskey Park game a month earlier. Sitting in the first row of the box seats down the third baseline, Liptak picked up something coming from the dugout.

"I heard someone singing," Liptak recalls, "nothing fancy, just a few bars. It was Lamar Johnson. I think the Sox lost 3-2 or 4-3, something like that. Johnson, if memory serves, belted a home run that day, I want to say in the eighth inning."

Liptak's almost 30 year-old memory is pretty good. The White Sox lost 4-3, and Johnson hit a solo homer in the eighth.

Johnson had been hitting .300 in the White Sox farm system for several years but had a hard time breaking into the major league club because of Dick Allen and then Jim Spencer. In fact, Spencer would have been the more natural choice for this game against the righty Mike Norris, but he was injured. Johnson got more chances in 1977 and ended up having his best year home run-wise.

Yet the real story was Wood. It had to be frustrating for Wood to sit on the sidelines after starting 40 plus games for five straight years. On this day, he assisted his team when a tough pitcher kept them from knocking the ball around the park. In doing so, he picked up his first win in over 13 months.

"The big thing for us today was Wilbur's performance," Bob Lemon said. "I told Wilbur he pitched nine innings as far as I was concerned—with all those boots behind him." (The Sox committed three errors in a game they could have easily lost.)

In game two, a young pitcher stepped up for the Sox. Francisco Barrios had psyched himself up by talking to the ball during his no-hitter with John "Blue Moon" Odom to during his 1976 rookie year. His win that day wasn't as dramatic but just as effective. Going the distance and having a little more offensive support, Barrios threw a seven-hitter and won 5-1.

The doubleheader sweep was sweet, but it wasn't your ordinary sweep. Comiskey Park wasn't over-flowing, but the crowd of 24,161 more than appreciated the Sox that day. The old stadium began to rock as the White Sox vaulted into first place. Minnesota had been in first place since April 27.

First place. No, division titles are not won in June. Yet, very few expected the White Sox to be anywhere near first place any time after spring. Just who were these guys?

The suddenly front running White Sox traveled to Minnesota the next weekend. In the three game set, the Hitmen came alive again as they scored 26 runs on 41 hits, knocking out nine home runs. But they managed only one win, and that came on the heels of the only good pitching they had in the series. Chris Knapp threw a complete game in an 8-1 victory. In the two Chicago losses, Sox pitchers got lit up for 26 runs on 28 hits. Even the Hitmen couldn't overcome that.

The ugliest game of all was the last game of the series on June 26. The Twins scored 15 runs in the first four innings and never worried about losing. Steve Stone couldn't last past the second inning giving up eight runs on six hits. Minnesota scored six in the second, sending 10 men to the plate. They added four in the third and three in the fourth.

The White Sox had a six run rally in the third when they hit two of their four homers for the day. However, the Twins scored in every inning except the fifth and sixth, and won the game rather easily, 19-12.

The Minnesota series exposed the Sox somewhat as a one-dimensional team. And, even with the excitement of the doubleheader sweep of Oakland a week earlier, the fans still didn't totally believe in the Sox even though the team was more entertaining than many preceding clubs. Other than the New York series and the Oakland Sunday doubleheader, the Sox didn't break the 20,000 mark in a June home game. Their 15-13 record for the month wasn't a June swoon but was far from awe-inspiring. Giving up 19 runs in a game wasn't inspirational, either.

But as the month came to an end, the White Sox were 40-32. This was a good but not great record. On the plus side, they were in second place, but one game behind again front-running Minnesota. Summer had officially arrived, and Minnesota was coming to Chicago for the first four games of July. When had Chicago last truly played a meaningful game this close to the All-Star break? It had been too long, and usually the Sox saw their division hopes torpedoed by some calamity. The Minnesota series would be a far, far different story, starting an incredible month that would be a highlight show of the entire 1977 season.

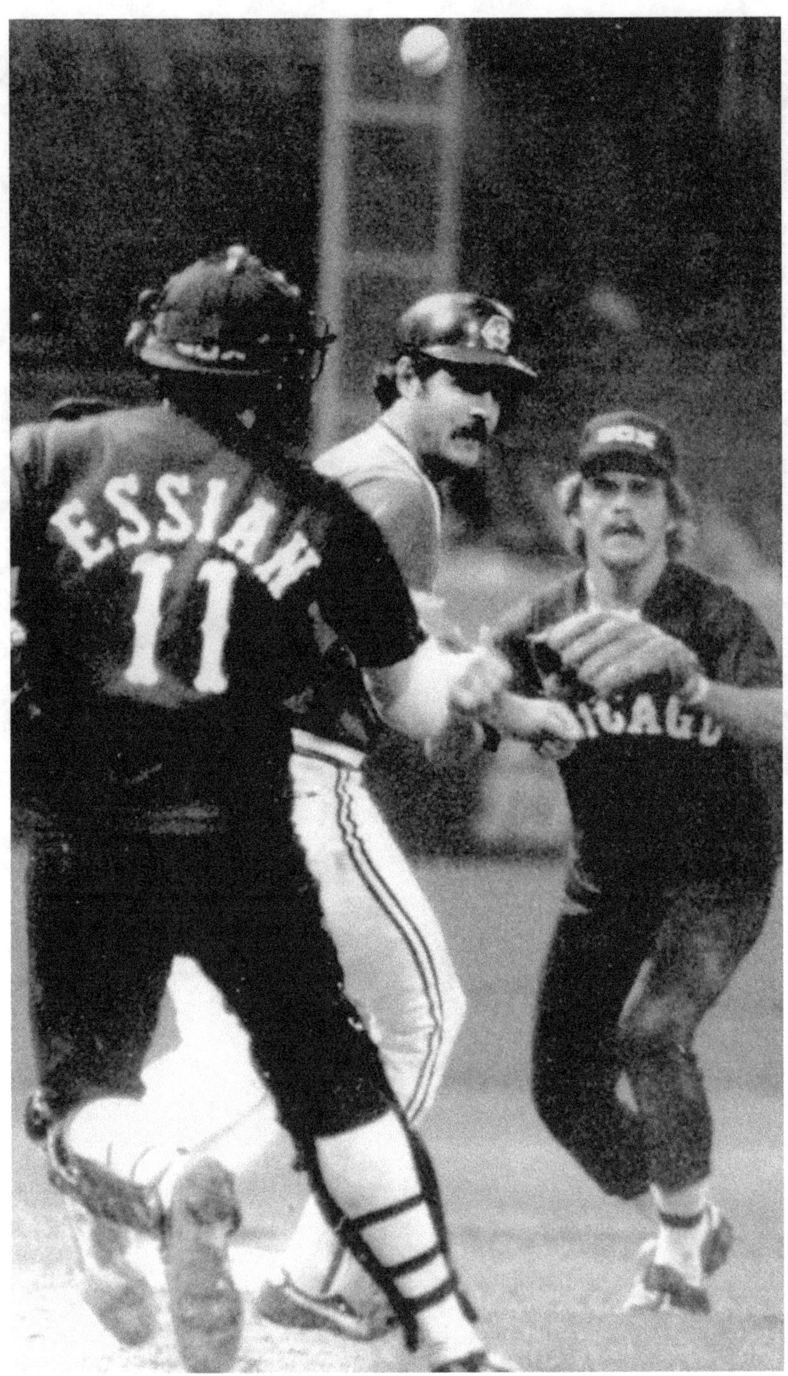

Caught in a rundown between Jim Essian and Eric Soderholm, former White Sox Bill Melton looks like he has nowhere to go. Ironically, Melton, who was booed loudly during the 1975 season, picked up his 1,000th career hit against the White Sox during the Hitmen season. (Leo Bauby collection.)

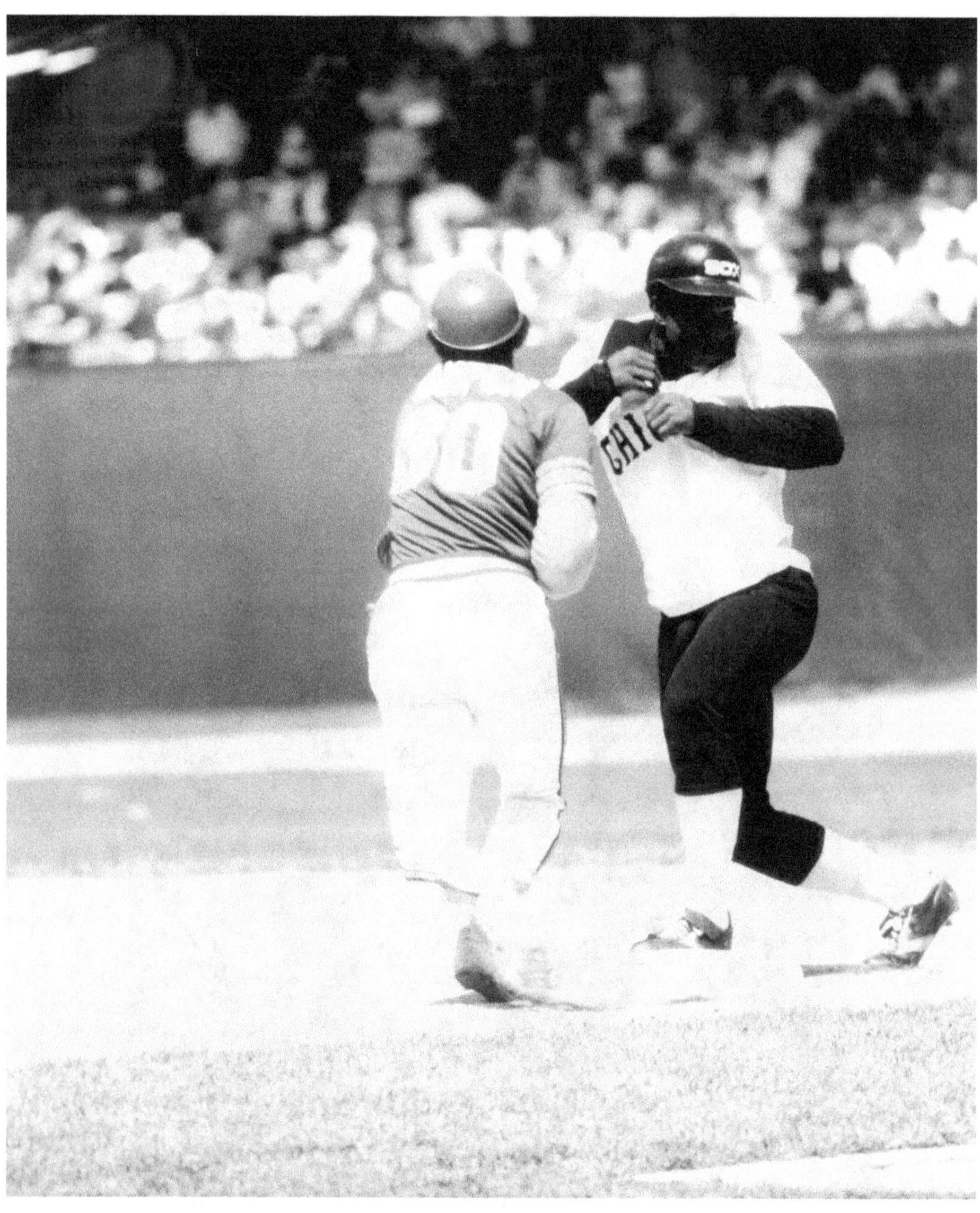

Pick off attempt goes awry as A's Dick Allen reaches around Ralph Garr. Garr scampered to second and eventually scored. It was one of the last games of Dick Allen's career, and was one of the first weekends that Sox fans began believing in the South Side Hitmen. (Leo Bauby collection.)

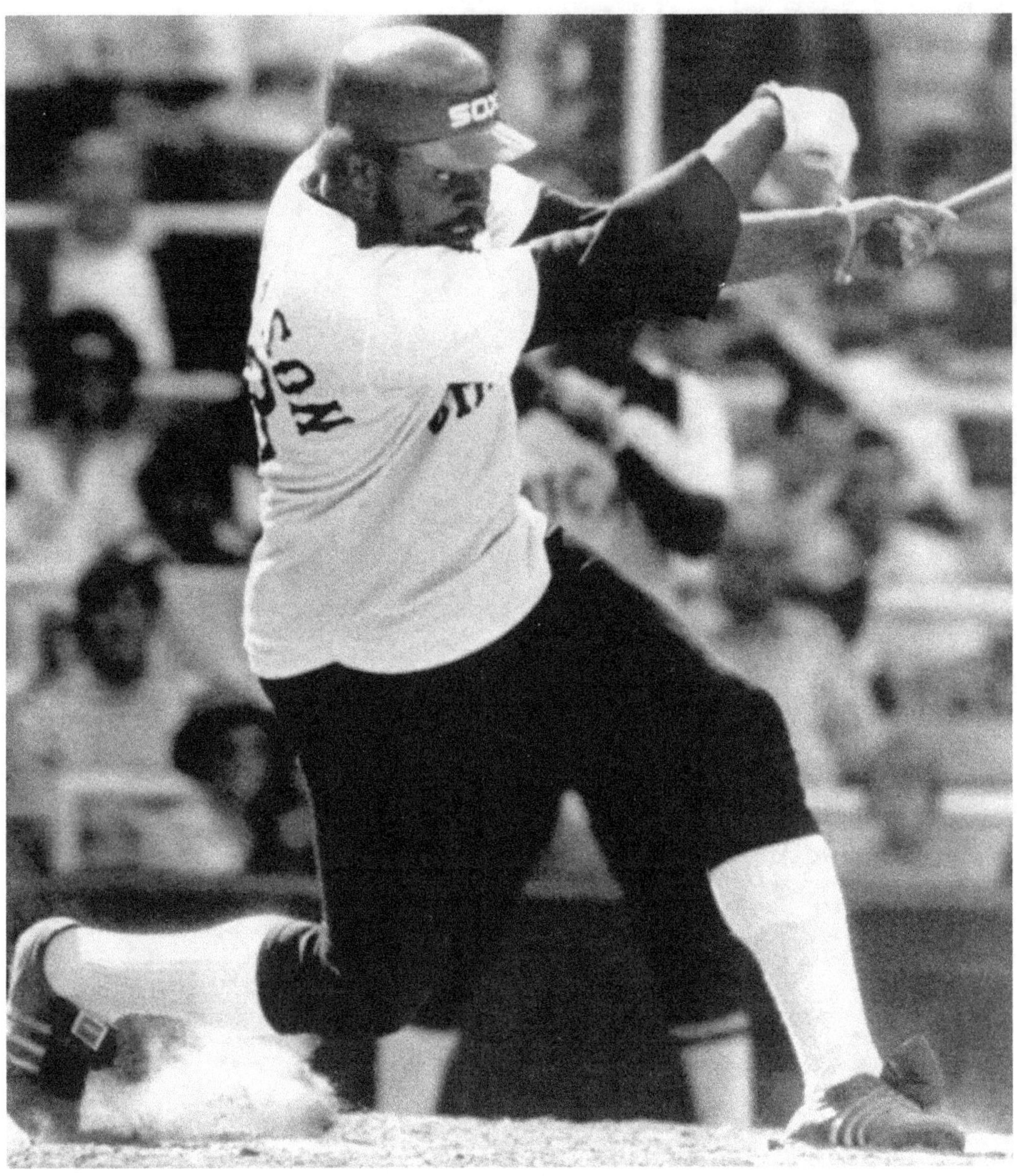

Lamar Johnson hits one of his two home runs against the A's in the first game of a doubleheader on June 19. His homers provided the winning margin in a 2-1 victory. The White Sox went in first place that day as they swept the A's. (Leo Bauby collection.)

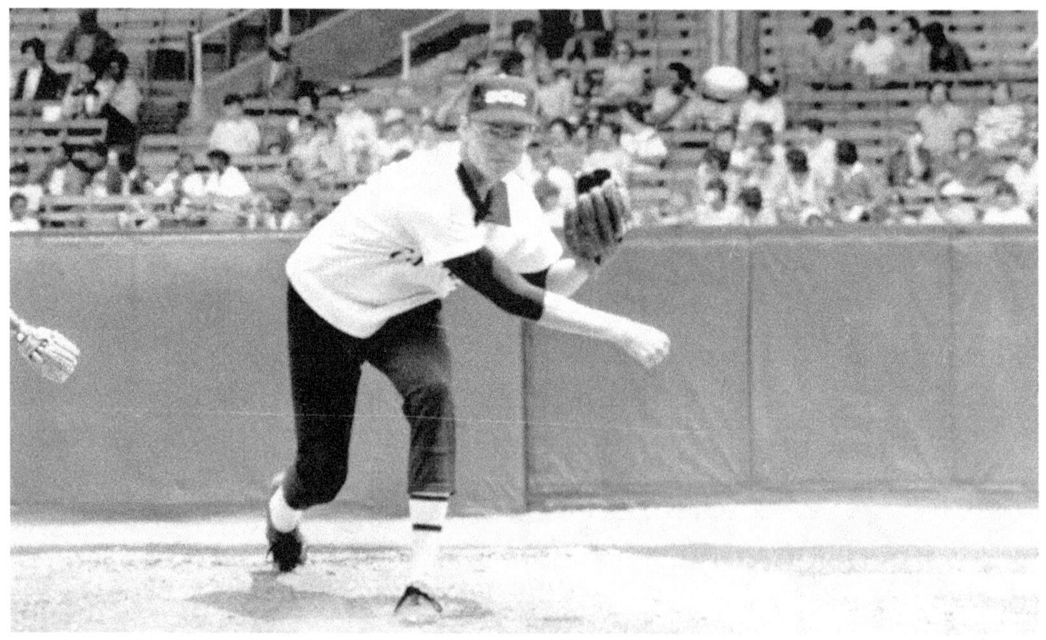

Chris Knapp, one of the young pitchers on the Sox staff in 1977, won 12 games during the Hitmen season. (Leo Bauby collection.)

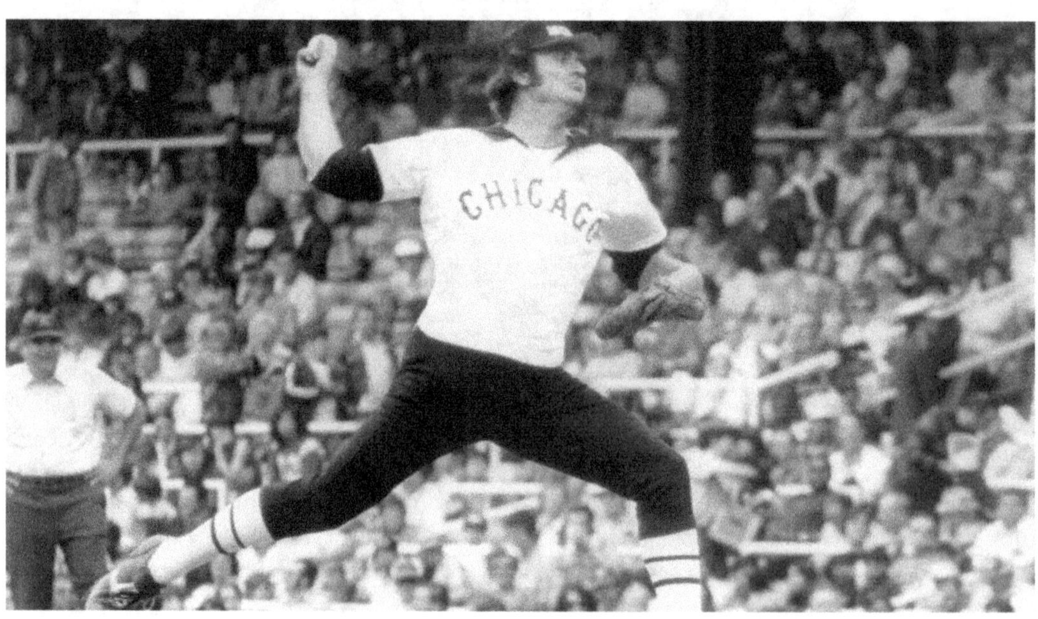

Lerrin LaGrow was another unlikely Sox hero in 1977. Acquired just before the season started, LaGrow had his best season as a reliever, saving 25 games. Very few would have thought of him as a closer but the righty did it time and again for the Sox as he posted a 2.45 ERA. (Leo Bauby collection.)

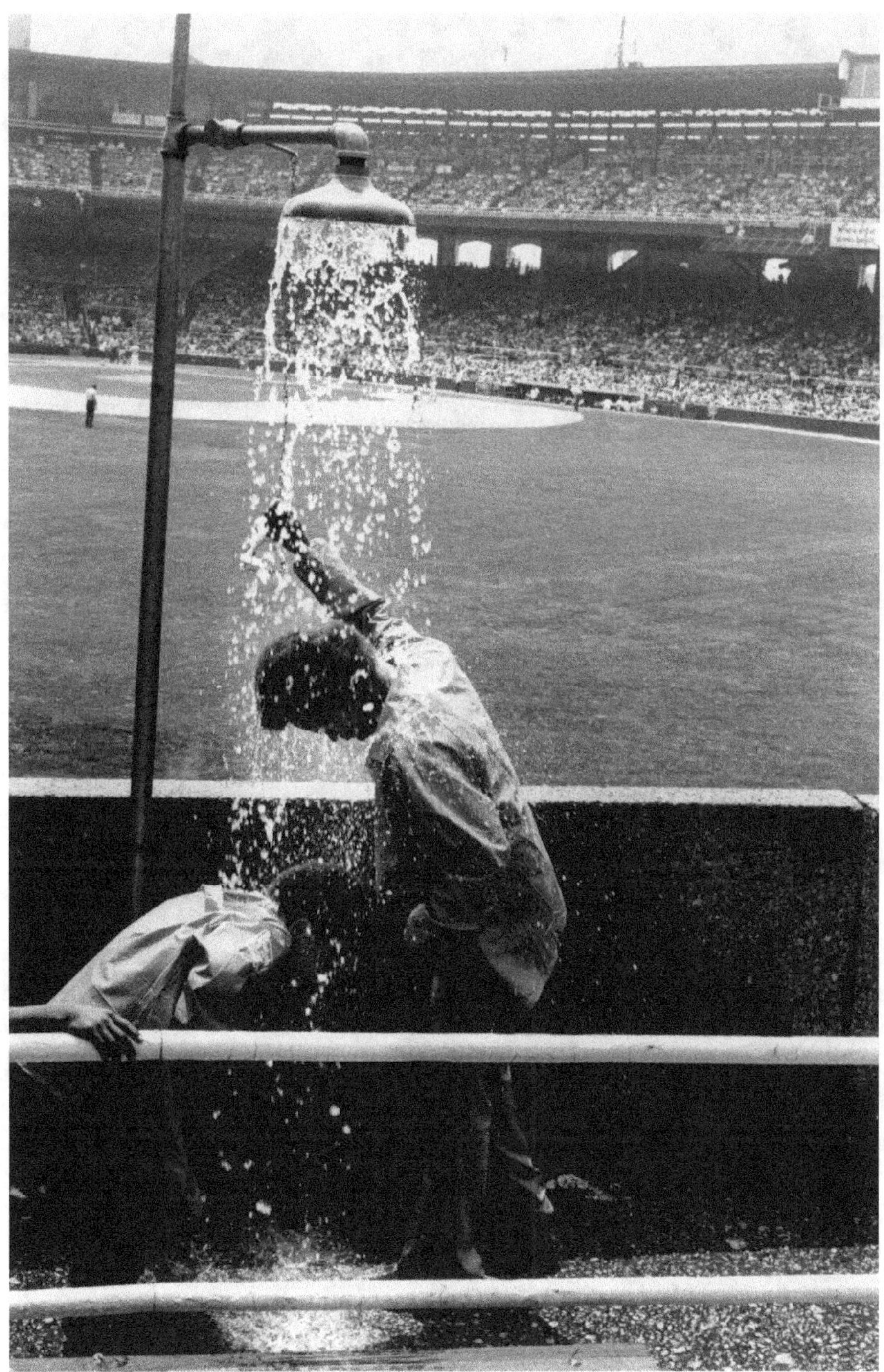

A fan cools off during the hot summer of 1977. The shower was one of the big symbols of the Hitmen year. It was situated in front of the center field bleachers, the spot where Richie Zisk hit one of his long home runs. (Leo Bauby collection.)

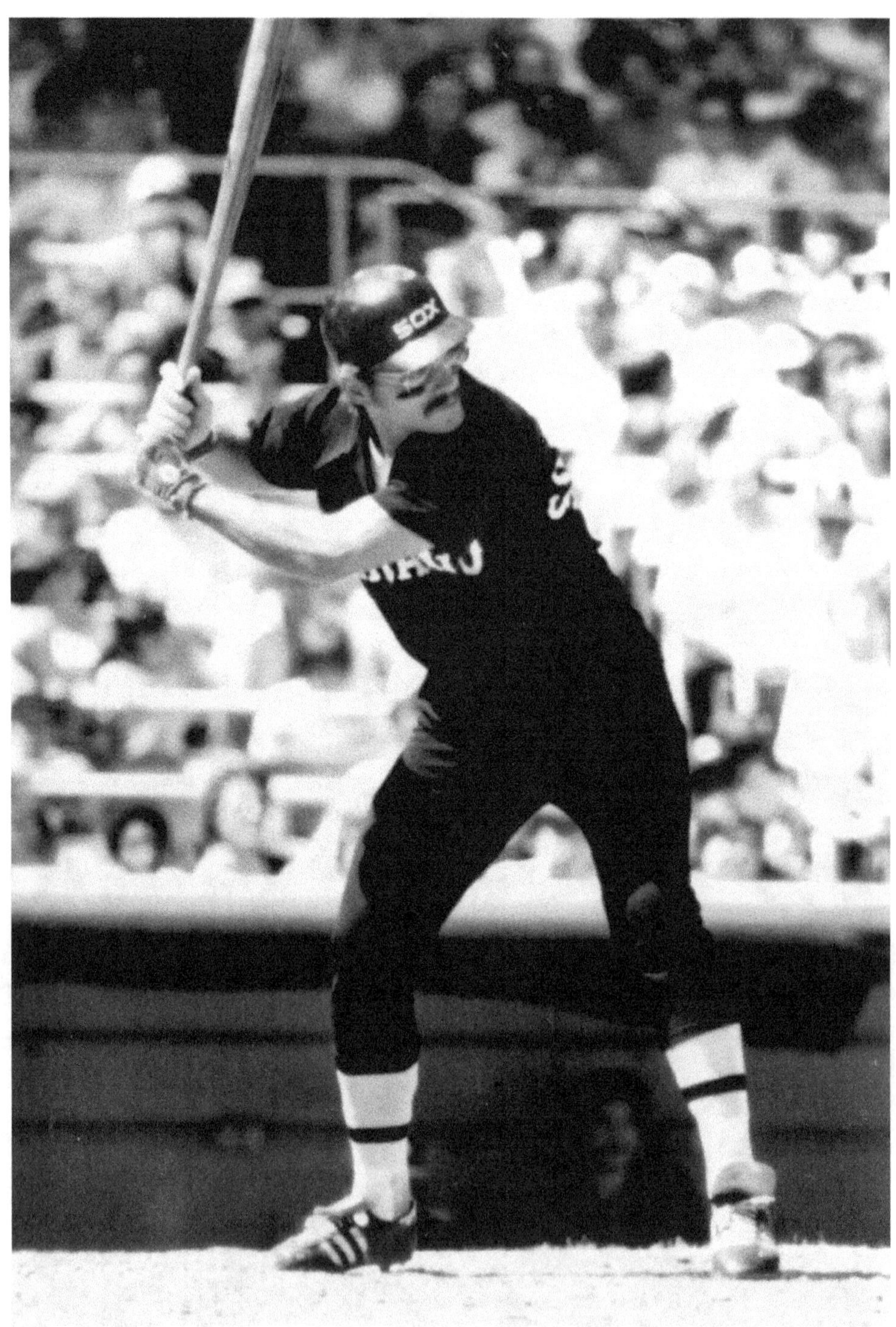

Eric Soderholm faces the Yankees in June of 1977. The White Sox lost the season series to the New Yorkers, but fought them tough in almost every game. The Yankees learned that most leads were not entirely safe from the South Side Hitmen. (Leo Bauby collection.)

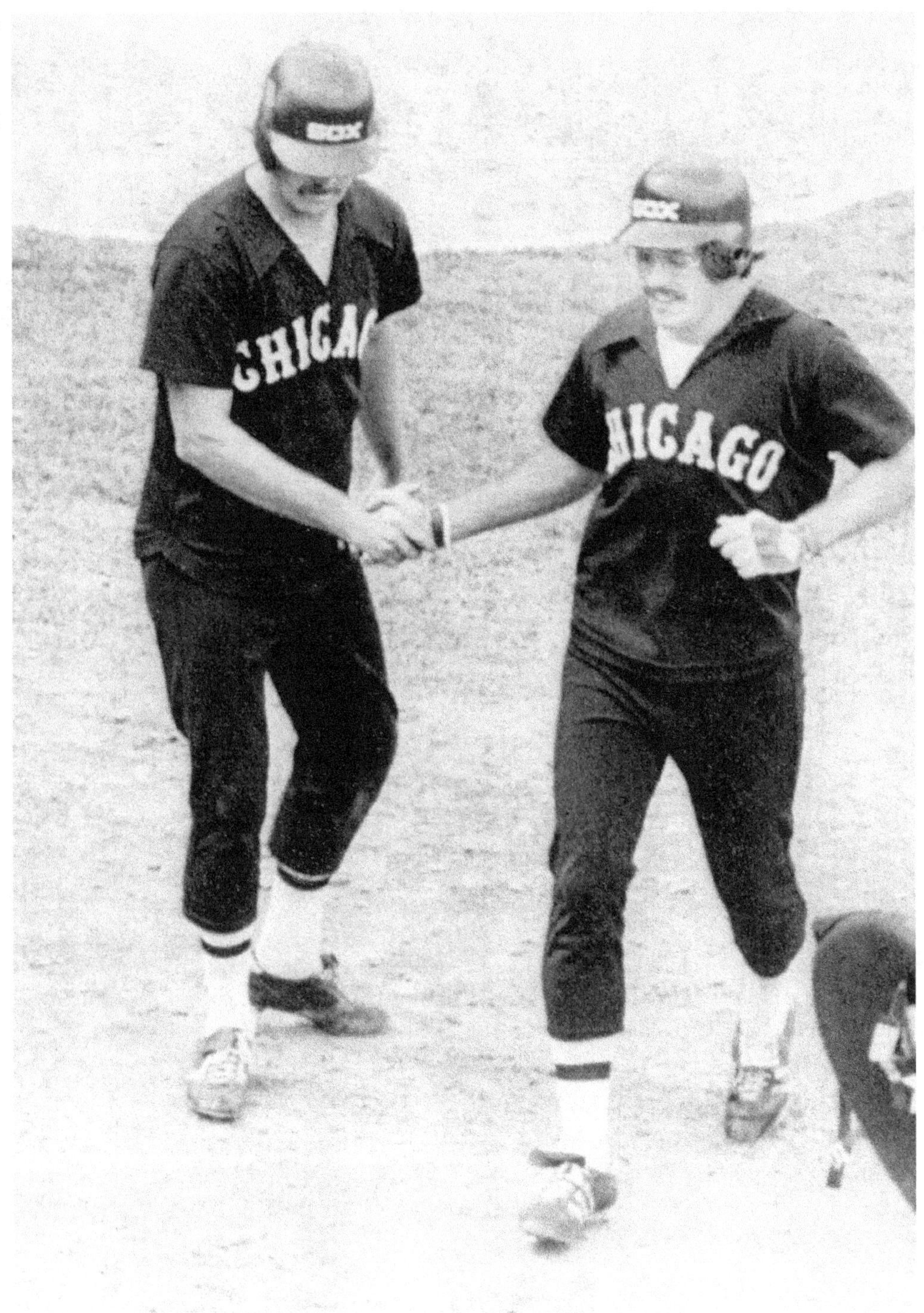

A very familiar scene at home plate in 1977, Jim Spencer (left) congratulates Eric Soderholm. This run is being scored on the road. (Leo Bauby collection.)

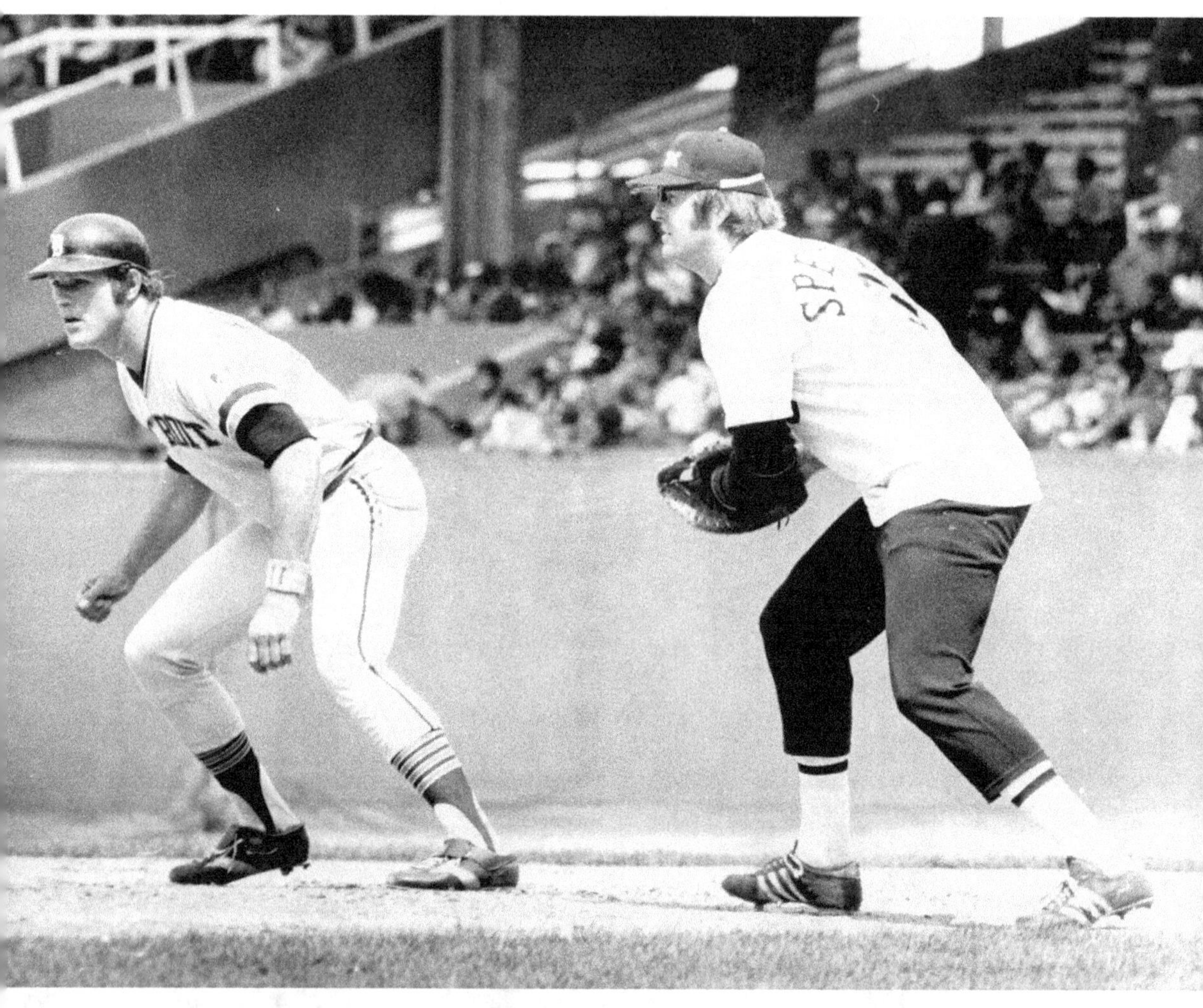

Jim Spencer holds a runner at first. Spencer was one of the few players who could play defense for the White Sox in 1977. His abilities were needed since throws from the infield that year had the potential to go just about anywhere. (Leo Bauby collection.)

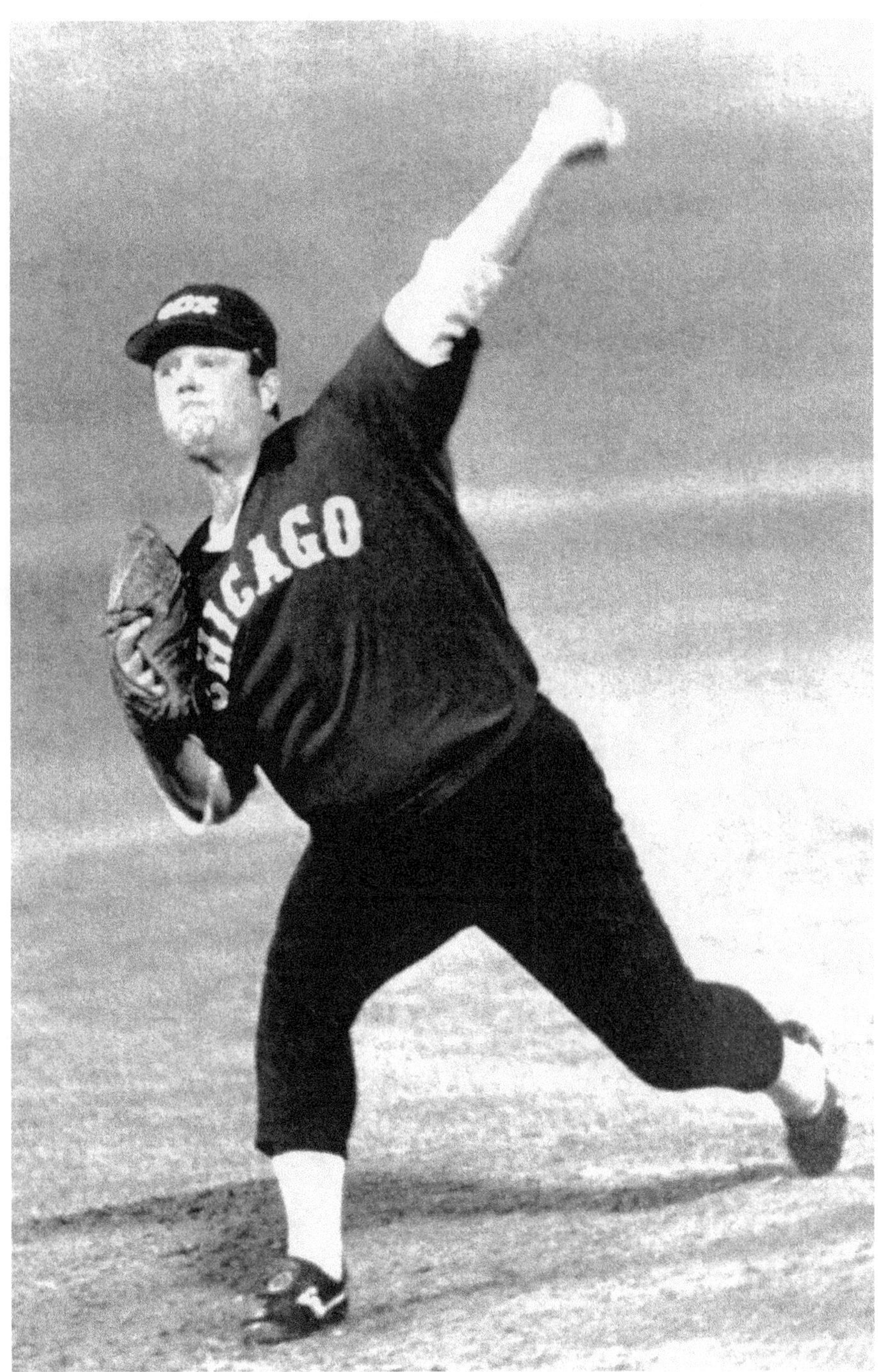

Wilbur Wood shows off his form on the road. In June, he won his first game in over a year, briefly giving fans hope that a pennant was possible. Unfortunately his ERA ballooned to nearly 5.00, and he won just seven games in 1977. He pitched his final game in 1978. (Leo Bauby collection.)

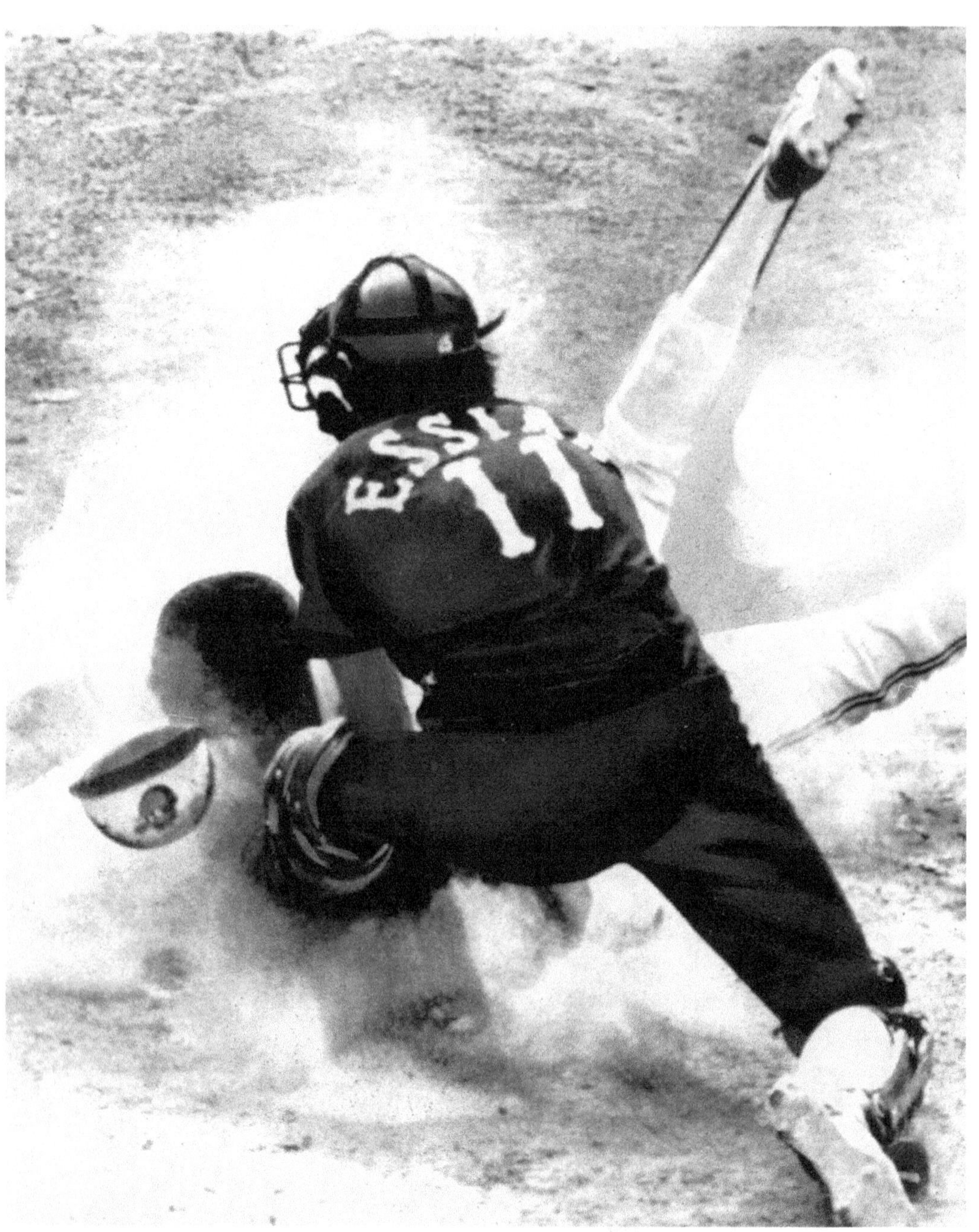

Sox catcher Jim Essian tags out would-be home plate stealer Pat Kelly. Kelly had supplied speed to the Sox during the early part of the decade when he played for the South Siders. The Sox ended up winning this June 12 game 6-4 in 11 innings. (Leo Bauby collection.)

5

July

A Fast, Furious Ride to the Top

A playoff atmosphere. July 1 is still a little early to get hyped for the playoffs. Then again, White Sox fans had had nothing to cheer for since the Allen 1972 MVP season. Injuries ruined the 1973 club. The 1975 and 1976 teams contended for nothing. And July 4 is one date when fans begin judging their team. Are they for real or not? Ten years earlier the White Sox were in first place on July 4 and ended up only three games out at the end of a crazy pennant race. Even a split against the first place Minnesota Twins would leave the Sox within a game of first after the holiday weekend. Sox fans could feel free to have some hope after nearly a decade of almost total futility and frustration.

Minnesota had a formidable ball club, at least offensively. Although they would hit almost 70 fewer homers than the Hitmen, the Twins would score 23 more runs. They had the likes of Hall of Famer Rod Carew (who came into the series with a .411 average), slugger Larry Hisle, and up and coming star Lyman Bostock. The Twins led the Sox in hitting by a microscopic margin of .2844 to .2835. Their team ERA was slightly better by a .10 difference. No one could blame White Sox fans for having a bad case of nerves when the Twins came to Chicago for a four-game series. With these two evenly matched teams, a split would have been nice, demonstrating that the White Sox could play with the best of them.

Instead fans got more than what they bargained for in the series against the Twins, and during the month of July. In fact, July 1977 was one of the greatest months, winning percentage wise, in the history of the franchise. It was also a month that forever bonded fans with the South Side Hitmen.

In game one, the Friday night game, the Twins took a 1-0 lead on triples by Carew and Bostock. They never led again for the remainder of the game.

The White Sox responded in the first and the fans responded with a deafening noise from the very start. Alan Bannister picked up a bunt single and then Jorge Orta doubled Bannister to third. Then newly found hero Richie Zisk came to the plate.

Zisk brought the house down with a three run opposite field homer. He at first thought it would be a sacrifice fly caught against the wall in right center, but right fielder Bostock just watched as it landed in the seats. Zisk thought he had been a lucky, and that the wind had helped a little. The fans didn't care if luck was involved or not. They just roared right along with the exploding scoreboard.

"These folks," Zisk said referring to Sox fans, "are caught up in a pennant race. I've been through this with the Pirates, but later, in September."

Zisk got the fans revved up again in the third when he hit his second home run of the night. According to Bill Jauss of the *Chicago Tribune*, it was "no more than 20 feet off the ground, probably set a record for the least time zooming from home plate into the eighth row of the left center field stands."

The White Sox won 5-2 on the Zisk's 5 RBIs. Fans showed their appreciation later in the game, giving him standing ovations when he struck out twice.

"Every time I think I have Chicago fans figured out, they amaze me," Zisk said.

Chris Knapp, the righty who went the distance that night against Minnesota, was greatly affected by a crowd that only cared about the Sox climbing into first place, even if it was only by two percentage points as they did two weeks earlier.

"When I heard all those people in the ninth inning going, 'We're number one,' that made me want to go stronger," Knapp said.

The White Sox widened their lead against the once first place Twins the next day, thanks to the slugging of first baseman Jim Spencer.

"Jim was a real gentle type," Eric Soderholm recalled in 2005. "He was easy going, fun loving. When you [an infielder] released the ball and you knew it was too low or too high, you also knew Jim would get it. He was that good with the glove. He made infielders look good."

In 1977, he fit right in with the Hitmen because he was good with the bat as well. Fans began bringing banners that read, "C'mon Spence, Over the Fence." But who knew that Spencer would have an eight RBI day? On Saturday, July 2, the shell-shocked Twins found out.

Spencer hit his second grand slam of the year in the fourth. In the sixth, he singled to drive in Chet Lemon who had tripled. Finally in the eighth, Spencer hit a high homer in the right center field seats to drive in three more and put the game out of reach. The White Sox had actually been trailing 7-6 going into their half of the eighth, but in typical South Side Hitmen fashion, the offense exploded and made it look easy, winning 13-8.

Actually, it hadn't been all that easy. That seven run eighth inning might not have happened if Twins right fielder Dan Ford hadn't lost Alan Bannister's fly in the sun. As a result, all seven runs were unearned.

"This isn't the kind of team you give four outs or five outs," Bannister said. "These guys really hit with two outs."

In the first game of a Sunday doubleheader to close out the Twins series, Wilbur Wood dominated the hard hitting Minnesota club. The left hander gave up singles in the first, fourth, and ninth—and that was it. Again showing how they pile up runs, Chicago scored five in the second and won handily 6-0. Wood used only 93 pitches in a game that only took a little more than two hours.

"It was head high," catcher Brian Downing said in describing the movement of Wood's last pitch of the game to strike out Lyman Bostock, "but I caught it off the ground."

In the nightcap that mercifully ended the series for the Twins, the Sox used the big inning again to pummel the once first place Minnesota team. Jim Spencer did it again, this time with a first inning upper deck homer. His third homer of the series came after a Lamar Johnson triple, a Zisk double and Orta single.

The center field scoreboard, maybe because it was being used so much that summer, blew a fuse and didn't go off after the Spencer homer. It was repaired in time for later White Sox blasts that game. Yet, the fans made up for the silent scoreboard. *Chicago Sun-Times* reporter Joe Goddard called the ovation for the Spencer homer as one of the loudest of the season.

It also has to be said that one of the most memorable images of 1977 was Spencer standing right outside the Sox dugout acknowledging that ovation from the crowd. Many baseball people cringed at these "curtain calls" thinking the Sox were showing up their opponents with theatrics. However, others felt that the ovations were so loud and so long, that the players had to do something to acknowledge the fans. The fans and team reveled in it that Fourth of July weekend, even though the hard feelings caused by the curtain calls would cost them later.

In the midst of taking two that day and sweeping the Twins, few thought of any potential backlash. The Sox piled on more runs and Minnesota's pennant hopes took a real beating. Against Minnesota, Chicago scored 34 runs, hit seven homers, and now were in first place with a three game lead. The Twins had to leave Chicago talking to themselves.

All during the 1970s, the Sox struggled with attendance. They had some huge crowds like the record setting 55,555 on Bat Day on May 20, 1973. But inconsistency and dashed expectations had made things extremely difficult to keep a cynical fan base interested. For the series against Minnesota, they drew a paid attendance of 96,204 plus a little more than 9,000 who made their way in with a promotional giveaway. In addition to the numbers, the team had crowds that were emotionally charged. It would have been hard to believe, but the incredible month of July 1977 was just getting started and it would only get better.

"The series awakened the people," Bill Jauss said in 2005, remembering how he covered the four games for the *Chicago Tribune*. "They were beginning to think this team was for real."

Once Minnesota left town, Chicago kept winning, eventually extending their win streak to nine. One of their victims was Mark "the Bird" Fidyrich. Fidyrich had won 19 in his American League rookie year of 1976, and liked talking to the ball when he was on the mound. After this game Fidyrich wondered out loud to the media about what had happened to his stuff.

Detroit ended the White Sox win streak with a 6-5 win in 10 innings at Tiger Stadium. Chicago then split a two-game at home series against the Royals, but even in an 8-3 defeat began to believe in themselves. With that explosive offense, the South Side Hitmen felt they still had a chance even as they went into the bottom of the ninth trailing 8-1. But after scoring two runs, and loading the bases with one out, the Sox brought their fans back into to the game. Before Alan Bannister grounded into a double play to end the game, Oscar Gamble sat in the on-deck circle and dreamed about stepping up to represent the tying run.

"We've been bringing it all back," Gamble said after the loss. "Not all teams think this way. Last year's Yankees did." (The 1976 Yankees went to the World Series.)

A few days later, Boston came into town and, as was typical that year, the White Sox greeted their guests with a big inning, this one a six-run fourth. The Red Sox made a much needed pitching change in the middle of the fourth. Fan Mark Liptak was in attendance and recalls the "great atmosphere" and the feeling that along with it by seeing the White Sox in first place in the middle of July. (Over 41,000 were at Comiskey that night.)

"The entire lower deck was chanting, 'Red Sox suck, Red Sox suck,'" Liptak told the author in 2005. "During a pitching change, [Carl] Yastremski was talking to [Fred] Lynn. They looked at each other laughing because the fans were having such a good time."

The White Sox took that game 9-7 and won the series two games to one with a Sunday afternoon 3-2 win two days later. Steve Stone pitched one of his best games of the year, going eight innings, giving up two runs on a measly three hits. Stone walked two and struck out nine. The difference in this game was again provided by Jim Spencer when he homered in the right field upper deck directly over the auxiliary scoreboard. The game ended in dramatic fashion as catcher Brian Downing threw pinch runner Steve Dillard out trying to steal second. Lerrin LaGrow notched his 16th save.

One week later Chicago traveled to Boston and swept an oddly scheduled two-game series, scoring 17 runs on 23 hits which included six homers. Even the Red Sox were impressed.

Going into the last weekend of the month, the White Sox posted a 19-5 record for July. They faced the Kansas City Royals in a three-date, four game series. Kansas City, in second place, was the closest Sox pursuer. three and a half games out. They also had to be considered one of the teams to beat since they were the defending division champions. Could the Sox end the month in the same dramatic fashion as they began it?

July 29–31, 1977. There was nothing like it, not in that decade and very rarely duplicated before or since. Although White Sox fans can come up with other examples of great times at both ball parks, it is very doubtful that anything surpasses the last weekend of July 1977 (with the exception of the 2005 post season). It was a weekend that created high emotions and sent a strong message to the baseball world that something special was happening on the South Side of Chicago.

First, there was the attendance. Getting a ticket at Comiskey Park during the 1970s was not all that hard. Fans could arrive late and not worry about sitting behind a pole. During this weekend, Chicago drew 131,285, and for the month they drew a little more than 482,000. In contrast, the gate for the entire 1970 season was a little more than 495,000. Of course, it wasn't only the numbers; it was the noise and the intense fan emotion that created an incredible atmosphere typical only of 1977.

Secondly, the Sox won three out of four in the series, each time coming from behind. No, they didn't overcome huge leads, but they were playing a tough team in close games and it was never easy beating the likes of the 1977 Royals when they scored first. And naturally, Chicago used the long ball in dramatic style.

Finally, the four games capped an incredible month. The Sox finished July 1977 with a 22-6 mark, good for a .785 percentage. July 1977 ranks as a landmark 31 days. It was their best monthly showing since 1951, and the franchise third best winning record in team history. There is no question that the Chicago White Sox not only peaked that month for the year, but also for the decade, and almost for the century.

Game one on Friday night was so typical of South Side Hitmen contests. After giving up three Kansas City runs in the first, the Sox put together a six spot in the third, capped by a homer by Chet Lemon.

Not being wimps themselves, the Royals countered with a three run, George Brett homer in the fifth, and took the lead in the seventh with two more. But with the help of a hit batsman and an error, Chicago responded with four in their half of the seventh, and added another in the eighth. The Sox won 11-8, pounding out 17 hits and knocking around four Kansas City pitchers.

The White Sox trailed again the next day 3-2 in the seventh. Eric Soderholm turned the game around with a three run homer. When interviewed in 2000, Soderholm remembered that day as one of his best that season. He recalled touching second base and hearing and feeling the "roar" of the crowd. Although Old Comiskey Park had its many critics, there was one thing it had over many of the large modern stadiums: the then 67-year-old park was large but was enclosed and noise tended to stay in its confines. In 1977, there was plenty of noise at Comiskey and that day Soderholm not only heard it, he felt it.

Chicago won game two 6-4 with three more RBIs from Jorge Orta including a homer in the eighth. The nearly 35,000 in attendance went home very happy.

Sunday provided a usually unmemorable split for the Sox. However, game one provided an excitement that even went beyond 1977 standards.

Marty Pattin, generally considered a good but not great pitcher, started for the Royals. But Pattin had everything working for him that day, especially in the first five innings. He set down first 15 Sox in order, something completely unheard of in 1977. Fortunately for the Sox, Steve Stone continued his good pitching that month and Chicago trailed only 1-0 going into the bottom of the sixth.

Chet Lemon picked up the first hit of the game for the Sox leading off the sixth. The center fielder hit his 13th homer of the season to tie things up. Lemon would be heard from again later.

On two occasions it appeared that the Royals would win the game and take the crowd of a little over 50,000 out of it. Amos Otis homered in the seventh to give Kansas City a 2-1 lead going into the ninth.

But Jorge Orta singled in Alan Bannister who had reached on an error to send the game into extra innings. The normally powerful Sox had only three hits off the luckless Marty Pattin, but were still in the game.

Once more the Royals looked like they were going to win when they picked up two runs after two were out and no one was on in the tenth. In 1977, however, no lead was ever safe from the South Side Hitmen.

Jim Spencer singled and that man Chet Lemon came through again. Lemon lined a two-run homer into the lower deck in left to tie the game one more time. One out later, Ralph Garr singled in Eric Soderholm with the winning run. It had to be one of the most exciting wins during a month with nothing but exciting wins.

Now no matter what happened in game two, the Sox had won another four-game series against a contender that month, and with the sweep of the Twins in the beginning of July, provided victorious bookends for that historic 31 days. It was quite a transformation from the previous year when the only anticipation the end of July brought was a game in August where players wore short pants.

Kansas City averted the sweep, winning game two 8-4 by slugging three homers. The Royals left Chicago in an angry mood, and losing three out of four was only part of it. They had little respect for the White Sox as a team and even less for the curtain calls. The Good-bye song only soured their mood further. In short, the Royals thought the Sox fans and players were making fools out of themselves with the ovations and the singing. Kansas City vowed they would catch and pass the White Sox.

This type of bitterness didn't take anything away from the euphoria that accompanied July 1977. The South Side Hitmen were in first place, by a comfortable but not an overwhelming margin. They seemed to be alleviating the disappointment and letdown in the entire Chicago sports city. The crybaby Royals, a team Sox fans liked to call annual pennant chokers, couldn't dampen the spirit of 1977.

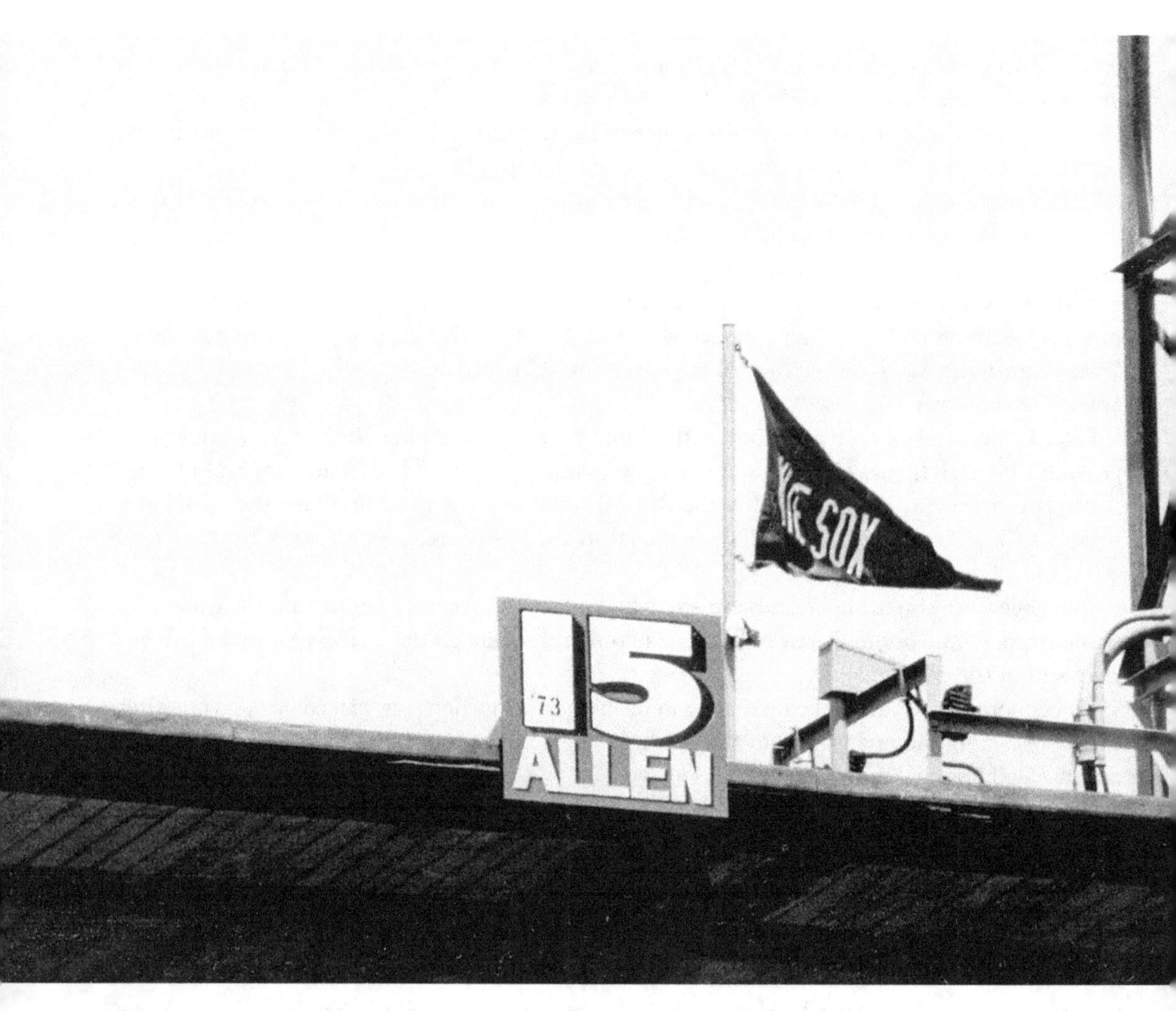

Plaques were placed where roof shots were made. Zisk added to the rooftop history in 1977. It was amazing only one blast made it up there during the 1977 season. Leo Bauby collection.)

Spencer holds Twin Dan Ford on first. Ford made a huge error in the second game of the exciting July four-game series at Comiskey. Spencer made him regret it with a three-run homer that broke open a tight game. Sox won the contest 13-8. (Leo Bauby collection.)

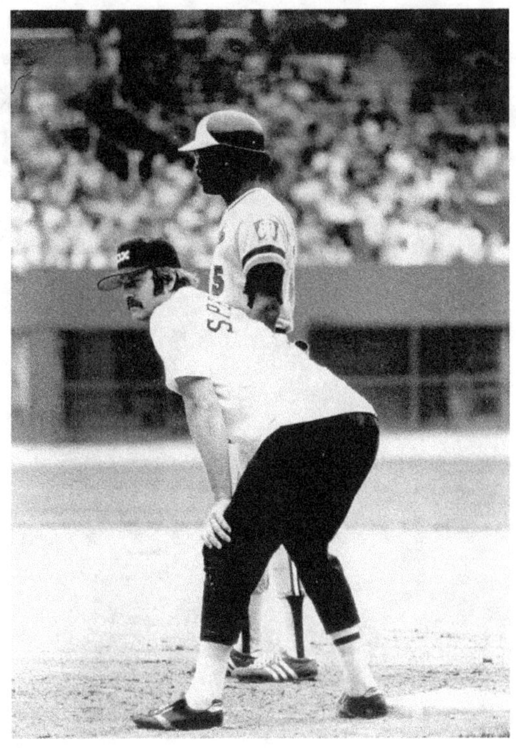

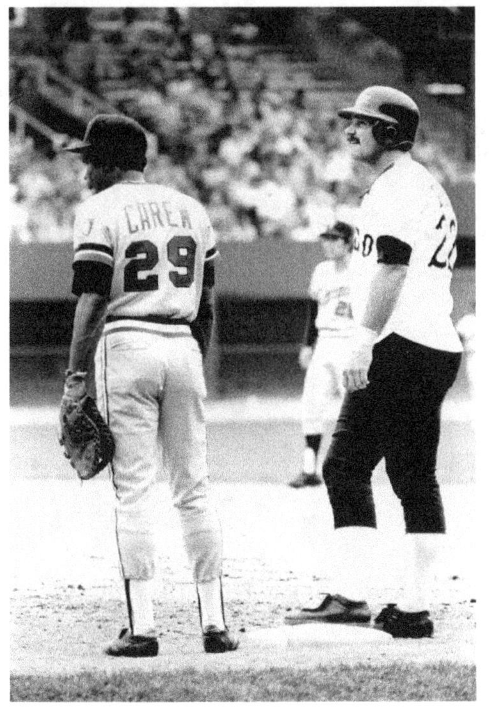

The Twins' Rod Carew does the honors of holding the not-do-fast Richie Zisk at first base. Carew was elected to the Hall of Fame in 1991. Richie Zisk, at this writing, is the manager of the Daytona Cubs in the Florida League. (Leo Bauby collection.)

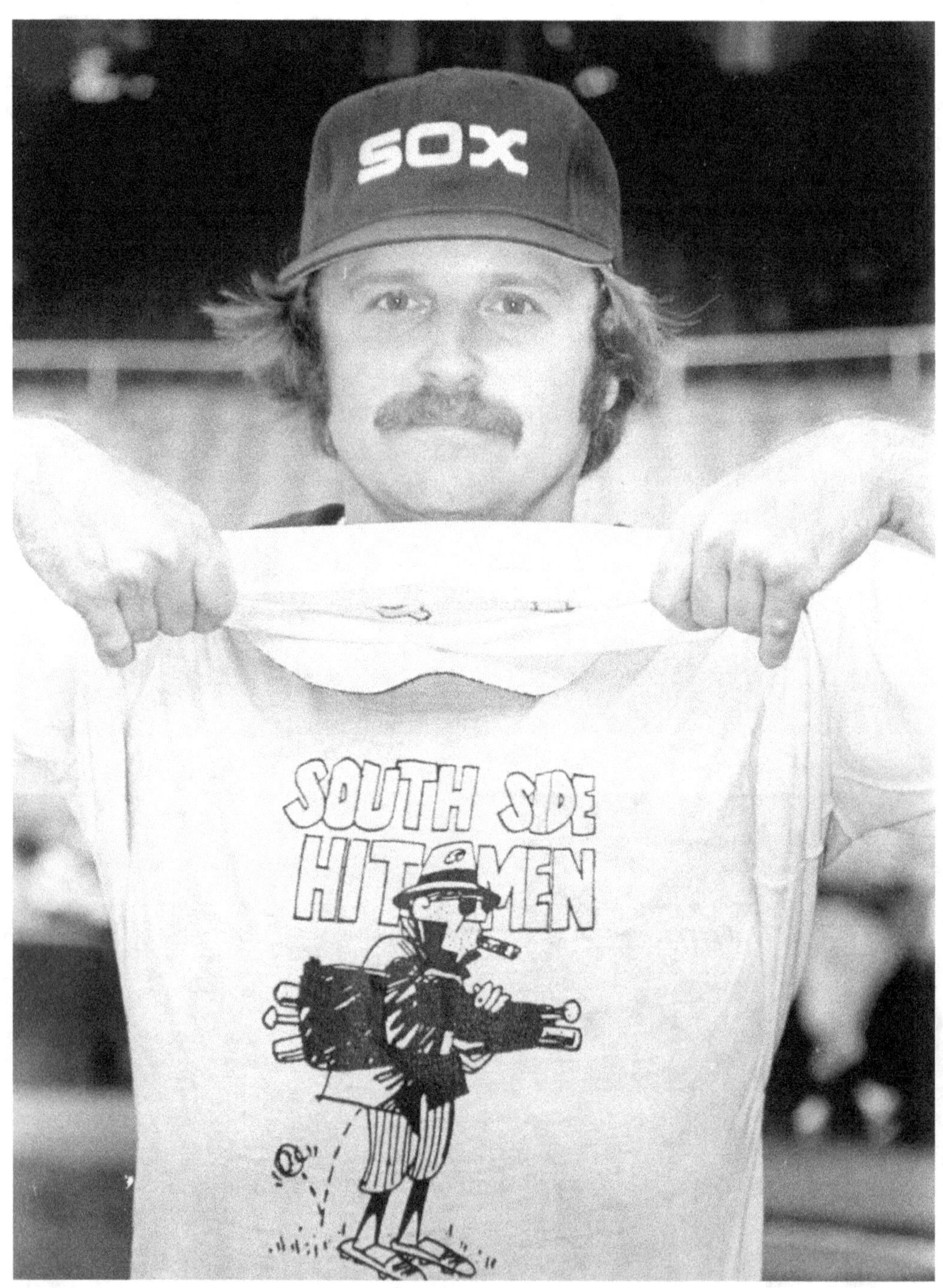

Jim Spencer holds a 1977 souvenir T-shirt bearing the "South Side Hitmen" nickname. The shirt was very popular, as was the team. The name has its own meaning with Sox fans and its mere mention brings back memories of the White Sox offensive onslaught of 1977. (Leo Bauby collection.)

Jorge Orta does some mean looking hitting at Fenway Park. Boston was one of the few teams that didn't scoff at the Hitmen in 1977, and actually got a kick out of Comiskey Park fans. The Red Sox were also impressed with the hitting prowess of the White Sox. (Leo Bauby collection.)

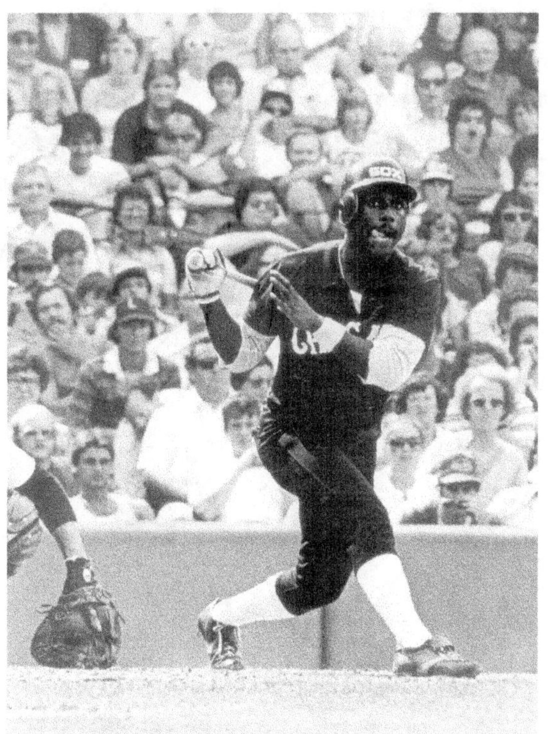

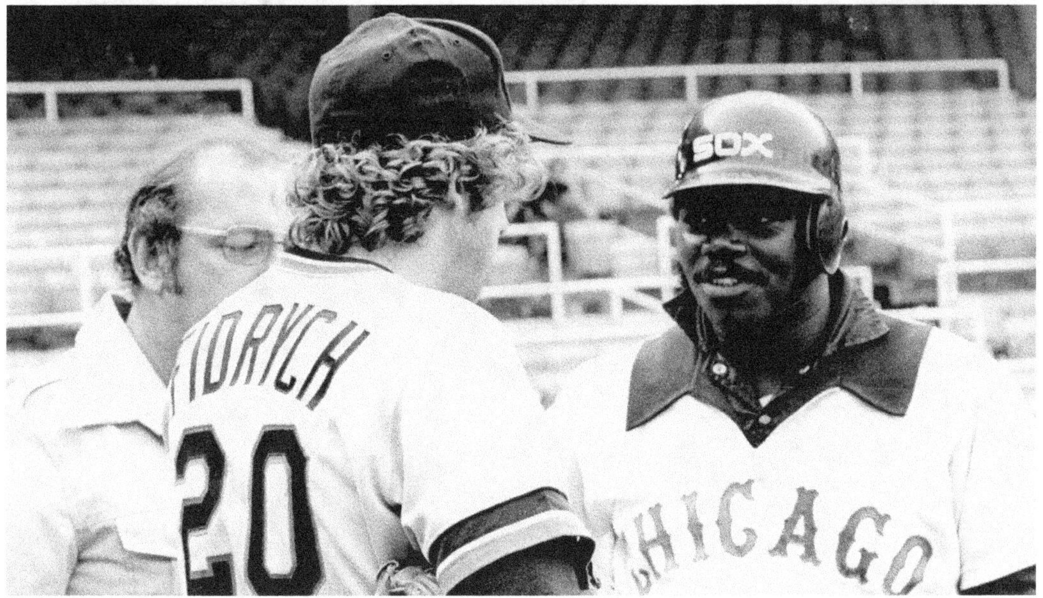

Pictured here, from left to right, are White Sox radio announcer Lorn Brown, Tiger pitcher Mark "the Bird" Fidrych, and Sox first baseman/singer Lamar Johnson. The Sox tamed Fidrych in a July 8 game 10-7, leaving the poor guy wondering what happened to his stuff. (Leo Bauby collection.)

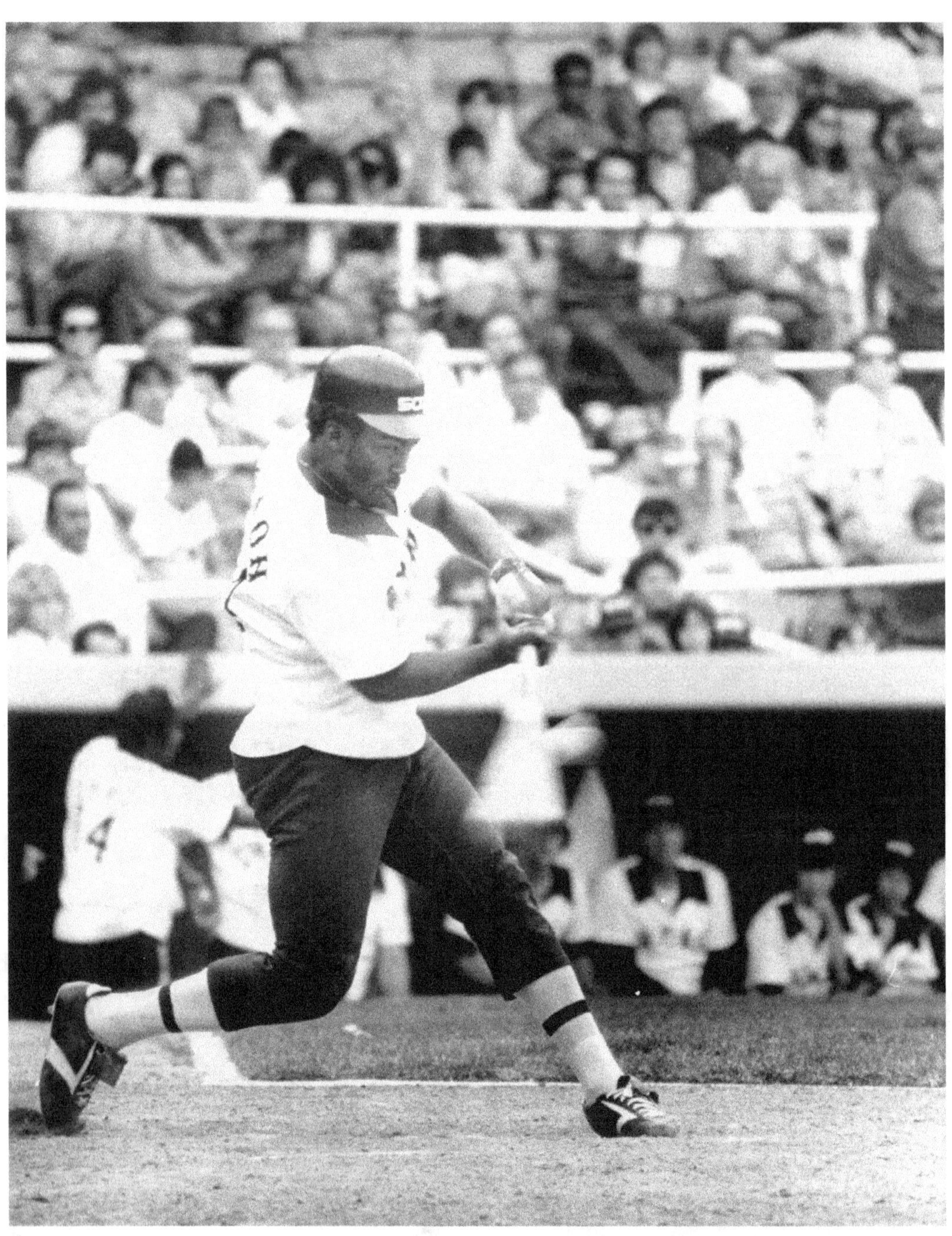

Chet Lemon unloads a powerful swing during July. The young center fielder began to come into his own during the summer of 1977. His two home runs in the first game of a July 31 doubleheader against Kansas City capped off an incredible month. Fans didn't know it, but his second homer that game, which tied the game in the tenth, would turn out to be the last great moment of the decade. (Leo Bauby collection.)

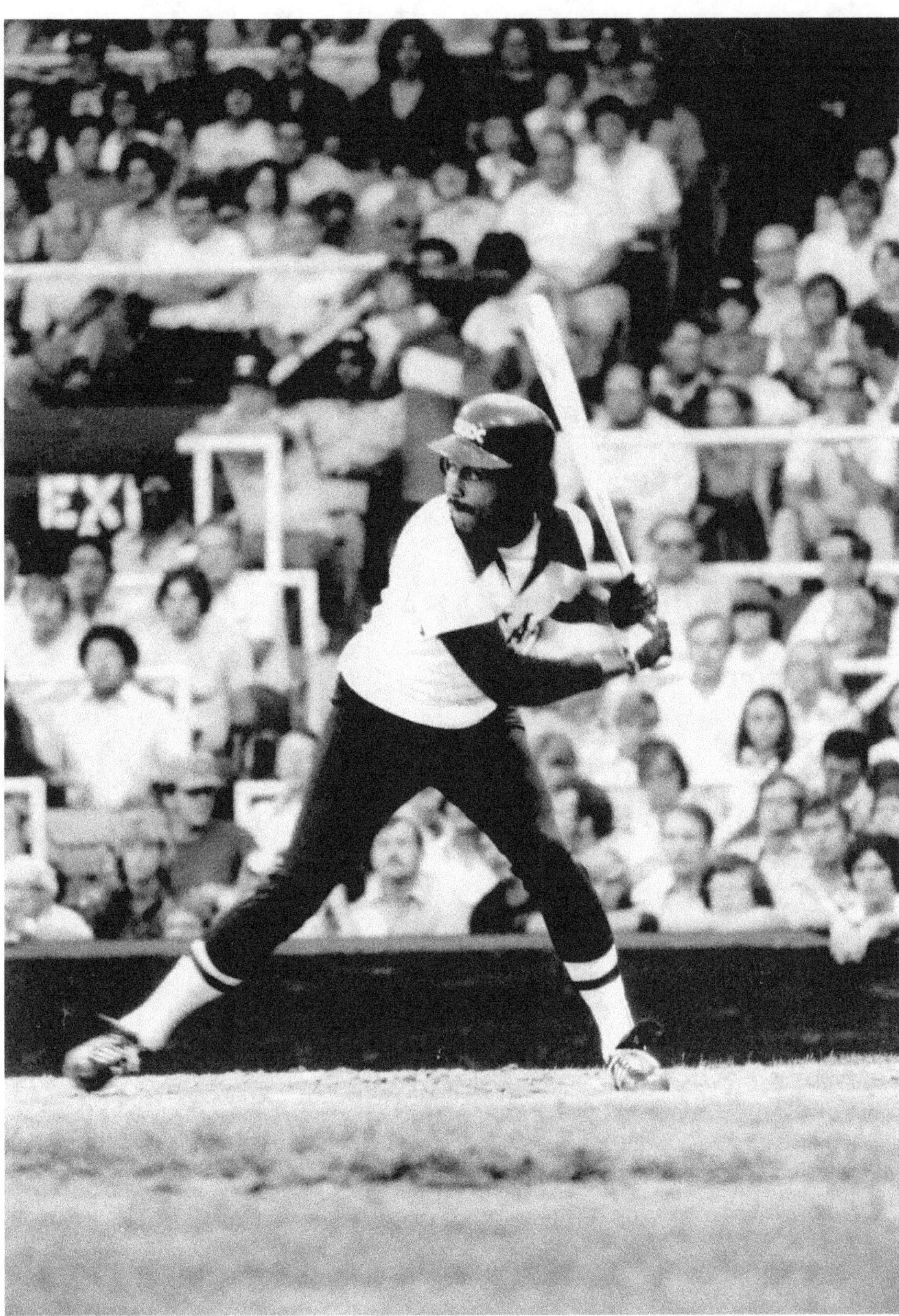

Oscar Gamble stands at the plate. Gamble became the first White Sox left handed hitter to knock out 30 homers in a season. Though he would only play two seasons with the White Sox, South Side fans will forever link his name with the team and the summer of 1977, as if Gamble had spent his entire career in Chicago. (Leo Bauby collection.)

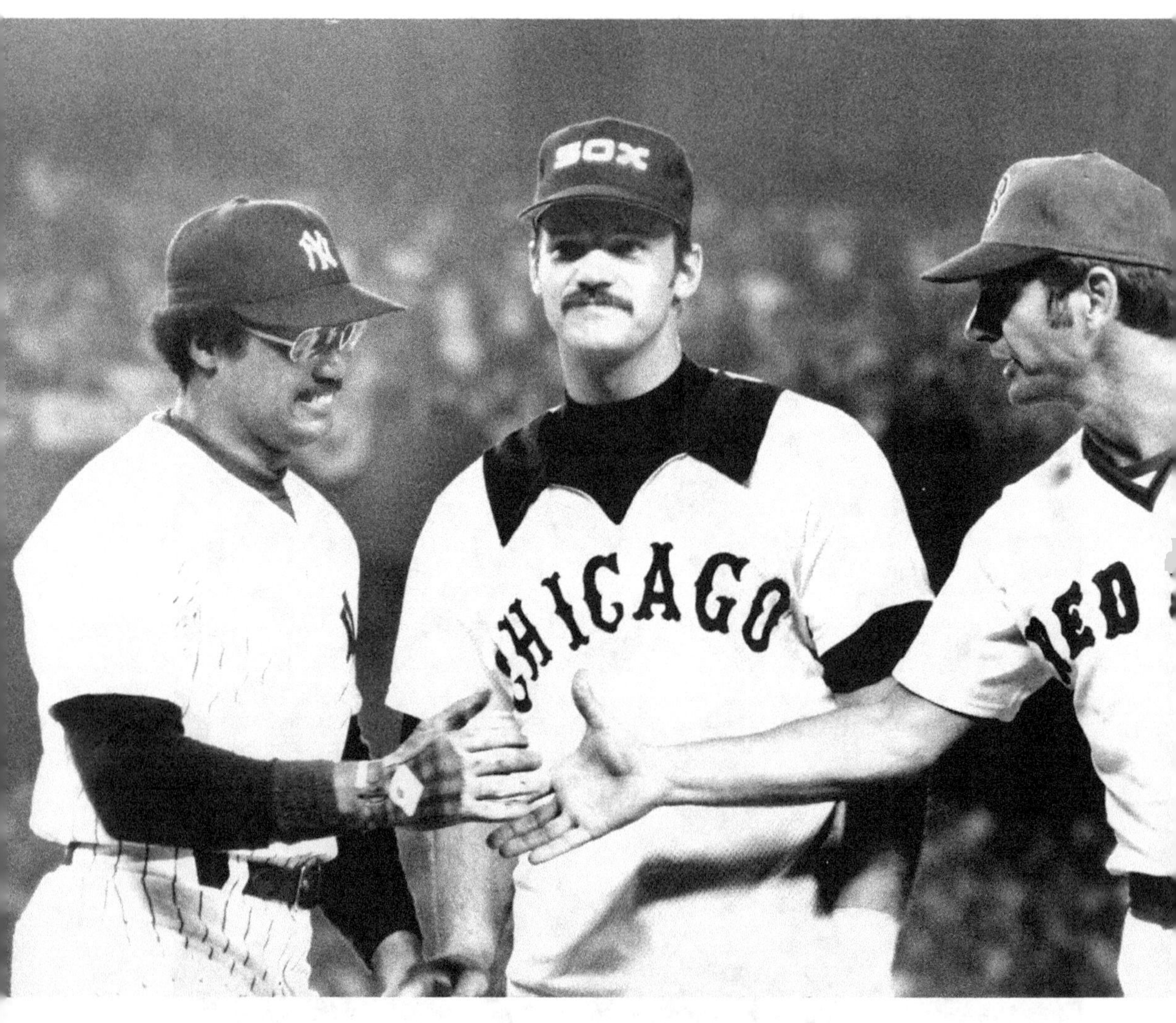

Richie Zisk was the only representative for the White Sox on the 1977 All-Star game. Here he is standing next to Reggie Jackson (left) and a Red Sox player. The American League lost the game 7-5. The game was played in Yankee Stadium. (Leo Bauby collection.)

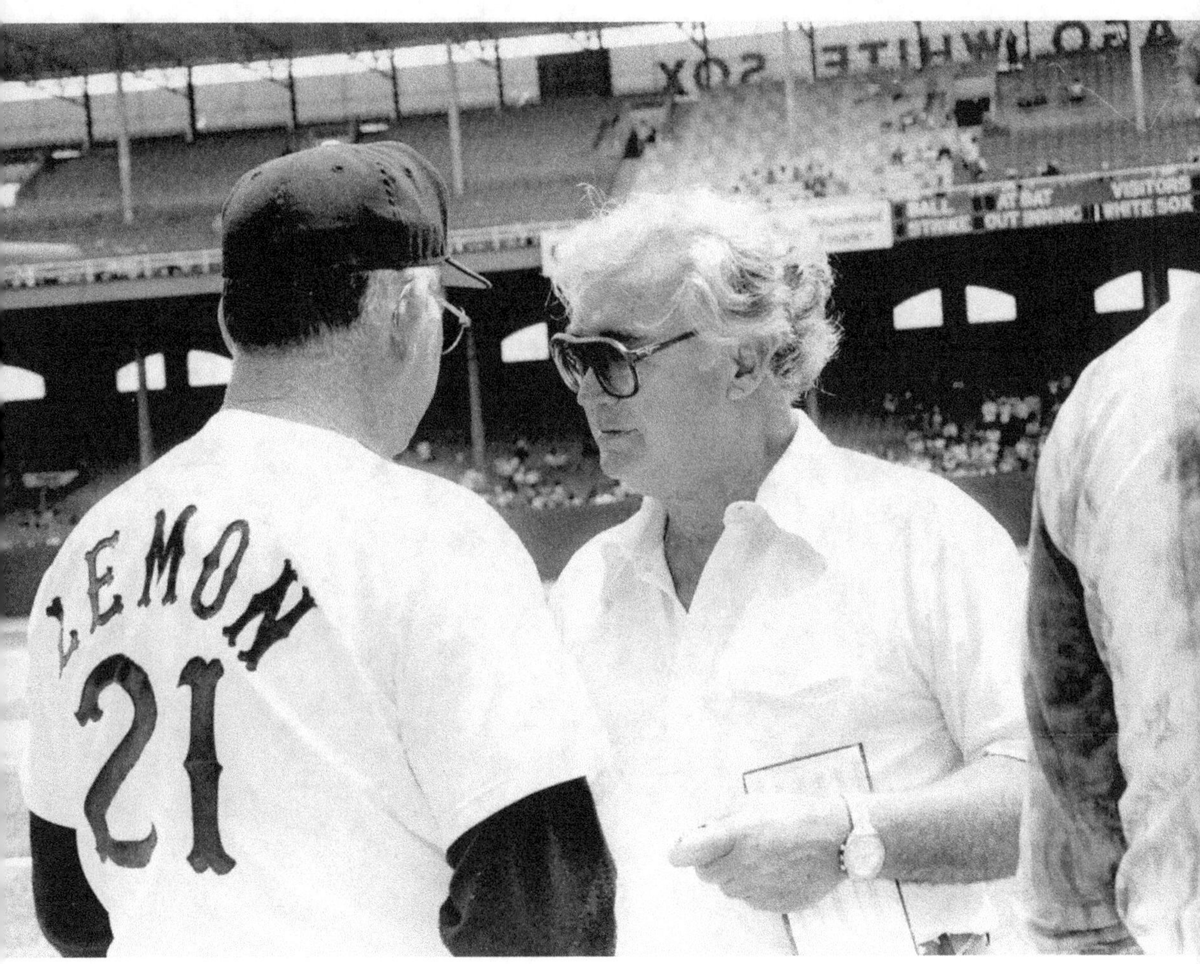

Manager Bob Lemon and play-by-play man Caray enjoy Comiskey on a nice summer day in 1977. It was a great summer for baseball on the South Side of Chicago. With his statue in front of Wrigley, it is sometimes forgotten that Caray began his Chicago broadcasting career with the Sox. (Leo Bauby collection.)

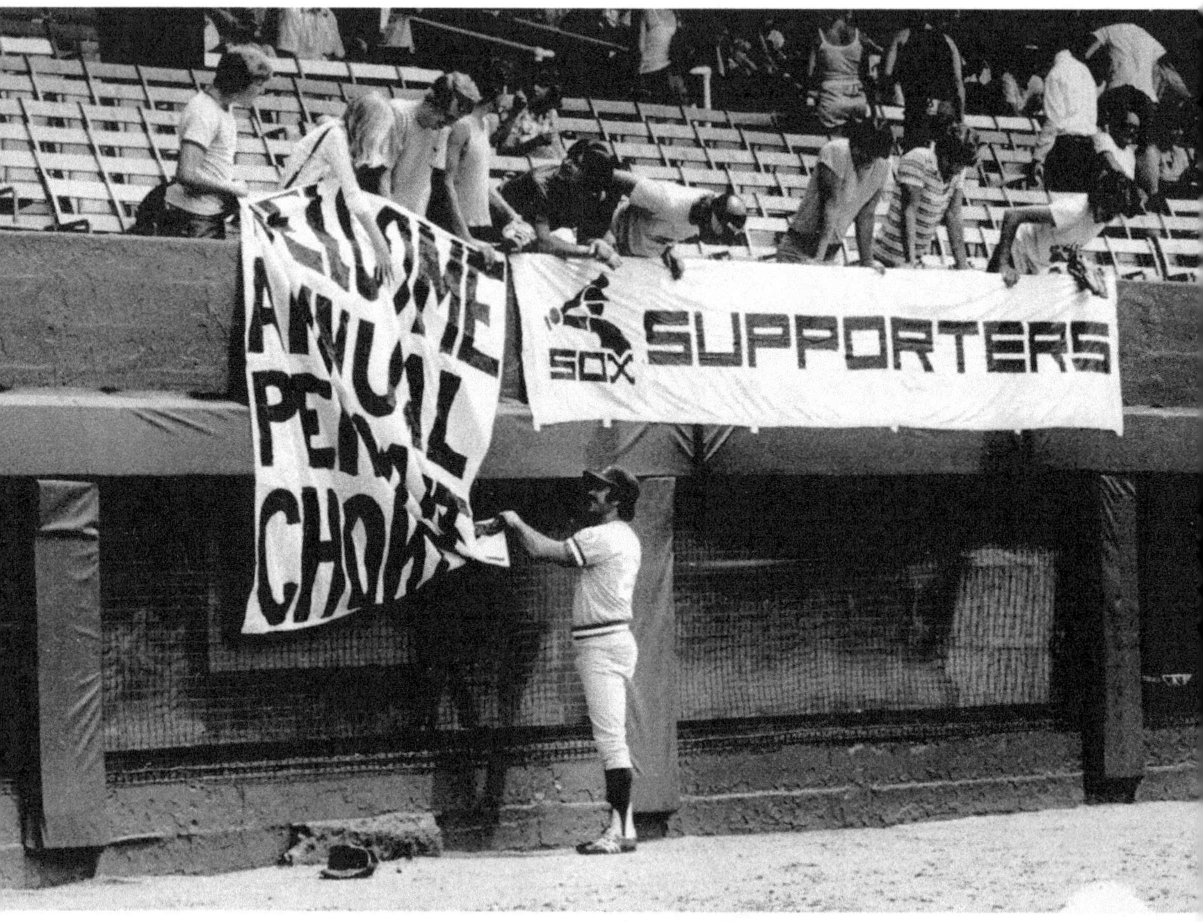

Banners were popular in the left field seats during the 1977 season. This one was not exactly a love note to the Kansas City Royals. It read, "Welcome Annual Pennant Chokers," for Kansas City's inability to win a playoff series. According to Sox fan Paul Duffy, the Royals confiscated the banner and destroyed it. The Royals were not impressed and even resented the success of the South Side Hitmen. Duffy is one fan who to this day cheers for a Kansas City last place finish. (Leo Bauby collection.)

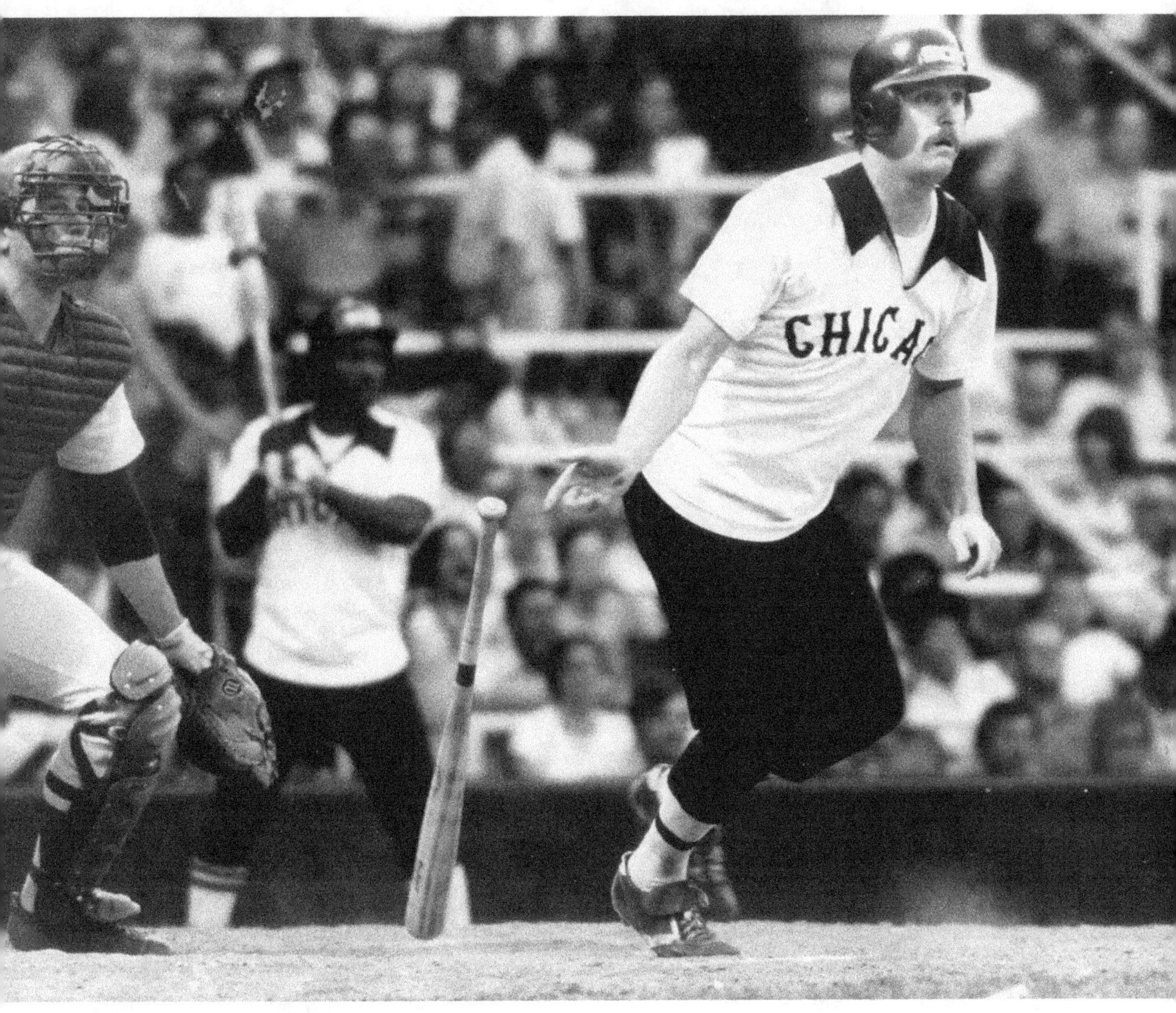

Jim Spencer follows through on a swing. Spencer had a big month in July, starting with the exciting series with the Twins. He also hit a game winning home run against the Red Sox in the July 17, 3-2 contest. Sadly, he died way before his time in 2002. (Leo Bauby collection.)

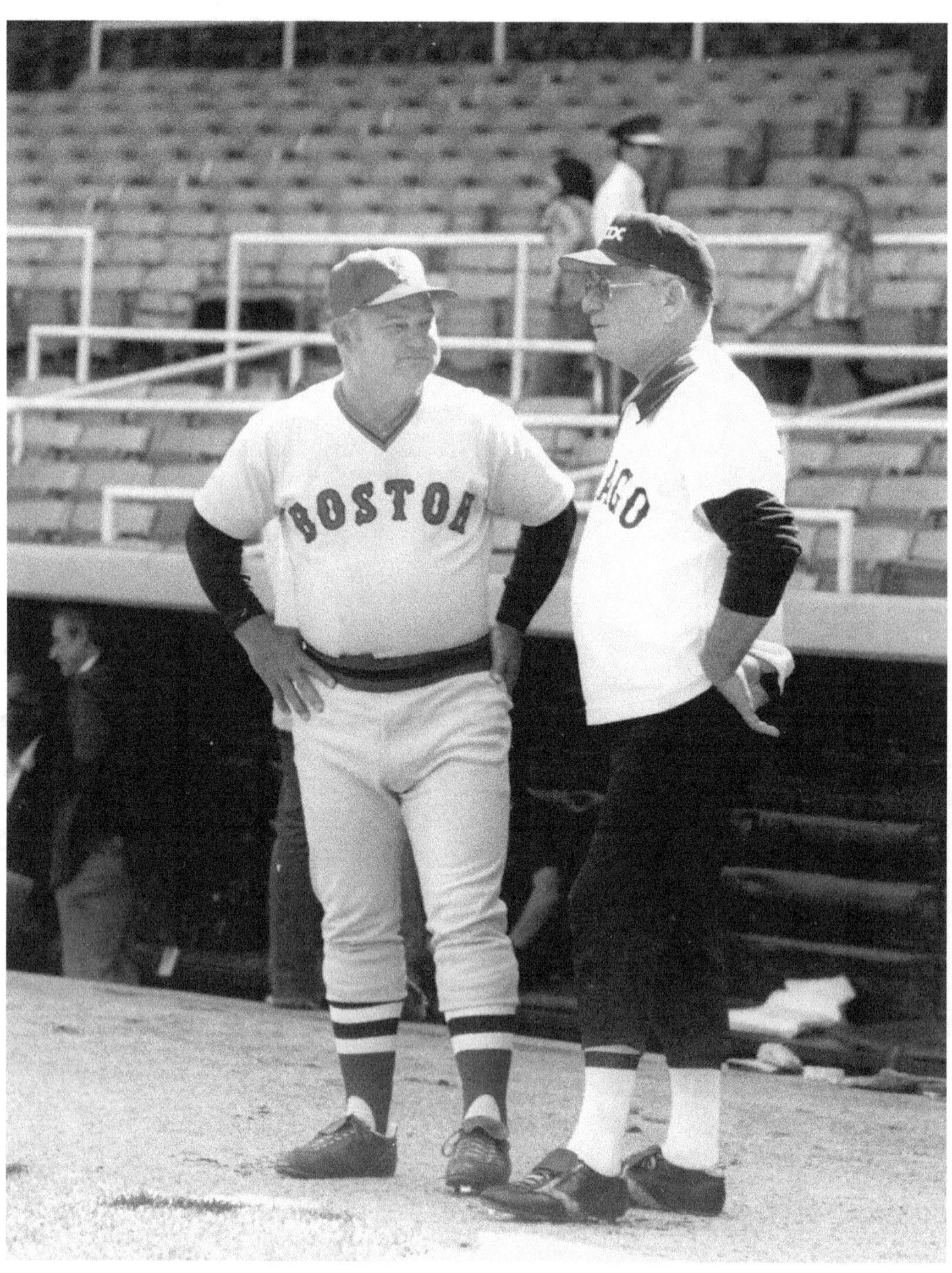

Bob Lemon chats with Boston manager Don Zimmer. Zimmer, unlike the angry Kansas City Royals, actually respected the 1977 Sox. The Hitmen had traveled to Boston that month and knocked the ball all around Fenway. They did the same when the Red Sox had visited Comiskey. (Leo Bauby collection.)

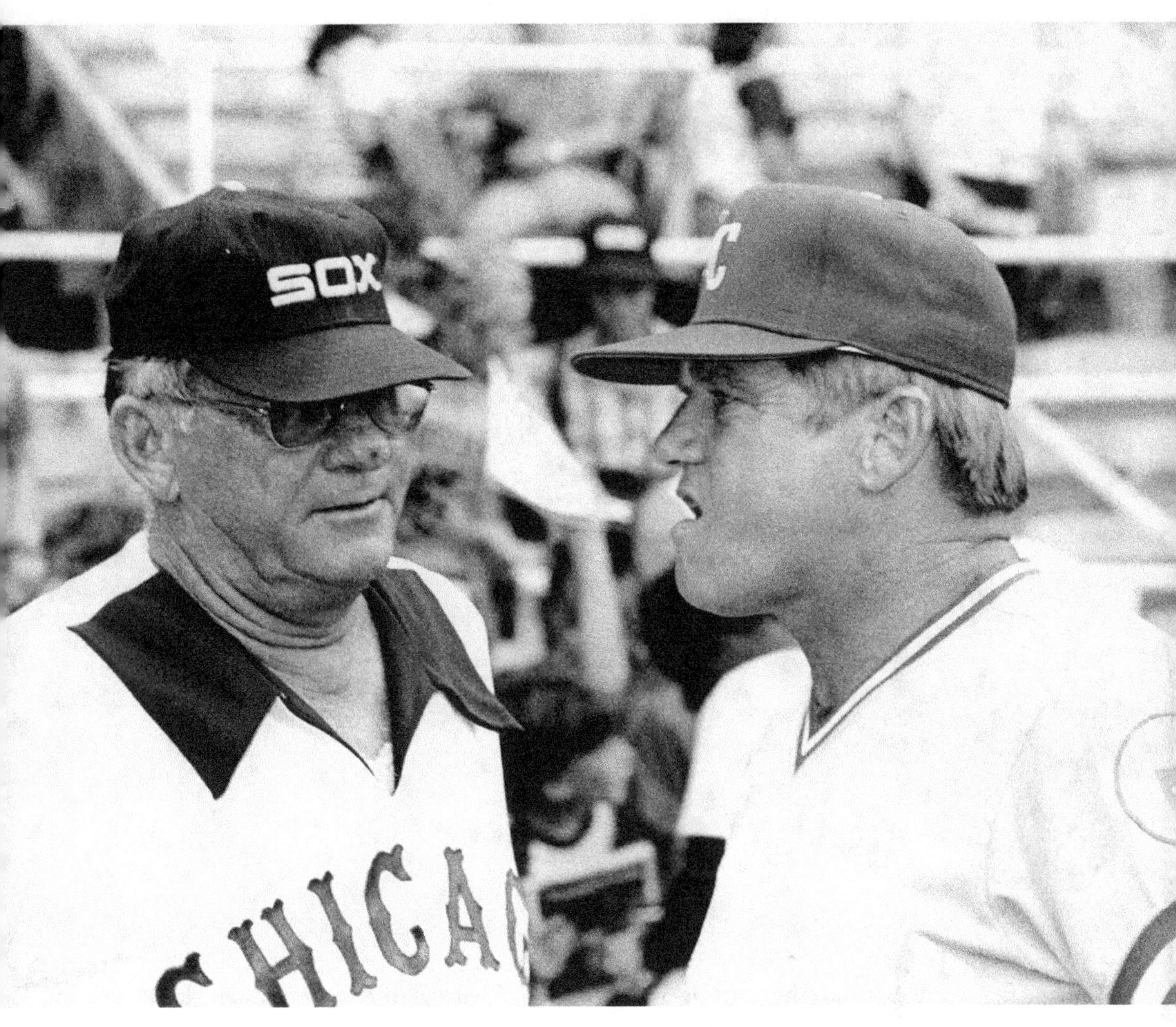

All looks great here between Bob Lemon (left) and Royals manager Whitey Herzog. The same can't be said for the feelings between their players. (Leo Bauby collection.)

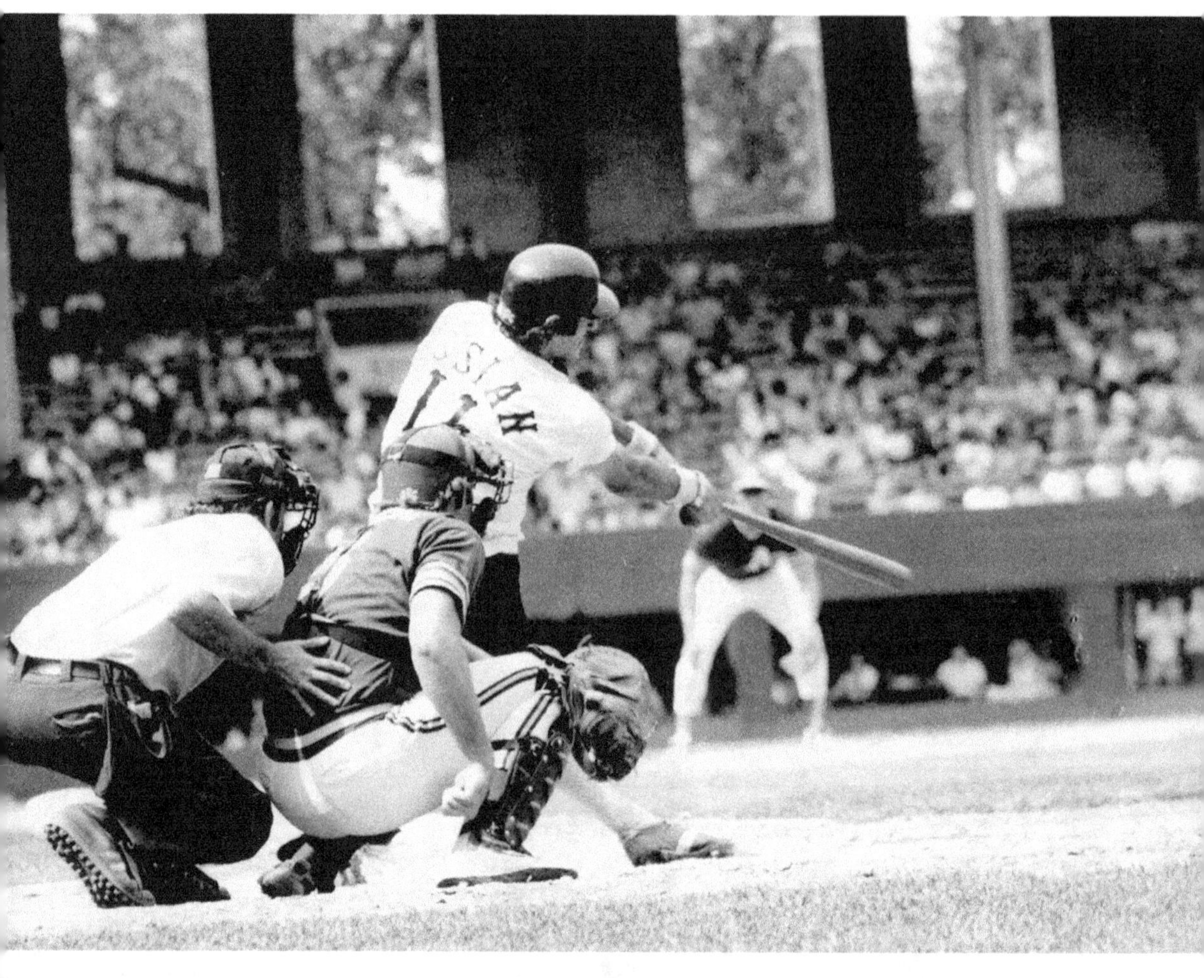

Jim Essian takes a healthy cut. He was part of back-to-back homer combination in the emotional Fourth of July weekend series against the Twins with Alan Bannister. He was one of nine South Side Hitmen to break into double figures for home runs. (Leo Bauby collection.)

6

August to September

Winding Down

Bonafide contending teams contend in the last part of the season. Though technically later season games don't count any more than games in April or May, their importance is magnified as top teams play head to head and there is less time to bounce back from slumps and losing streaks. Teams in mid-season form must turn it on during late-season hysteria or they return to the middle of the pack from whence they came.

After the exciting three of four series over the Royals to end July, the Chicago White Sox seemed ready to go where no Sox team since 1959 had been. They were in first place, 5 ½ games in front of the second place and defending division champion Royals. Everybody on the club seemed to be veterans having career years or young players coming into their own. The story looked like it was going to be a great one; one where a once financially strapped and talent-impaired team had a great chance to get into the post-season.

Before facing an angry Kansas City team again, the Sox were scheduled to finish a 10-game home stand with a four-game set against the fourth-place Texas Rangers.

Winning Ugly would become the battle cry of the 1983 Sox. The first week of August 1977 was plenty ugly with winning only a small part of it. Chicago dropped three out of four to the Rangers, lucky not to be swept in their own ballpark as they salvaged the last game 5-4. With Texas amassing 36 runs in the four games, the Sox were lucky they didn't let the last game get away from them as they almost blew a 5-1 lead in the late innings. Their lead in the American League West was beginning to shrink.

Playing on the road is tough. The visiting team has to face a variety of disadvantages including not being able to sleep in their own beds, playing in a park that is not tailored for them, and the always hostile atmosphere of someone else's hometown crowd. The hostile atmosphere was the biggest obstacle they faced heading into Kansas City for a three-game weekend series.

The Royals were still seething. Not only were they angered by good-bye songs and curtain calls, Kansas City had little respect for the unexpected and first-place holding Sox. Before leaving Chicago, Royals outfielder Amos said he wasn't impressed with the overall Chicago lineup except for a few hitters. "We'll catch them," he predicted.

The first game on August 5 set the tone for the series. Young pitcher Chris Knapp came in with a 9-5 record, but the right hander was knocked out in the second inning. The Royals did some South Side hitting of their own with Otis and catcher Darrell Porter hitting back-to-back homers in a five-run second inning. John Mayberry homered to lead off the third and tipped his cap to the crowd as he returned to the dugout. Before the Sox knew it, they were down 8-1. The final was 12-2 in one of the most humbling losses of the season for the South Siders. Three Sox pitchers had been pounded for 17 hits.

Kansas City won games two (6-3) and three (3-2) to finish the sweep. The worm had begun to turn. Manager Lemon was left in the dugout after game three to ponder the powerful shift in momentum. Over 118,000 Royal fans had come to see their hometown heroes take the air right out of the surprising White Sox. Chicago was still in first place, but their lead stood at a half game ahead of the second place Twins, and one and a half in front the vengeful Royals. Fourth place Texas was not too far back, three games behind. The four-team race brought back memories of 1967.

By August 13 things began to look bleaker. For the first time since July 1, when they beat the Minnesota Twins in that memorable series, the White Sox were no longer in first place. Blowing a two run lead in the eighth, the Sox lost to the Rangers 10-7. And while the Sox had endeared themselves to their fans with an unexpected pennant run, opposition in their division continued to show lack of respect for them and their fans.

"I haven't seen too many teams bludgeon their way to a pennant," Ranger manager Billy Hunter said.

"It's catching up with them—finally," said Texas reliever Darrold Knowles. "It's a little surprising to me they were up there this long. Even if you hit the ball like they do, and score seven or eight runs a game, you gotta get hurt in the long run if you can't catch it that good or throw that good."

The White Sox climbed back into first place with a 6-5 win in the second game of this three game series, but lost the finale as they were again beaten by their own tactics losing 12-9. And again the South Siders felt the backlash as a result of their fan celebrations. Ranger fans had a sing along to serenade the Sox. The good-bye song was played over the loud speaker and the Ranger faithful gladly joined in.

"Whatever happened to that Chicago World Series?" wondered Ranger reliever Dock Ellis. "The Cubs have gone down the tube. You don't suppose the White Sox will be next, do you?"

The Cubs, uncharacteristically, had been playing well but went into their usual slide and would end up dead even for the season. Unfortunately for the White Sox, they were next, as the entire Chicago baseball scene went down the tube as Dock Ellis so eloquently put it.

In an August 16 game against the Yankees, it looked like the Sox would pull out a win in 1977 South Side Hitman style. Chicago went into the top of the ninth down 9-4. They then rattled a barrage of hits. Chet Lemon started off things with a single and was homered in by Spencer. Brian Downing singled to left and one out later Bannister doubled Downing to third. Orta singled in Downing and a Zisk sacrifice fly brought in Bannister. Lamar Johnson singled and Soderholm walked to load the bases. Gamble batted for Lemon and singled in two. When it was all said and done, the Sox had piled on six and took a 10-9 lead.

But as Texas manager Billy Hunter said, not too many teams bludgeon their way to a pennant. The Yankees won the game on a two run homer by Chris Chambliss in their half of the ninth. The inspiring ninth inning rally was rendered meaningless by a heartbreaking loss when the relief pitching couldn't hold the lead. Randy Wiles was the losing pitcher for the White Sox. Wiles never pitched in another major league game.

August 20 was another benchmark in the 1977 season. The Kansas City Royals, as many of their players had predicted, moved into first place. They would never relinquish that position.

By the end of August, the White Sox were still in the hunt, two and a half games behind the Royals. But August had been a terrible month, their only losing month of the season. (Other than the three games in October.) Just what had happened in those dog days?

In an article for http://www.ESPN.com in 2003, writer Keith Scherer analyzed what had gone wrong for the White Sox. His statistics and analysis pretty well mirrored what so many others had been saying about the South Side team.

The ugliness began with the pitching. White Sox hurlers allowed almost six and half runs per game that month. Obviously any team, even a team with great hitting would have a hard time winning over any long stretch if it needed to average seven runs a game to do it.

Even uglier, the Sox staff gave up at least 10 runs eight times. That fete had occurred only three times in the three previous months. Giving up runs in double figures will do it to you most of the time.

The maligned defense lived up to its criticism in August 1977. The Sox gave up 30 unearned runs during the 11-18 month. That is one unearned run a game, and that is pretty hard to overcome. Scherer put it this way: "Balls were slipping through and dropping in, double plays weren't being turned –the pitchers were under constant pressure, and under duress they allowed 33 home runs, again the worst for any month."

Scherer also believes that Orta and Bannister made for a terrible double play combination. The White Sox were last in the number of double plays turned that year.

And on the days the team wasn't knocking the hell out of the ball, they were having a hard time manufacturing runs. Scherer pointed out that the Sox were last in number of steals and stolen base percentage in 1977. They stole a meager 42 while being caught 43 times. Bunting was also a big problem for White Sox. They had but 33 sacrifice hits, again the least in the major leagues.

In essence, their lack of balance caught up with the team in August 1977. Their fans' enthusiasm was thrown back in their faces, and used as a psychological ploy against them. The most lovable thing about them—that they could hit and do nothing else—had exposed the Sox as a team that could not go wire to wire. A foreboding September awaited them.

Much has been said about winning games in September. Being in contention in the last full month of the season is an excellent indicator of how that season has gone and just how good a team is. The 1977 White Sox entered September 73-56, their best record for starting that month since 1965. For a pleasant change, White Sox fans looked forward to that stretch month of September and had some hope of a championship. The White Sox did have one huge disadvantage. Since they no longer had any games with front running Kansas City, they would have to depend on weaker teams in the Western Division to beat the Royals to help the Sox gain ground.

Contending teams make late season acquisitions to push themselves over the top. The Sox went out and picked up ex-Cub Don Kessinger to shore up their not-so-good infield defense. They then re-acquired reliever Clay Carroll from St. Louis. Carroll had valuable post-season experience, winning the decisive game of the classic 1975 World Series for Cincinnati by throwing two hitless innings including a three-up three-down ninth inning in Boston.

Bill Veeck felt he did all he could with his limited resources to shore up his ball club and give Chicago fans a chance to experience their first World Series since 1959.

September 8 was a day that helped seal the fate of the South Side Hitmen. The White Sox started the month with an okay 4-3 mark, but they continued to lose ground to the Royals. The euphoria and hope of July 31 now seemed like it had happened in another season.

First there was symbolism. In the first game of a doubleheader against the California Angels, and in the 137th game of the season, the South Side Hitmen were shut out for the first time. Nolan Ryan, author of many shutouts and no-hitters, earned his 19th win of the season by throwing six and one third innings of three-hit ball. Chicago actually had a great opportunity to score in the first inning when Ralph Garr led off the game with a double and advanced to third on a fly out to right by Alan Bannister. Jorge Orta came up needing only a decent fly to the outfield to score Garr. But before Orta could even attempt to deliver, Garr got himself picked off third by Ryan. Orta did fly out to right but it only ended the inning.

The Sox actually chased Ryan in the seventh when Zisk and Orta singled with one out. Lefty Dave LaRouche relieved Ryan, and got Gamble to fly out to center. Lamar Johnson, pinch hitting for Spencer, fouled out. The last threat of the game for the Sox produced a goose egg.

Game two went beyond symbolism. The Sox blew a 2-0 ninth inning lead and lost 3-2. A wild pitch by Lerrin LaGrow brought in the winning run. Lefty Ken Kravec had given up three hits in eight plus innings, but a succession of three relievers couldn't protect the lead. The hard-hitting Sox had been held to two runs and 12 hits in the doubleheader which was enough to evoke memories of Black Wednesday, 1967.

To compound the misery of this double loss, Kansas City won by knocking out five homers and easily beat Seattle 7-2. The Royals now had a seven game lead over the Sox with 24 remaining. In recalling how the Royals netted a 12 ½ game gain in the standings against the Sox in a little less than six weeks, Steve Stone used the old cliché in 2005 saying they "passed us as if we were standing still."

The Sox were not actually standing still. They had it in reverse, now playing eight games under .500 since the historic July 31 doubleheader. In the reversal, the defending division champs had a foot on the throat of the White Sox.

Chicago rebounded a little with a win the next day. However, Wilbur Wood tied a major league record by hitting three batters in one inning on September 10. None of them were really hurt by the slow moving knuckle ball, but the White Sox felt the pain of a 6-1 loss. A three-run homer by Bobby Bonds provided the Angels with more than enough runs against the suddenly offensively impaired White Sox.

Four days later, the Hitmen were shut out for the second and last time. They again had an opportunity to score when they loaded the bases with one out in the fifth. But Garr forced Bannister at the plate with a grounder to first and Lemon forced Garr at second with a grounder to short. Twins pitcher Dave Goltz went all the way for the win, the only pitcher to throw a complete game shut out against the Sox that year. More importantly the Sox fell to nine games behind the now runaway Royals with only 15 left to play. Only a person with a Cubs fan view of the world would think the Sox would have any chance at a division championship.

All that was left was a little team history. On September 17, Oscar Gamble became the first left-handed White Sox batter to hit 30 homers in a season and only the third South Sider to perform that feat. (Bill Melton and Dick Allen had been the others.) Chicago was down 3-0 in the seventh when Gamble tied the game with a three run shot after Lemon and Orta had walked. No one seemed to care that Gamble took a curtain call for the 15,378 in attendance. Unfortunately the White Sox lost the game when the Angels pushed a run across in the ninth and then made it hold up. Regardless, it was somewhat fitting that Gamble came through in the clutch to get the Sox back into the game. Gamble's final homer of the season came on the next day, giving him the team lead for the season.

On September 27, just days before the season ended, Zisk joined Gamble in the 30-homer club when the Sox exacted a little revenge on Dave Goltz. Zisk's eighth inning solo shot proved to be the difference in a 4-3 win. It was also the first time in the 77-year history of the franchise that the White Sox had two 30-homer players in one season.

But personal achievements were all that was left for the South Side Hitmen. Two days earlier Kansas City clinched their second consecutive Western Division title. While the Sox had cooled down considerably during the last two months of the season, the Royals had an even more incredible month in September than the Sox did in July. Kansas City went an amazing 25-5 in September. They, without a doubt, proved they were the best team in the division, and one of the best teams in baseball. Because of Kansas City's surge, the division race was not even competitive. Even second place Texas finished eight games behind the Royals.

Chokeitis. Many Chicago sports fans thought their teams were forever inflicted with it. But on the last day of the 1977 season, White Sox fans didn't think their team had let them down or choked away a great chance to go to the playoffs. The White Sox, which had been at the top or near the top of the standings since July 1, had actually fallen to third. Texas, with a near Kansas City type September, had taken over second place. No matter what the Sox did that day, they were going to end up in third.

Eric Soderholm recalls how he wanted to achieve two little milestones. He wanted to end the season with a .280 average and have 25 homers. He was able to do both, picking up his 25th homer in the fifth inning. He also remembers the ovation the crowd gave him after his last round tripper. It was as if the White Sox were still in the division race.

The White Sox clowned around and enjoyed the crowd of a little over 20,000. As they took the field for the last inning and when they came in for their last at-bat, they received ovations. As in the season opener, the White Sox finished against an expansion team, this time the Seattle Mariners. Seattle won the game 3-2 as the South Side Hitmen hit very little that dark and rainy afternoon.

No matter. The fans didn't want to leave Comiskey once the game was over. They cheered and Bill Veeck cheered right along with them. It was such a rare day since the decade of disappointment that began in late September 1967. The South Side Hitmen were just different. They knocked the hell out of the ball like no other Sox team before them and allowed their fans to actually think a Chicago World Series was possible. The fact that they didn't get to the Promised Land didn't matter. After the game, White Sox fans chanted, "We want the Sox, we want the Sox."

"Bill Veeck and I were in the depths of despair at this time a year ago," Soderholm said after that final game. "The Sox were in financial trouble and I didn't know if I would ever play again. We both had great comebacks." (Soderholm would win the American League Comeback Player of the Year Award.)

"Win, lose or draw, we put on a show," Alan Bannister chimed in. "Then again the fans put on a show, too."

At mid-season, Richie Zisk had made it clear that he wanted to stay with the White Sox.

"I would love to make my home here and raise my family here," Zisk said. "I'm hopeful something can be worked out. I honestly mean that. But at the same time I realize that with each day that goes along puts me closer to free agency—not that I am looking forward to that."

Unfortunately that last game of the season was the last for Zisk as a White Sox player. It would be the last for others, too. And also unfortunately, the reign of the South Side Hitmen would last for just one year.

"People don't realize what offensive balance we had," Oscar Gamble recalled in 2005, referring the power from the right and left as he ticked off the names of Zisk, Spencer, Lemon, and Soderholm. "If we could have stayed together when the pitching came later, we would have been in the Series."

Looking back in 2005, Soderholm summed up the team in a different way. He referred to himself as a "step and dive" at third, alluding to his reduced range. Alan Bannister had "to sling it at short" because of his bad shoulder. He also remembered that Jorge Orta was not too hot at turning double plays. Soderholm described Lamar Johnson as "a big target at first," and recalled Zisk's non-range in right. He felt Ralph Garr was at the end of his career and had a hard time chasing down fly balls. But the combination of this rag tag bunch was just the right mix—at least for one year.

"We felt we had something to prove," Soderholm says now. "People told me and Bannister that we would never play again. Zisk felt as if he wasn't wanted in Pittsburgh."

At the center of the improbability of the South Side Hitmen was owner Bill Veeck. The baseball powers that be had speculated that Veeck and his group didn't have the resources to run a major league franchise. As free agency began in the late 1970s, that was probably true. Veeck didn't have the ability to sign a marquis star like Reggie Jackson to a long-term contract. Instead, Veeck tried to buy time by trading a player or players that he wouldn't be able to sign for other players he wouldn't be able to sign. This rent-a-player strategy didn't work in the long run. But in 1977, some players may never have been available to Veeck if it wasn't for the dynamics of free agency. It certainly was the case regarding Soderholm and Stone and probably in the cases of Zisk and Gamble. Today Stone and Soderholm are grateful for the faith Veeck had in them when others had been skeptical.

Yet the newly found freedom of players exploring the market place worried fans as they enjoyed the summer of 1977. From all indications, the South Side Hitmen were not going to stay together. Most of the speculation centered around Zisk and Gamble, the team's leading home run hitters. In the middle of all the excitement, it was becoming apparent that a winning team was going to be intentionally split apart once the season ended. Fans appealed to the players to stay, but it wasn't a matter of loyalty. Gamble said in 2005 that the Sox did make him an offer as he tested the free agent market after the 1977 season. In comparison to other offers he received, Gamble said the Sox offer "wasn't even close."

There was a parallel to the early 1960s when bitter Veeck critics savaged him for trading away talent and potential costing the Sox future pennants. During the late 1970s, the Sox had a net loss when they traded one player they couldn't sign for another whom they also would not able to resign. As a result, the success of the 1977 Hitmen was short lived.

Still, the South Side Hitmen have to be credited with helping the Sox remain in Chicago. Couldn't anyone imagine what kind of interest Chicago would have had in a team that in any way resembled the 1976 squad? In 1978, the White Sox drew a little over 1.4 million and in 1979, they had a little more than 1.2 million. By 2005 standards, that isn't overly impressive. In comparison to the Sox attendance in the early part of the decade, it was quite an achievement. The afterglow of 1977 had to be partly responsible.

Even the most cynical and hard boiled fan will get defensive if anyone accuses the South Side Hitmen of "choking." Most will say that the 1977 White Sox didn't have the depth to win a division championship or World Series. Fans know that the defense wasn't there, and the pitching was only so good. They knew that, in the end, good pitching stops good hitting in the long run. So many fans felt they got what they paid for. The 1977 South Side Hitmen gave them the most exciting moments of the decade, and that was enough to endear the team to its faithful for decades afterward. Only the passage of time and a World Series team like the 2005 edition will push the memories of 1977 to the back burner.

"They didn't want the whole field, they wanted the whole grandstand," says Bill Jauss who many times covered the Sox for the *Chicago Tribune*.

Jauss referred to the resentment and anger the Kansas City Royals felt toward the Hitmen after that season-defining series at the end of July. Jauss said that he understood the resentment the Royals felt since they looked at themselves as a team that paid its dues and weren't ready to take a back seat to the upstart White Sox. Kansas City followed the philosophy of batting instructor Charlie Lau (whose last batting coach job was with the White Sox before he died in 1984) and used the whole field to pick up hits. It irked the Royals to see this one-dimensional team swing from the heels and then bow to their fans like an actor who was just too full of himself.

The Royals may have used that resentment to rally themselves, but they were wrong if they thought the Sox were grandstanding. The Hitmen had awakened a slumbering fan base that had not been impressed with .500 records or .241 hitters. The decade between 1967 and 1977 had been a long one with only a few highlights. The year 1977 was different in that it was unexpected and thus exceeded the hopes of fans who had grown tired and frustrated with a team that sometimes played like a contender but finished as an also-ran. More importantly, there was an excitement at Comiskey Park that lasted the whole summer when other White Sox teams could only occasionally stir such emotion. A case can be made that the 1977 White Sox are more loved and revered than the division winners of 1983, 1993, and 2000, and that only the 2005 World Series squad will produce a team that can generate similarly charged emotions.

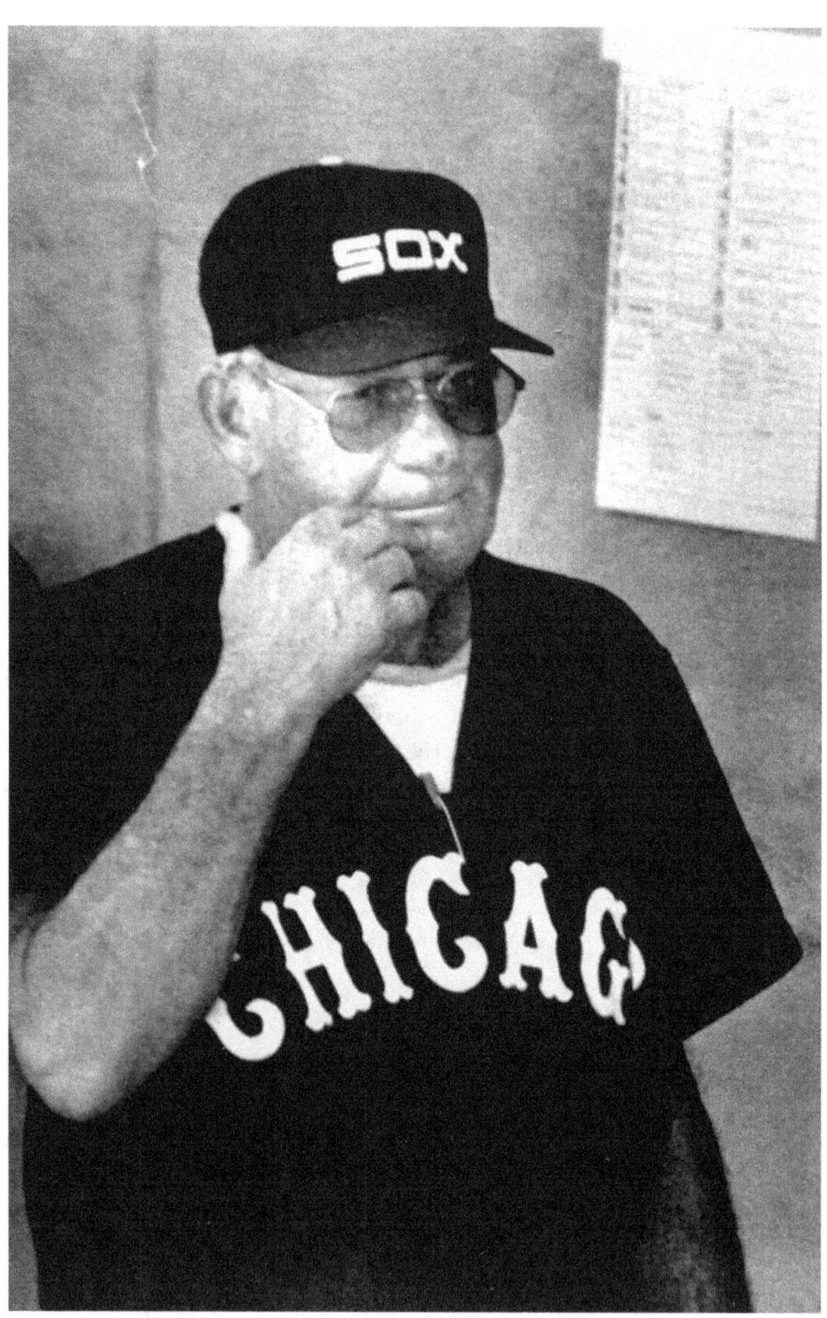

Almost in a state of shock, Bob Lemon muses in the dugout after the Royals had swept the Sox in a three-game series during the first weekend of August in Kansas City. The White Sox were crushed in game one, and couldn't win close games two and three. The Royals had their revenge for the previous weekend in Comiskey when White Sox fan hysteria was at its 1977 peak. Worse yet, Kansas City was on its way to division championship. (Leo Bauby collection.)

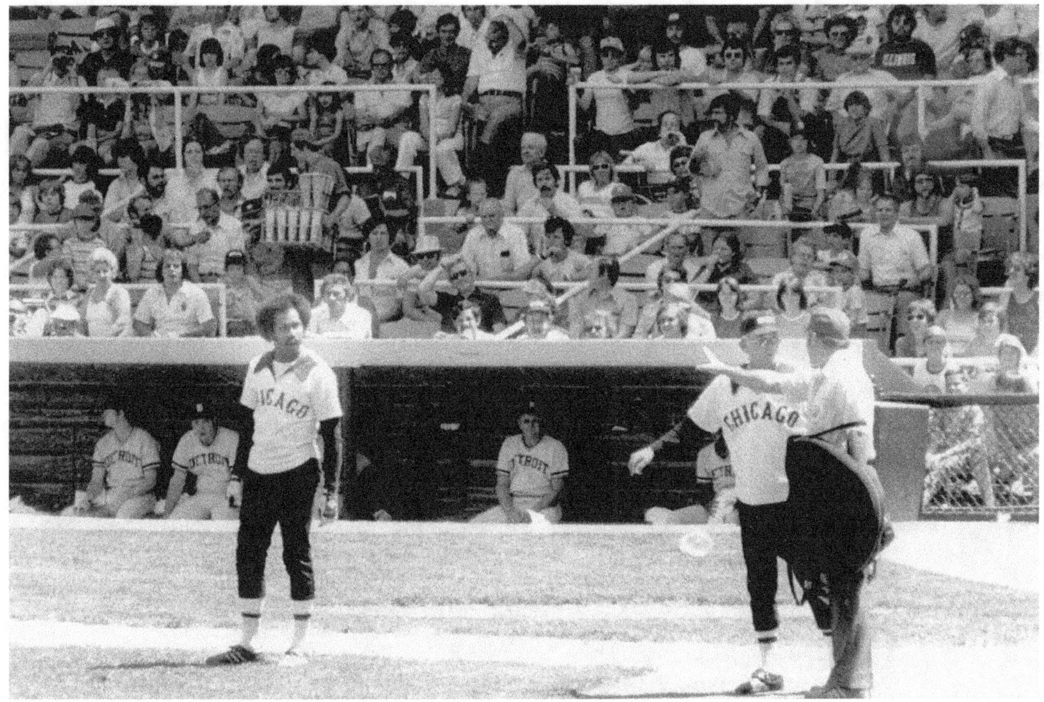

Oscar Gamble (left) and Bob Lemon have a disagreement with the umpire. Nothing much went right during the month of August. (Leo Bauby collection.)

There is one other thing that went right in 1977. The White Sox signed Harold Baines after making him the overall first pick in the amateur free agency draft. A key member of the 1983 Winning Ugly team, Baines could always be counted on for a late inning hit that drove in a big run. Fans loved Baines because the quiet guy let his bat do his talking for him, finishing his career with 2,866 hits. He received a long-standing ovation during his last career at bat on September 27, 2001, at Comiskey Park, now called U.S. Cellular Field. (Leo Bauby collection.)

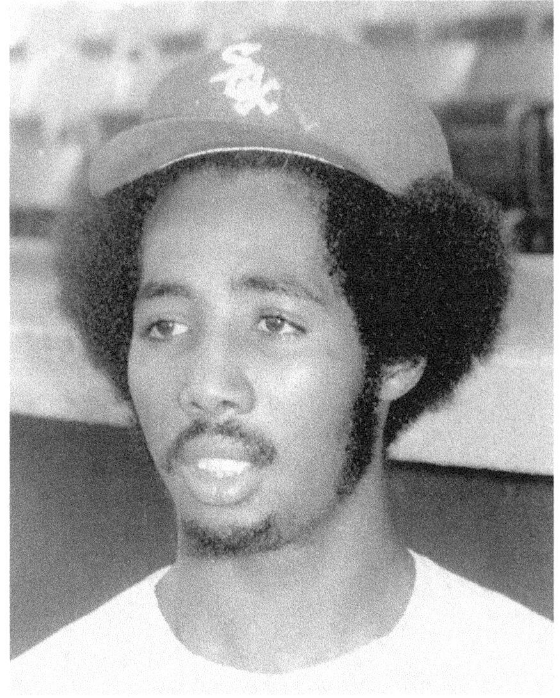

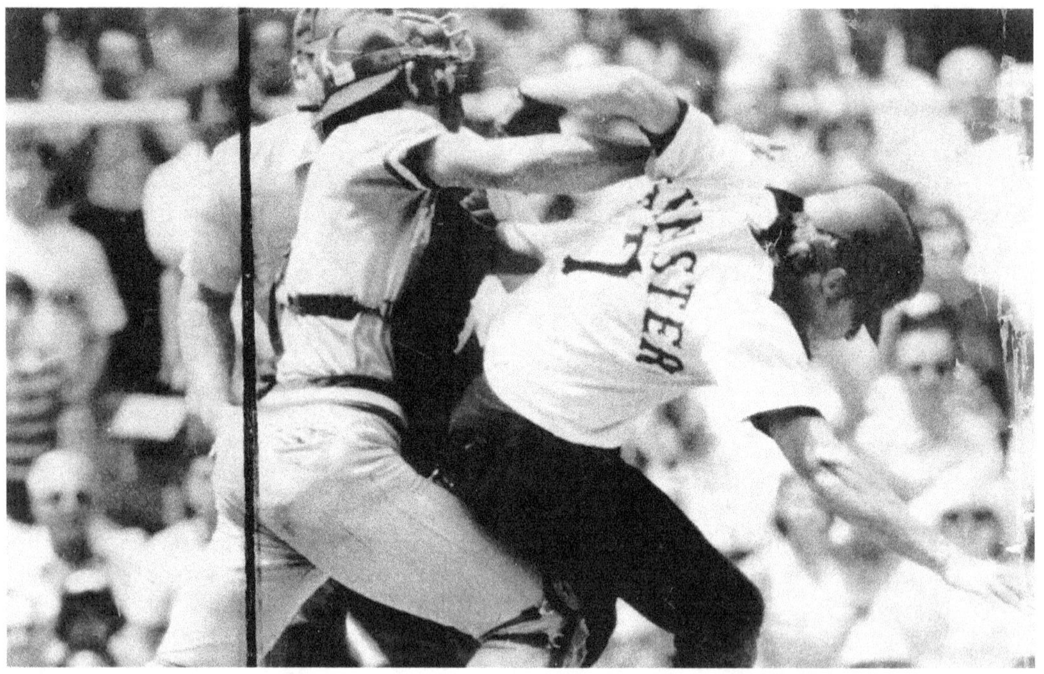

Darrell Porter puts a rough tag on Alan Bannister. Tension between the White Sox and Royals was high during the summer of 1977. Porter ended up getting into an altercation with Sox pitcher Bart Johnson during the momentum changing series in Kansas City. (Leo Bauby collection.)

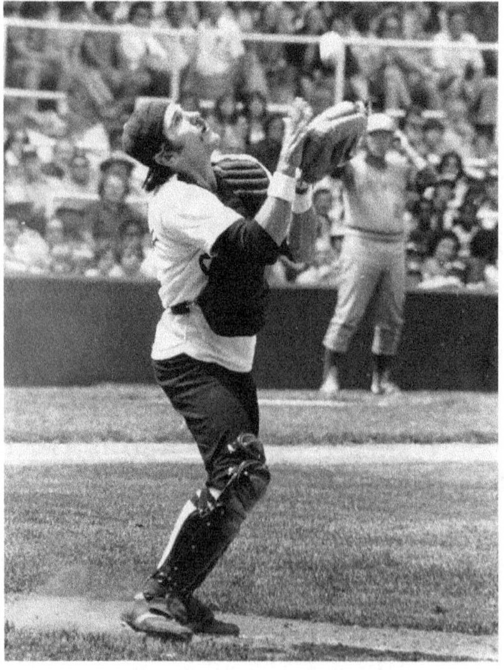

Catcher Jim Essian gets under a pop-up. The White Sox could have used a few more plays like this in August. Instead their pitchers got hit around for over six runs a game and their defense didn't help matters much. They paid for it with their 11-19 record that month. (Leo Bauby collection.)

Harry Caray poses with broadcast partner Mary Shane. Veeck, who liked to be different, broke ground by bringing a woman into the booth. Her Sox broadcasting career was short. (Leo Bauby collection.)

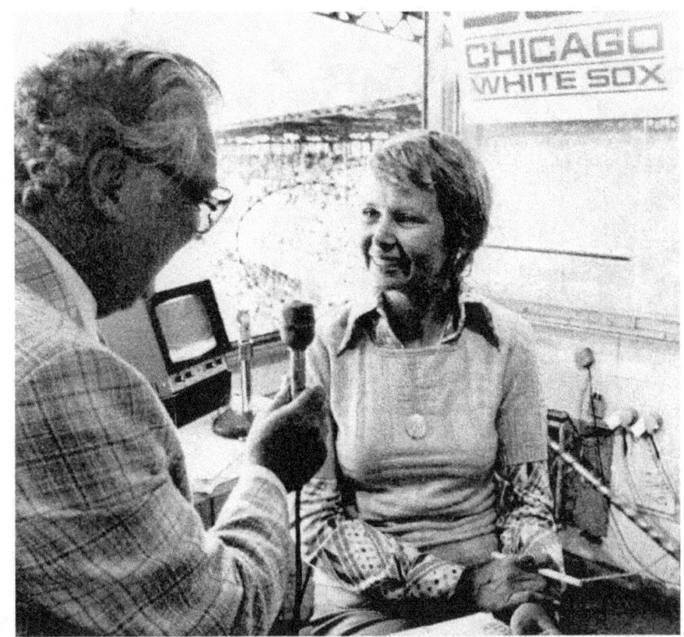

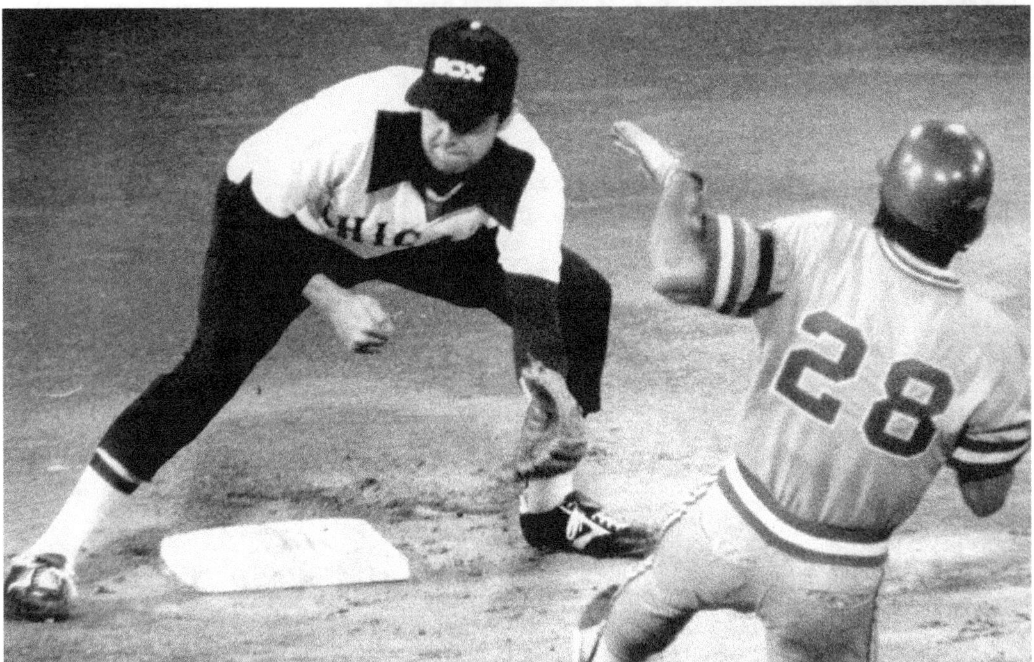

To shore up the weak White Sox defense, Veeck went out and got Don Kessinger in August 1977. Kessinger, a key component of the 1969 Cubs, was known for his great range at short and his incredible off balance throws from deep in the hole. He would later manage the White Sox until the beginning of August during the not-so-memorable 1979 season. (Leo Bauby collection.)

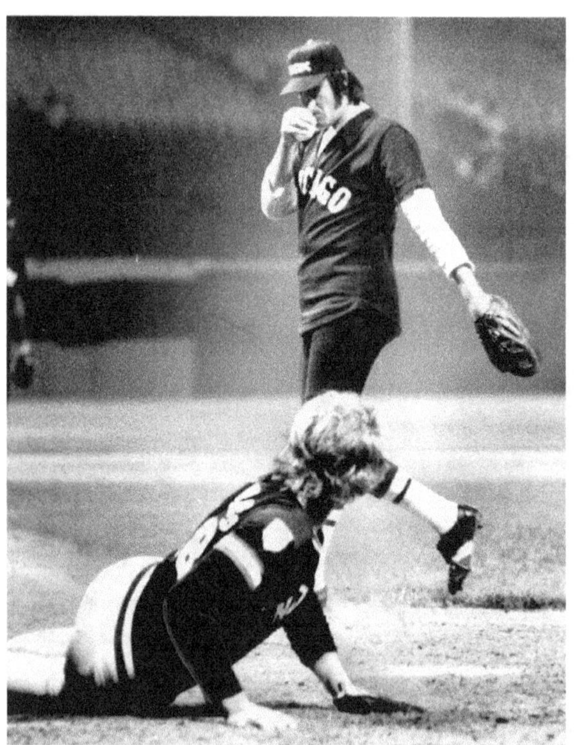

The mercurial, but talented Francisco Barrios won 14 in 1977. Here he is gesturing to an opposing player in a kind of un-sportsmanlike way. Barrios never came close to fulfilling his potential after the 1977 season. He died of a heart attack in 1982 two months short of his 29th birthday. (Leo Bauby collection.)

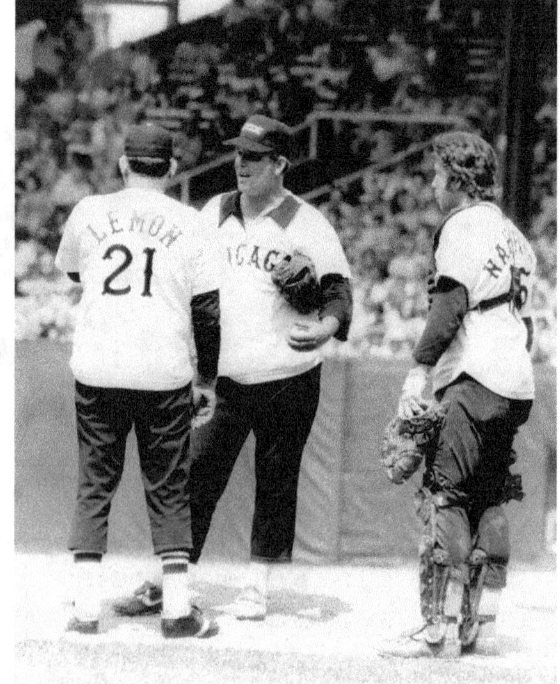

Unfortunately, in a too familiar scene in August of 1977, Bob Lemon comes out to the mound to make a pitching change. (Leo Bauby collection.)

7

The 1977 Hitmen Remembered

Fan Memories of the South Side Hitmen

David Sheputis: This is my favorite all time Sox team and the best games I ever attended were that season. I was 13, we were living in southern Illinois at the time, and I listened to almost every game on the radio. My most memorable game was July 31. The Sox played a doubleheader against the Royals wrapping up a four-game first place showdown of which they had already won the first two. It was banner day and my brother, stepfather, and I stayed up all night making a banner for the doubleheader. We had to leave around 4:00 a.m. and basically slept all the way to Chicago. We got there before the gates opened and there were already big crowds outside the ballpark. We ended up sitting in the right field upper deck, halfway up, against the rail looking down into the center field bleachers. It was extremely hot that day, and the whole atmosphere in the park was electric. I can remember when the Sox took the field for the first game; they were given what seemed like a ten minute standing ovation delaying the state of the game. The crowd was just at a fever pitch that whole first game, without a scoreboard telling them to cheer. It was the loudest I can ever remember it being in the old ballpark. Marty Pattin started for the Royals, and I seemed to remember he had a perfect game for six innings. Then in the seventh someone for the Sox (I think Chet Lemon or Alan Bannister) hit a homer to break up the perfect game. Then in the tenth Chet Lemon hit a homer and I swear the upper deck was shaking it was so loud. It gave me goose bumps. We went down to the field between games to line up for the banner parade, and it was like an English soccer game with spontaneous chants/cheers just breaking out. By the time the second game started, the heat and probably a lot of booze has just taken it out of the crowd. I remember the Royals won it easily. Hal McRae and Al Cowens incited the crowd by tipping their caps to the crowd mocking the Sox curtain calls during the first game. I watched a lot of fights in the center field bleachers in the second game and security continually getting pelted with garbage when they would try to break it up.

Richard Brook: I typically attended at least 20-25 games annually. Back in 1977, with a surging, exciting team on the field, I attended over 40 home games. One of the most vivid memories I have of that season, while usually seated in the left field stands, was how Sox fans started singing, "Na, Na, Hey, Hey, Good-bye." It was the last week of July and the Sox were heading into a weeklong home-stand against the Twins and a four game weekend series against the Royals. The left field grandstand fans started taunting the Twins by singing, "Na, Na, Na, Na, Na, Na, Na, Minnesota, good-bye." That carried over when the Royals were here, and as they were being knocked from first place, the left field fans again sang, only this time saying "Royals." By Saturday, Nancy Faust picked up the song and played it all weekend long. The rest is history, and the song remains a fixture today whenever an opposing pitcher is removed. As usual, the fun didn't last past August, and we continue to wait for a championship season. [Fan quoted before the 2005 playoffs.]

Paul Duffy: I was in high school and my dad took my brother and sisters and me to a Friday night game on May 13. It was "Anti-Superstition Night" because it was Friday the 13th. It was one of Bill Veeck's ridiculous over-the-top pre-game carnivals. They had 13 people who called themselves "witches" on the field before the game to put a "spell" on the other 13 AL teams. People broke mirrors on the field with baseball bats. They set up a ladder and announced beforehand that they'd make the visiting Cleveland walk under before the game, but I think the Tribe players refused. The Sox beat the Tribe easily. [Actually it was a 5-3 Sox win.]

Bill Veeck was like a rock star in 1977. I saw him arrive in a cab at the park a couple times that summer and people always yelled nice things to him and wanted to shake his hand or get him to sign something. He always looked happy to be talking to people and was very nice. He'd walk around the ballpark during the games and there was a buzz when he was nearby. He co-hosted the "Mary Frances Veeck & Friend" show with his wife Sunday mornings and we'd never miss it; often we were on our way to the ballpark when it was on the radio. Mary Frances Veeck was a very gracious and intelligent person and they were great together.

Howard Cosell was doing Monday Night Baseball for ABC and Harry Caray did an interview with him (I think on radio) before a game. Cosell was effusive in his praise during the Caray interview and both basically complimented each other. Then Cosell went on the national telecast and just savaged Caray, calling him unprofessional for being a cheerleader, etc. Caray ripped Cosell afterwards about being a back-stabber. It became fashionable for national announcers, players, and others to rip on the behavior of the Sox fans, Veeck, and Caray/Piersall. I took offense to it; the Sox had never won anything in my life and what was wrong with having fun with it?

Leo Bauby: The early season Sunday doubleheader vs. the A's. I watched all five hours on my grandparents' TV as the Sox won the first game 2-1. Lamar Johnson cracked two homers in game one and the Sox had a well-pitched game. The Sox won game two and I specifically remember Dick Allen pinch hitting [for the A's] in a key situation and striking out. After the game Harry did his post game recap from the Channel 44 booth and the Sox fans were loud. He repeatedly waved his microphone in an attempt to let the fans voice themselves on the air. [So he could resume his recap.] The noise actually got louder and Harry was having a ball. Soon the "We're Number One" chant began and Harry commented how the best fans in the world have waited a long time for this. The TV crew caught Harry's interaction with the fans a good five minutes after he was through recapping the game. I believe this was a defining moment in 1977, as the fans' excitement for the Sox became infectious from this point on.

I caught Greek Night Vs the Red Sox on the radio as there were terrible thunderstorms where we lived. The White Sox bashed the Red Sox and cruised to a big lead. Wilbur Wood again held a very potent Red Sox lineup to a couple runs until he tired. Our radio crackled with every bolt of lightening. I remember Harry Caray asking the audience to stop by Comiskey Park that night if they wanted to earn money. There were not enough beer vendors to service the 45,000 person crowd.

A fan next to us offered my friend and me sips from his whiskey bottle. We declined as we were only eight years old. [Bauby and his friend were at the July 31 doubleheader. He vividly remembers Chet Lemon's first of two homers in game one going into the left field upper deck.]

Nancy Faust—The Person Entertaining the Fans

In two interviews that she has given the author, Nancy Faust never claimed to be a lonely woman. To the contrary, with all the attention fans have given her during the past 35 years, it would be hard to believe that Faust would ever feel unpopular.

Yet when she was hired as the third organist for the White Sox in 1970, she may have considered joining a lonely hearts club, at least after spending so much time at the vast and sometimes lonely looking Comiskey Park. Stationed out in center field close to 500 feet from home plate, Faust played to an empty house most of that summer. Bill Melton once described that 106-loss experience as "hard to be humiliated in front of 5,000 people."

Sometimes the White Sox didn't draw that much, and there wasn't much applause for a team going down to one defeat after another. It couldn't have done much for a musician's ego to constantly entertain a small audience.

Then there was the White Sox organization's idea of getting fans involved in the game. Front office man Stu Holcomb gave Faust a list of players and their native state songs. They could be played when a player was at bat or entering the game. No doubt Chicago fans would feel the chills when they heard the state song of Oklahoma. (Oklahoma was the birthplace of Virle Rounsaville. Remember him?)

Additionally, Faust wasn't welcomed with open arms by some, expressing their belief that the ballpark was no place for a woman organist. A petition was passed around calling for her ouster.

"That has been the only negative thing about my job," Faust recalls.

But Faust became more known as attendance improved during the early 1970s. Not taking Holcomb's advice, Faust was a little more imaginative about entertaining White Sox fans. And in 1977 she cemented her place in team history by starting a tradition that has endured for almost 30 years with no signs of dying.

"It wasn't the first time I played it," Faust says, referring to a song that was a hit for a group named Steam. It made it to number one for two weeks in Billboard's Top 100 chart in December 1969.

The Kansas City Royals visited Comiskey Park almost eight years after Steam had its 15 minutes of fame. No doubt group members had no idea that their song, a ballad about a guy who is the third part of a love triangle and desperately wants to see the object of his affections kiss another guy good-bye for good, would ever become a theme song for a major league baseball franchise.

"The mood at the park was at a fever pitch," Faust recalls. "The Sox were vying for first and it was a free for all at the park. The fans were into the game and they started singing. You can't dictate something like that.

"Later on people asked me, 'What was that song?'"

The actual title of the song is "Na, Na, Hey, Hey, Kiss Him Goodbye." It was played to serenade opposing pitchers as they left the game after being once again pummeled by the South Side Hitmen. Faust also played it at the end of White Sox victories when the opposition had no choice but say good-bye to any chance of getting a victory that day.

Mercury Records re-released the "45" and it became a hit once more. The record company presented Faust with a gold record as a token of its appreciation.

"Harry Caray told them to 'forget the record and just give her the gold,'" Faust said.

"He [Caray] promoted every side of the game," Faust added. "And that included me. When he sang during the seventh inning stretch, he always said, 'Let me hear you, Nancy.'"

Faust, who has missed only five White Sox games since 1970 due to the birth of her son, doesn't believe she ever alone caused any adverse fan reaction by playing a song, especially during the 1970s.

"In the old days, you didn't need any stimuli," Faust says. "It was a natural excitement. What I do is to enhance the emotion and prompt people to respond. There were times I got cues from the fans.

"There are still organists in five or six parks, and two or three are full time," Faust says, referring to the dying breed of organ players. "It is not a popular instrument. I have the edge. Not a lot of people are doing what I am doing."

Faust has added technology and other instruments to modernize her act, but she says, "I long for days and years that have gone by. You can never replace the good old days."

No, one cannot relive the past. However, Sox fans still feel an attachment to Faust and she remains a symbol of the team. How many organists are still remembered by a team's fans? Betcha you can't name one of them.

Steve Stone Remembers the South Side Hitmen

Every team has a defining game in a memorable season. Steve Stone, who led the Sox staff with 15 wins in 1977, thinks the second game of the July 31 doubleheader was the pivotal game that helped put an end to the White Sox division hopes that year. While third baseman Eric Soderholm believes that Hal McRae's slow home run trot and angry post-game remarks to the media put the White Sox on the defensive about the curtain calls, Stone questions the lineup that manager Bob Lemon put on the field when the White Sox had a chance to sweep the defending Western Division champion Royals.

"When you have your foot on their throat," Stone said in the summer of 2005, "you better kill them."

Stone remembered Lemon using a great deal of the Sox bench in that game and thought it was not a good time to rest the team's players. (In fact, regulars Garr, Orta, Zisk, Gamble, Spencer, and Chet Lemon were in the contest. Regulars Soderholm, Essian, and Bannister didn't start though Bannister was late inning replacement and got one at-bat. These three regulars were replaced by part-time players Jack Brohamer, Brian Downing, and Tim Nordbrook. The three went a combined one for nine, although that hit was a two-run homer by Downing in the ninth that made the score a little more respectable.)

"I don't know why he did it," Stone said of Lemon, who died in 2000. "Managers didn't explain why they did things back then."

However, loss of momentum or no loss of momentum, Stone believes the best team won the Western Division Title in 1977. He described Kansas City as "a complete ball club," and the White Sox, even with nine players in double figures in home runs, didn't have the depth to be there at the end of a six-month season.

"We were short on skills." Stone recalls. "In a 162 game-season, whatever you have suspect will come out. You can't win the pennant with 10-9 wins. We were a bit shaky on defense. Jorge Orta is still waiting to complete his first double play of 1977."

Stone signed as a free agent with the White Sox after spending three seasons with the Cubs. He labeled himself as the cheapest of the first crop of free agents, making $60,000 a year. He quickly calculated that the White Sox paid $4,000 a victory, wondering out loud if the Cubs would like to pay Kerry Wood that much for each of his victories. Regardless, Stone was grateful to Bill Veeck for giving him a chance to perform for the White Sox, and credits the Sox owner for creating the excitement during the summer of 1977.

"Harry Caray talked about having fun at the ballpark," Stone said, "and that was Bill's idea. He lived that phrase. That is what he gave them that year. It was exciting."

Stone also recalled Veeck saying, "If you don't have money, you should err on the side of offense."

Stone also has fond memories of Caray who had spent 11 seasons on the airwaves describing failed White Sox attempts to go to the World Series.

"Harry would come up to me after a loss, and say 'what happened to you,'" Stone recalled. "I never made any excuse to him. He respected that."

As a result, Stone says, it was Carey who put Stone's name on a short list when the Chicago Tribune Company was looking for a color man in the WGN-TV broadcast booth for Cub games. And Stone felt that the relationship between players and announcers and the rest of the media was more healthy in 1977 than now when "thin skinned" players get offended about what is written or said about them.

"We viewed the media as our friends," Stone remembers. "There was no 24-hour sports cycle with people trying to uncover dirt."

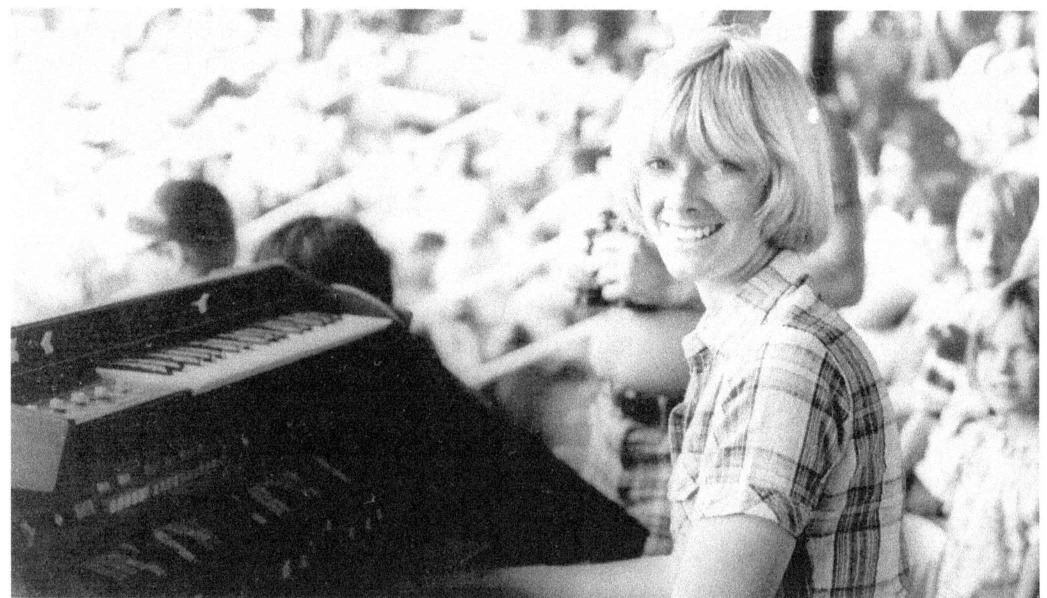

Nancy Faust is seen here one year before the Hitmen. Throughout the years, Faust has said, "I try to make myself accessible to the fans." It is one reason that she has been able to remain a fixture with the White Sox through two ownership changes, two stadiums, and over three decades. It is amazing how she is associated with the 1977 team almost in the same way the players are. (Leo Bauby collection.)

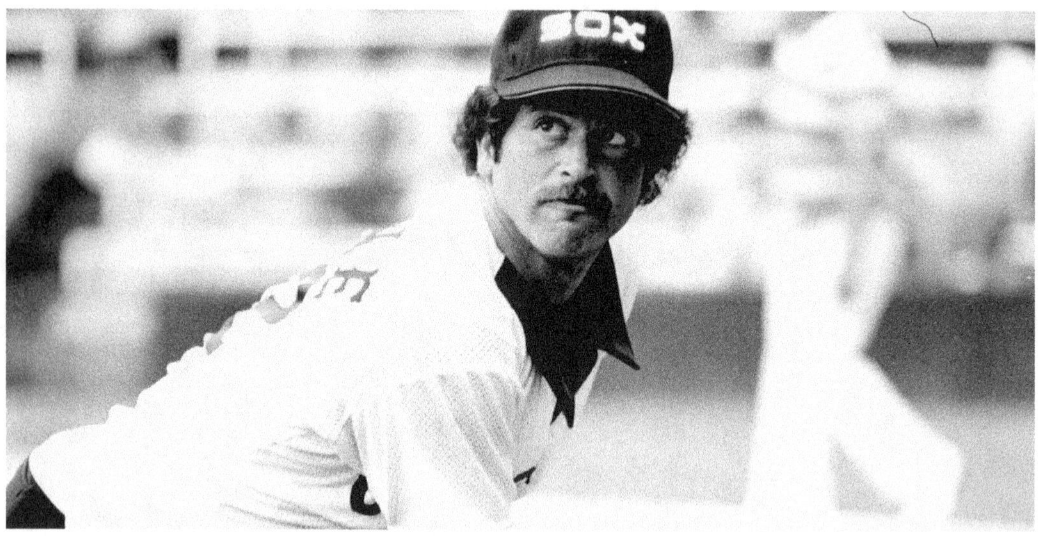

"But I didn't get any hits," Steve Stone said when contacted by the author in 2005. Like many others, Stone associated the 1977 White Sox with hits and homers and not pitching. He still led the White Sox with 15 wins that year. His best year was in 1980 when he won 24 for Baltimore and won the American League Cy Young Award. (Leo Bauby collection.)

Stone felt that Bob Lemon had not put in his "A" lineup against Kansas City in the second game of the infamous July 31 doubleheader. Brian Downing, shown here chasing a pop-up, started game two, which was one of 69 games he appeared in that season. He went on to have an "A" type career with the California Angels. (Leo Bauby collection.)

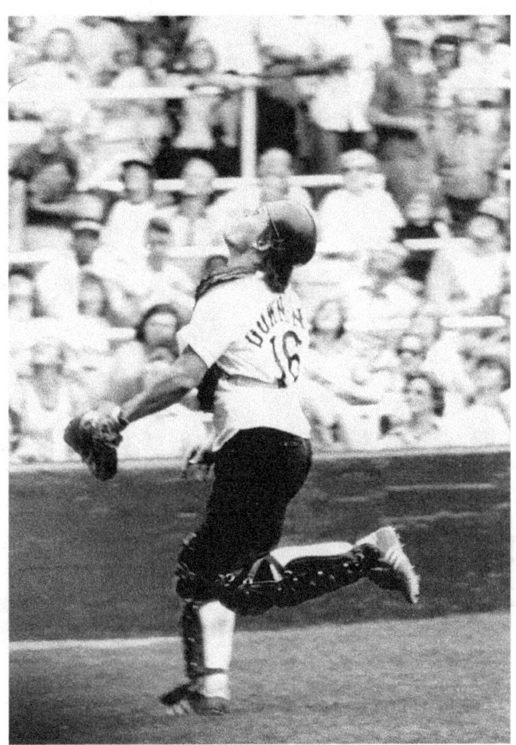

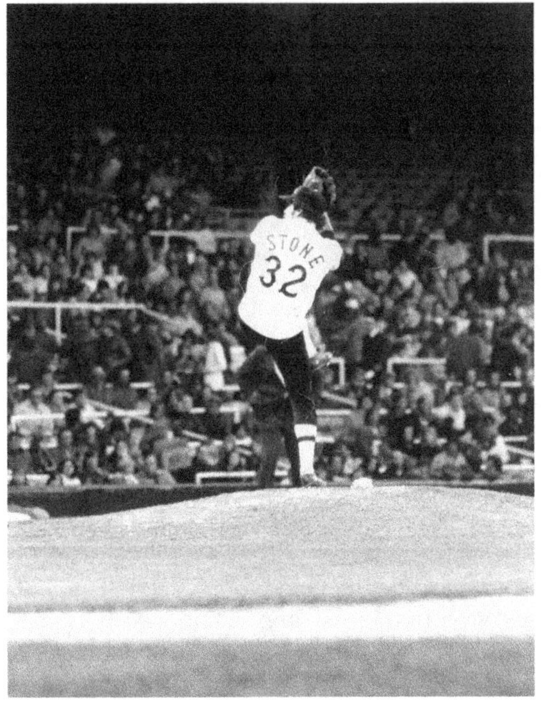

Steve Stone is in pitching form against the New York Yankees. Very few of the games between the Sox and Yankees were pitching duels in 1977. Stone and the Hitmen had their problems against the team that went on to win the World Series. Yet the Yankees always knew they had to come to the park to play when the White Sox furnished the competition. (Leo Bauby collection.)

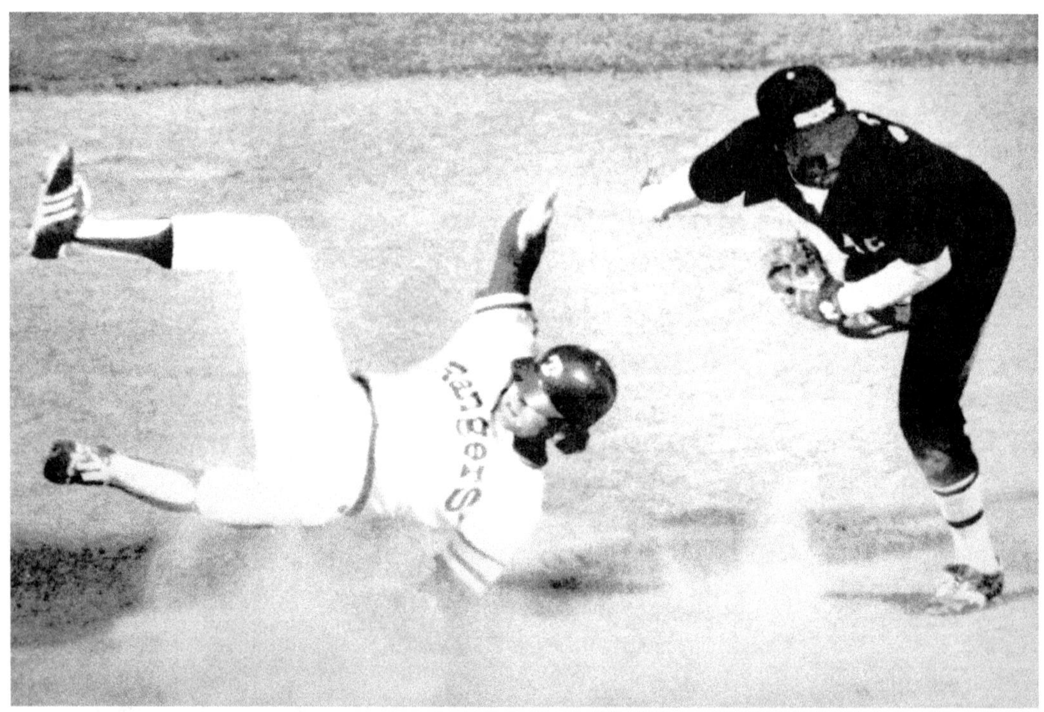

Stone jokes that Jorge Orta is still waiting to complete his first double play of 1977. Well, not quite. He is turning the trick here in May of that year. (Leo Bauby collection.)

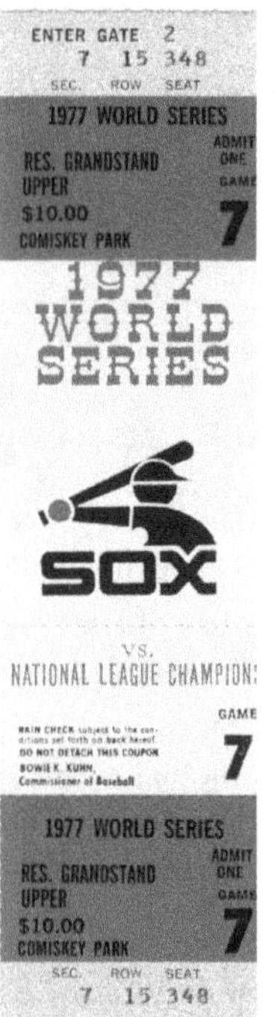

Another printed World Series ticket never used. It would have been a great series if the Hitmen had a chance to do their thing on the national stage, if only to get even with Hal McRae. (Leo Bauby collection.)

Chet Lemon was still swinging the bat well in September. However, it was all over pretty quickly during that month. The White Sox wouldn't play another meaningful September game until the Winning Ugly season of 1983. (Leo Bauby collection.)

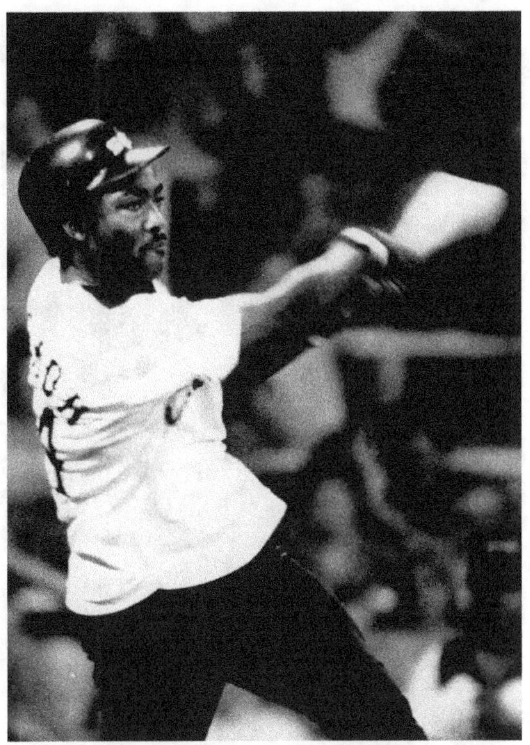

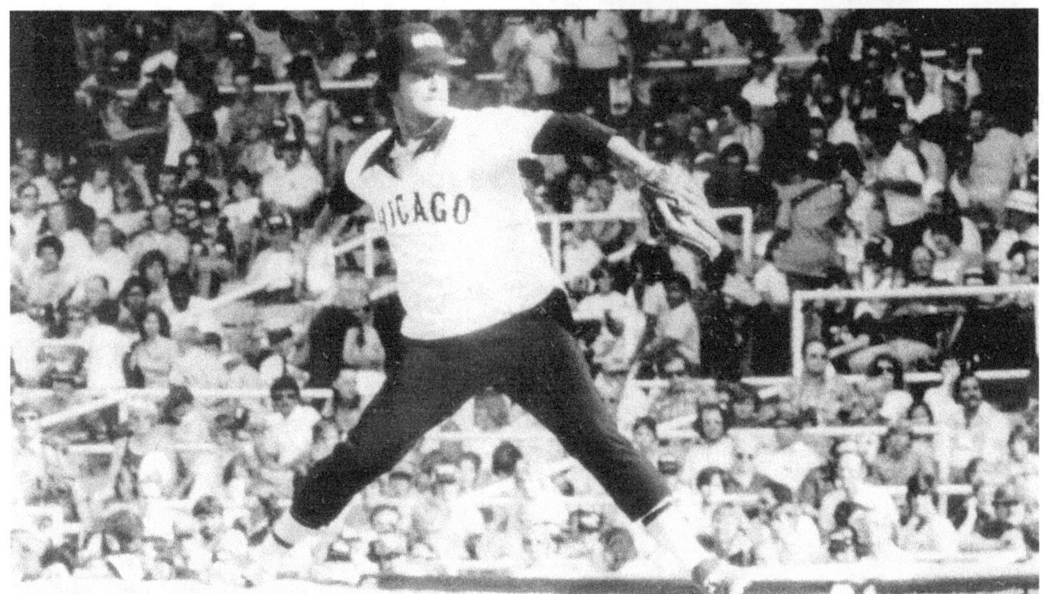

Clay Carroll looks to be in good form in September. He had been traded away right before the season started and re-acquired for the stretch run. His numbers were not that great for the month. It didn't really matter. Kansas City was so good that month that no one was going to catch them. (Leo Bauby collection.)

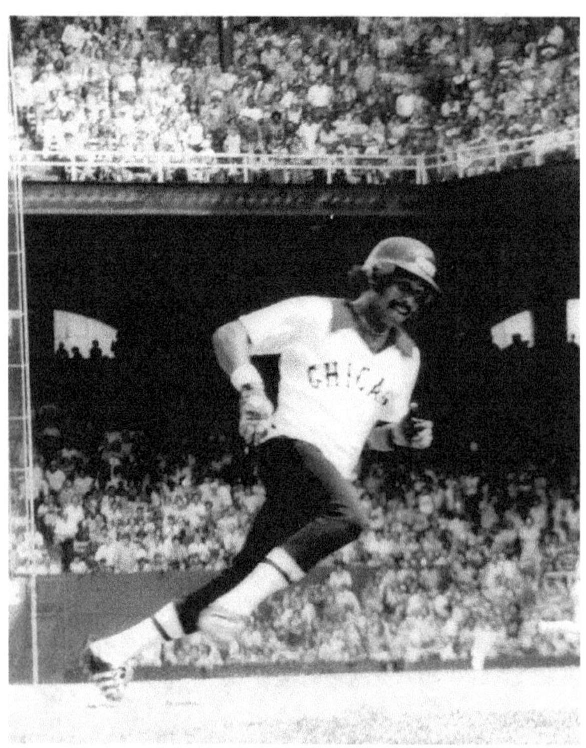

Oscar Gamble rounds third and heads for home. In the background is a pretty good looking crowd. The Hitmen brought many out to the park, because they were the most entertaining Sox team in a long time. Entertaining, yes. Championship winning, no. (Leo Bauby collection.)

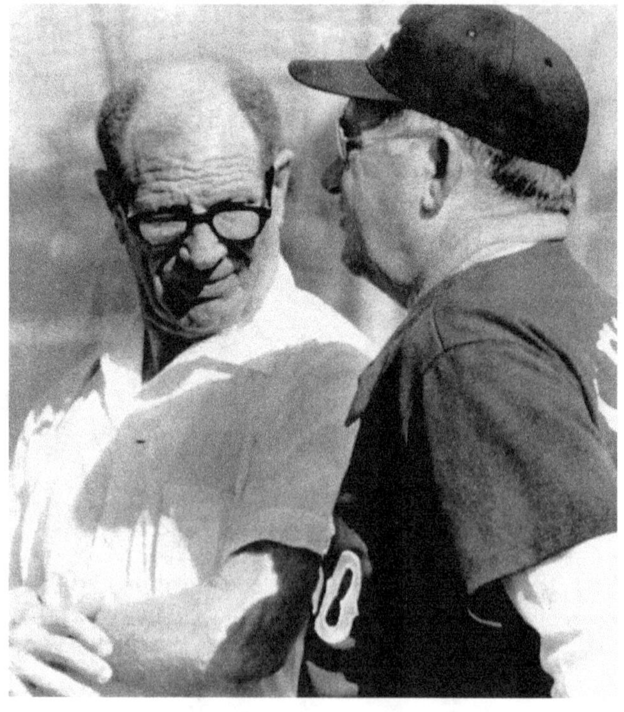

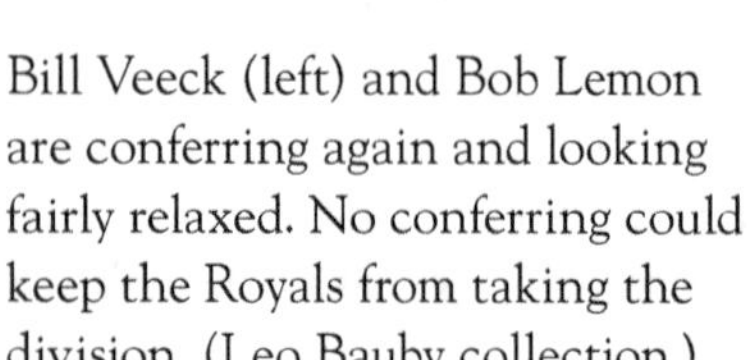

Bill Veeck (left) and Bob Lemon are conferring again and looking fairly relaxed. No conferring could keep the Royals from taking the division. (Leo Bauby collection.)

Richie Zisk was one of the most popular players during the Hitmen season. Here he is signing autographs for some fans. The last game of the season wasn't over for long when he cleaned out his locker and left, never playing for the White Sox again. (Leo Bauby collection.)

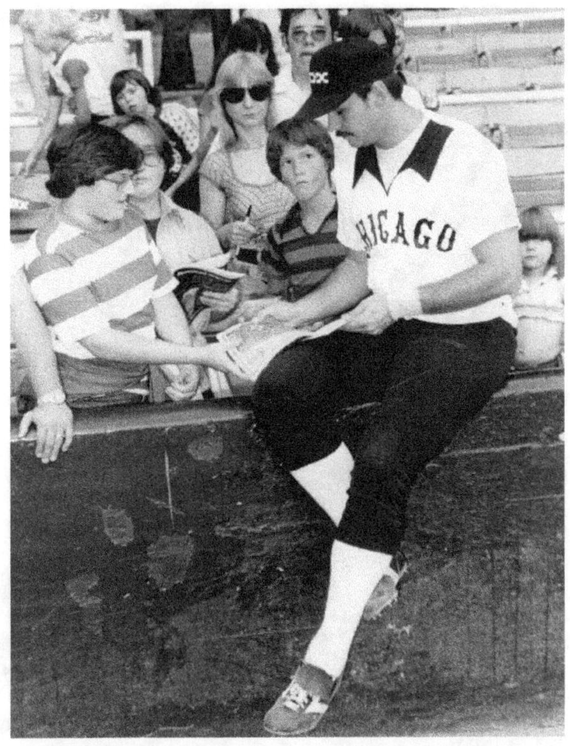

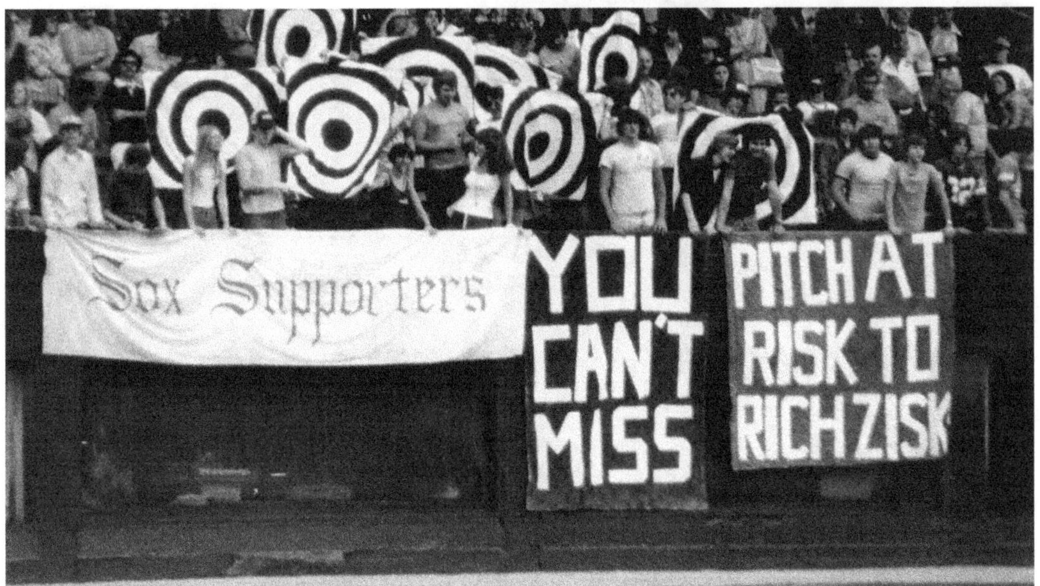

Banners were very popular during the 1977 season. Here we have the Sox Supporters, the bull's eyes, and the warning of pitchers of the risk of throwing to Richie Zisk. The emotion at the ballpark has been rarely matched since 1977, and in some ways, will never be matched. (Leo Bauby collection.)

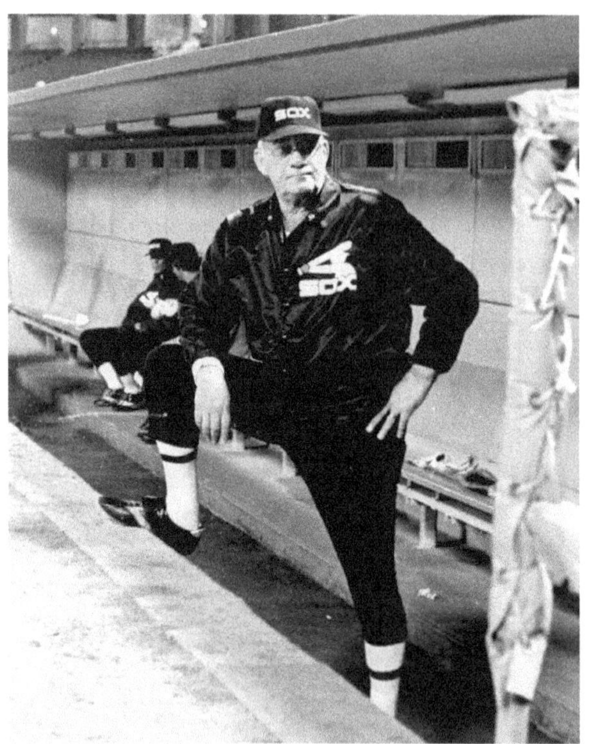

Bob Lemon sits on the dugout steps during an away game in September. The body language tells it all. (Leo Bauby collection.)

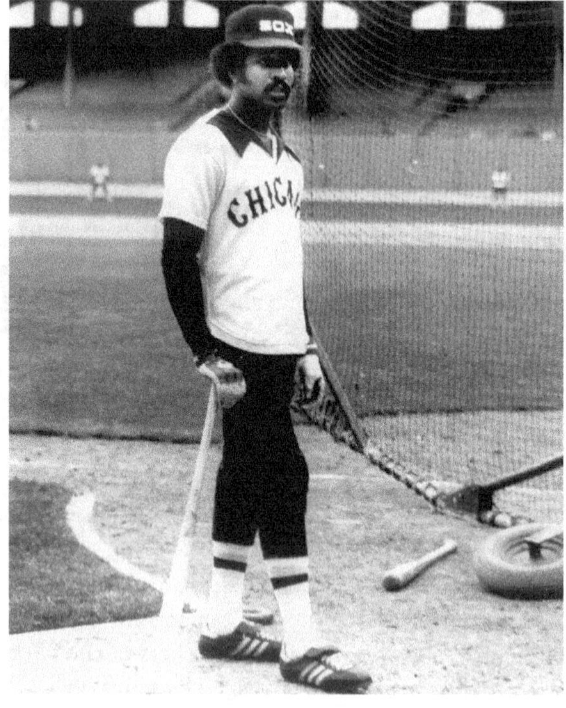

Oscar Gamble stands by the batting cage symbolizing the hit in South Side Hitmen. Gamble became the first left handed hitter for the Sox to hit 30 homers in a season and ended leading the team with 31 round trippers. (Gerry Bilek collection.)

8

The South Side Hitmen—Aftermath

There is no question that the 1977 Chicago White Sox left an everlasting mark on Chicago baseball history. No Chicago baseball team on either side of town that decade created the memories of the South Side Hitmen. Part of the charm of the 1977 team was that they had a different hero almost every game.

Other teams and their fans didn't understand the emotion that engulfed Comiskey Park that summer. They couldn't stand the curtain calls and the taunting good-bye song. Even six years later, after the bitter American League Championship series, the Baltimore Orioles taunted the Sox and their fans by singing the same song during their locker room pennant celebration.

There were several reasons why fans latched on to the team. The first has been stated many times in this book: the 1977 White Sox could hit. After decades of the go-go way of manufacturing runs, the 1977 team just hit the hell out of the ball. Reporter Bill Jauss recalled Veeck thinking he was a hitter or two short from winning it all in 1959 and vowed not to make that mistake again. Remember the 1990 White Sox? They won 94, but couldn't come close to the dominating Oakland Athletics. Many Sox fans look back at the 1990 team with great affection, but the atmosphere at Comiskey Park didn't have the emotion that was generated during the summer of 1977. The exception was the last game ever to be played at the old ball yard when fans bid Comiskey an emotional good-bye. The Sox won that day 3-2 when a bad hop single turned into a triple, plating the eventual winning run. That team of over-achievers hit a whopping total of 106 homers with old guy Carlton Fisk leading the way with 18. Nothing else needs to be said here.

Lack of expectations was another reason fans fell in love with the 1977 Sox. At season's start, no one picked the Sox to do anything but finish in the lower half of their division. Once the team looked like it was going to contend, a reverse psychology took place. The team became the blue collar Cinderella, taking on a different aura from recent Chicago baseball teams who were looked upon as choke artists and late season party-poopers.

Also there was the fan backlash to free agency. As was earlier stated in this book, free agent turned Indian pitcher Wayne Garland was booed mightily when he made an early season return trip to Baltimore. Though fans probably sympathized with players more then than now, purists abhorred the idea of buying a pennant. What happened to building a farm system and using one's guile to assemble a ball club? Why should someone like George Steinbrenner be able to take the Yankees to the World Series just because he had the money to do it? And the Yankees? Hadn't they been there before? The 1977 White Sox, seemingly a bunch of misfits discarded by the rest of baseball, were more lovable than a bunch of rich guy carpetbaggers.

Yes, it was old-fashioned baseball and a great change of pace at Comiskey. There was no hoping some little guy would steal a base and come home a sacrifice fly. Instead, the exploding scoreboard was used as never before.

Bill Veeck was praised for his "Rent-a-Player" scheme. Under this plan, Veeck would trade a player or players that he knew he was not going to be able to sign for another player he knew he would also not be able to sign. So instead of merely losing a player, he would gain the services of another player who just might have a career year before moving on. In the case of Richie Zisk and Oscar Gamble, it worked well enough to give the Sox one of the most exciting seasons ever.

"Nobody's asking about my finances now," gloated Bill Veeck in the middle of the July excitement.

No, no one was asking his financial picture that almost kept him from buying the team in late 1975. However, maybe someone should have because the fallout from the 1977 season was coming and another White Sox decline was on the way.

Rich Gossage, Terry Forster, Bucky Dent, Richie Zisk, and Oscar Gamble. These players were traded for each other, and so essentially when Zisk and Gamble were not resigned, the White Sox lost five players. Then, in December of 1977, Jim Spencer was traded to the Yankees in an essentially cash deal that netted the Sox two players (Stan Thomas and Ed Ricks) who never played one inning for the team. The South Side Hitmen had been dismantled before the fans' eyes.

To offset the loss of Zisk, the Sox acquired Bobby Bonds from California. To replace the left handed hitting hole created by the departure of Gamble, Ron Blomberg was signed as a free agent. Blomberg had been first player to play the role of designated hitter in 1973, but had only two at-bats in 1976 and none in 1977. Even in 1975, Blomberg had only 106 official plate appearances. He was signed to a four-year guaranteed deal.

Additionally, the White Sox felt that Lamar Johnson was ready to fill in as the every day first baseman. From appearances the Sox had the firepower to replace the combined 79 homers of three players (Zisk, Gamble, and Spencer) who had played such a vital role in the 1977 season.

The good feelings of the South Side Hitmen carried over to the beginning of the 1978 season. Veeck ran commercials of happy fans singing the good-bye song. The gloom and doom of an almost move to Seattle and an embarrassing 1976 season was gone.

A total of 50,754 fans came to welcome the new season on April 7 against the Red Sox. And for a day, the 1977 excitement was back, and there was the good feeling generated by an underdog player, all of which was so typical of the previous year as the Sox won 6-5.

Yet, the chemistry and excitement were not back. Bonds, heavily relied upon to replace the popular Zisk, got off to a slow start. After hitting only his second homer of the year in a May 16, 8-3 loss to the Yankees, Bonds learned he had been traded to Texas for Claudell Washington. Washington inspired fans to hang "Washington Slept Here" signs in right field while playing nearly three uninspired baseball seasons in Chicago.

The Blomberg gamble didn't pay off. The former Yankee hit .233 for the Sox in 1978 and was released just prior to the 1979 season. The team chose to pay him the remaining three years of his contract without benefiting from his services. And with Steve Stone leaving for free agency in November 1978, the 1978 team was dismantled as quickly as its 1977 counterpart.

One 1977 South Side alumnus did quite well for himself. Manager Bob Lemon was fired on June 30, 1978, and landed on his feet by taking over the New York Yankees. By late July, the Yankees were 14 games behind division leading Boston. New York caught the Red Sox, forcing a one-game playoff for the Eastern Division Championship. Ironically, it was ex-Sox Bucky Dent who hit one of the most memorable homers in playoff race history to help the Yankees into the playoffs and eventually the World Series. Bob Lemon's team vanquished the annual pennant-choking Kansas City Royals in the American League Championship Series and beat the Dodgers in a tough six-game World Series.

The most memorable thing about the White Sox 1979 fifth-place finish was, of course, Disco Demolition. Most White Sox fans of that time know the details about the promotion that drew a great crowd for a July 12 doubleheader against the Detroit Tigers. Films depicting the atmosphere in Comiskey show that an eruption was just waiting to happen. While the crowds of 1977 carried an excitement because of an entertaining club, the electricity before the blowing up of disco records between games was a different type altogether. In 1977, Sox fans held up banners like "Pitch at Risk to Rich Zisk." The disco haters flagged the upper deck railings with "DISCO SUCKS" signs. While the 1977 crowds cheered on the Sox to demolish the opposition, the July 12, 1979, crowd attempted to demolish Comiskey Park.

The Veeck era was coming to a close. His sale of the White Sox to a group headed by Eddie Einhorn and Jerry Reinsdorf was completed on January 30, 1981. (This was after a failed attempt to sell the franchise to Edward DeBartolo when the American League owners looked down on DeBartolo's gambling interests.) The popular shower was ripped out of center field. Einhorn made comments about the new ownership running a class organization, taken by some that Veeck had not. The new owners also claimed Comiskey was in deplorable condition, and thought the team's TV contract was a disgrace. Free TV would still be available to fans but not like before.

Stung by the criticism, Veeck stayed away from Comiskey Park for a good deal of the time during the last couple years of his life. He appeared on a local PBS TV show about baseball produced and aired on WTTW-Channel 11. Veeck sat with other guests, drinking beer and criticizing Major League Baseball. He died on January 2, 1986, having spent his last years as a true baseball outsider.

Whatever can be said about Bill Veeck, one accomplishment cannot be taken away from him. Veeck was the architect of the 1977 South Side Hitmen. The crowds were large and loud. Even if a fan wasn't at the game, he could still feel the adrenaline and excitement engulfing him as if he were sitting in the left field seats. Unlike past Sox teams, the Hitmen pasted one hit after another, with few bloopers or grounders sneaking through in the infield. Line shots were fired all over Comiskey which could rip a fielder's face off if he was stupid enough to get in front of it. The scoreboard went off time and time again, blowing fuses and firing duds from exhaustion. Sometimes the smoke from the fireworks hung over the field, no doubt stinging the opponents' eyes and rubbing salt in the wound. In 1977, Sox fans reveled in it, because after all, the scoreboard fireworks had been used so rarely in the past.

It all seemed to be in defiance of White Sox critics everywhere. You don't like the home run fireworks? You don't like the fact that the 1977 Sox contended longer than anyone thought they had a right to? You don't like names on the backs of uniforms? You don't like curtain calls and serenades? You don't respect a team that hit and not do much else? Then the hell with you, for the 1977 Chicago White Sox gave their fans an excitement and hope that had been missing for so long, and what other people thought didn't matter.

And in the Channel 44-WSNS-TV broadcast booth, Harry Caray pounded Budweisers or whatever was available. He sang "Take Me Out to the Ballgame" during the seventh inning stretch. He led the cheers with his main rallying cry, which, more often than not, was portentous of excitement to come. This cry was echoed by a banner held by fans in the left field seats that read, "Oh-H, For The Long One."

Yet, in 1977, the fans didn't need Harry Caray or anyone or anything else to get them excited. The noise and the intensity of the emotion fed on each other and provided memories that have lasted decades. No round the clock coverage from ESPN or rooftop seats were needed.

Bill Veeck was sometimes called the PT Barnum of Baseball. His promotions and gimmicks were often criticized, frowned upon or scoffed at as a con game to divert the fans from remembering how bad the team was. But, unlike some of Goose Gossage's laments, baseball on the South Side of Chicago in 1977 was no circus. The 1977 Chicago White Sox were not just the Chicago White Sox. They were the South Side Hitmen.

Banners were again popular at Comiskey Park during the beginning of the 1978 season. This one could have been right if Bonds hadn't been traded away to Texas. (Leo Bauby collection.)

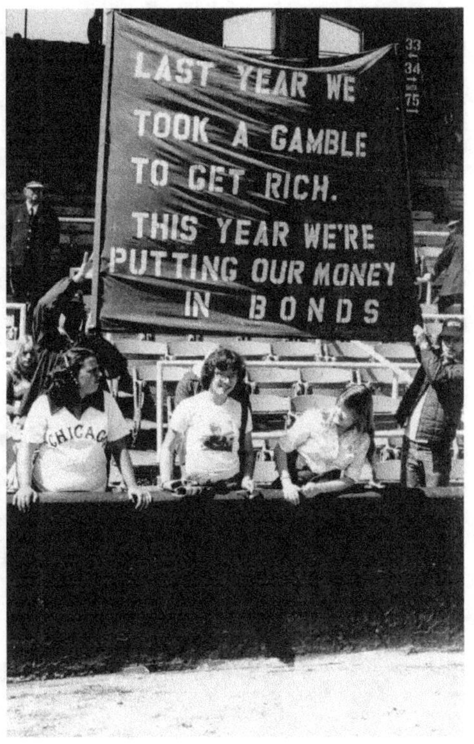

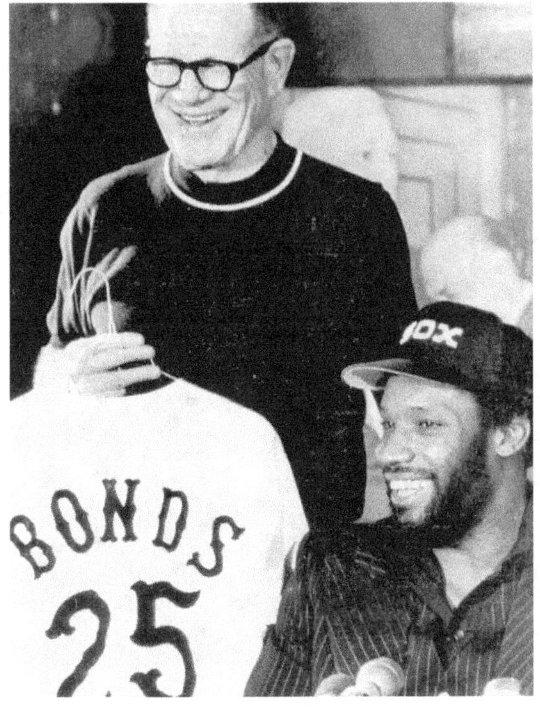

Bill Veeck (left) and Bobby Bonds look happy after the trade that brought Bonds to the White Sox. Bonds hit 31 home runs in 1978—too bad that 29 of them were with Texas. (Leo Bauby collection.)

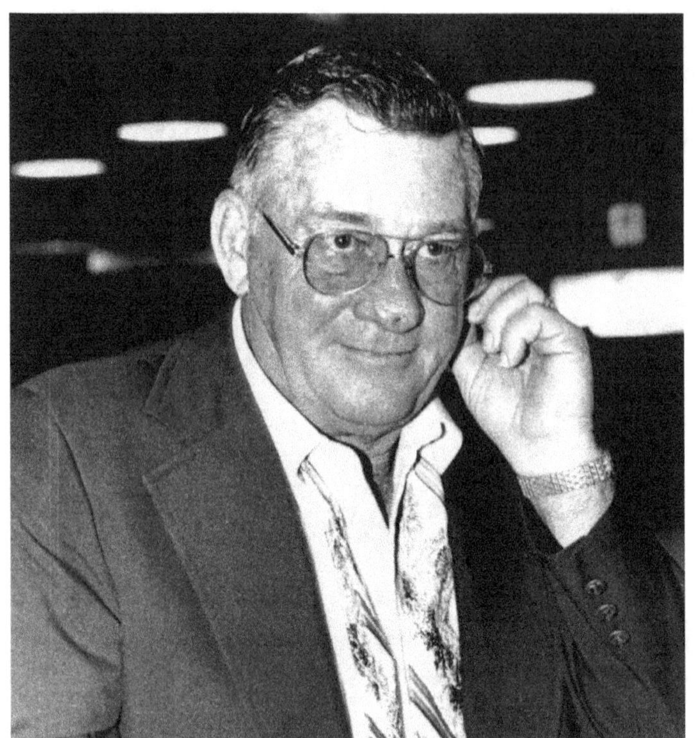

Bob Lemon was let go on June 30, 1978, after it was becoming obvious that the Sox season was going nowhere. He landed on is feet and is shown here after being hired by the Yankees. New York again won the World Series. The White Sox finally did the trick in 2005. (Leo Bauby collection.)

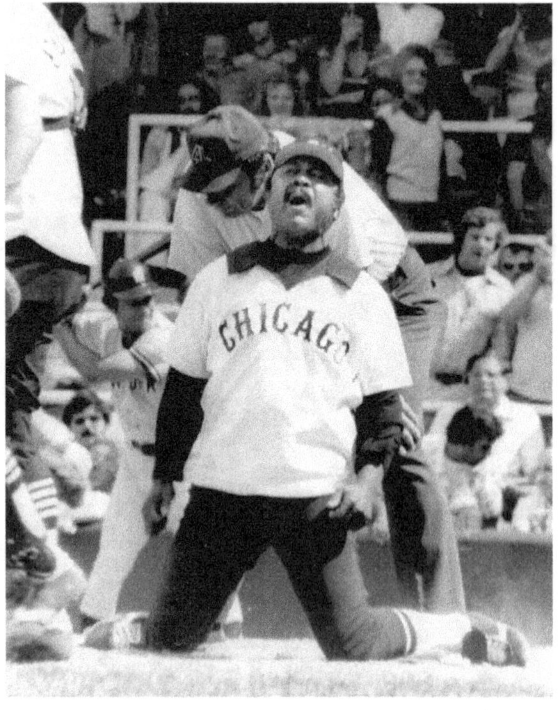

Larry Doby took over after the departure of Bob Lemon. He is taking issue with an umpire here, not that it did any good. Doby lost this argument, but more importantly, the Sox lost many more ball games. Their record was almost a complete reversal of 1977 as they lost 90. Doby wasn't around for the 1979 season. He should have been thankful for that. (Gerry Bilek collection.)

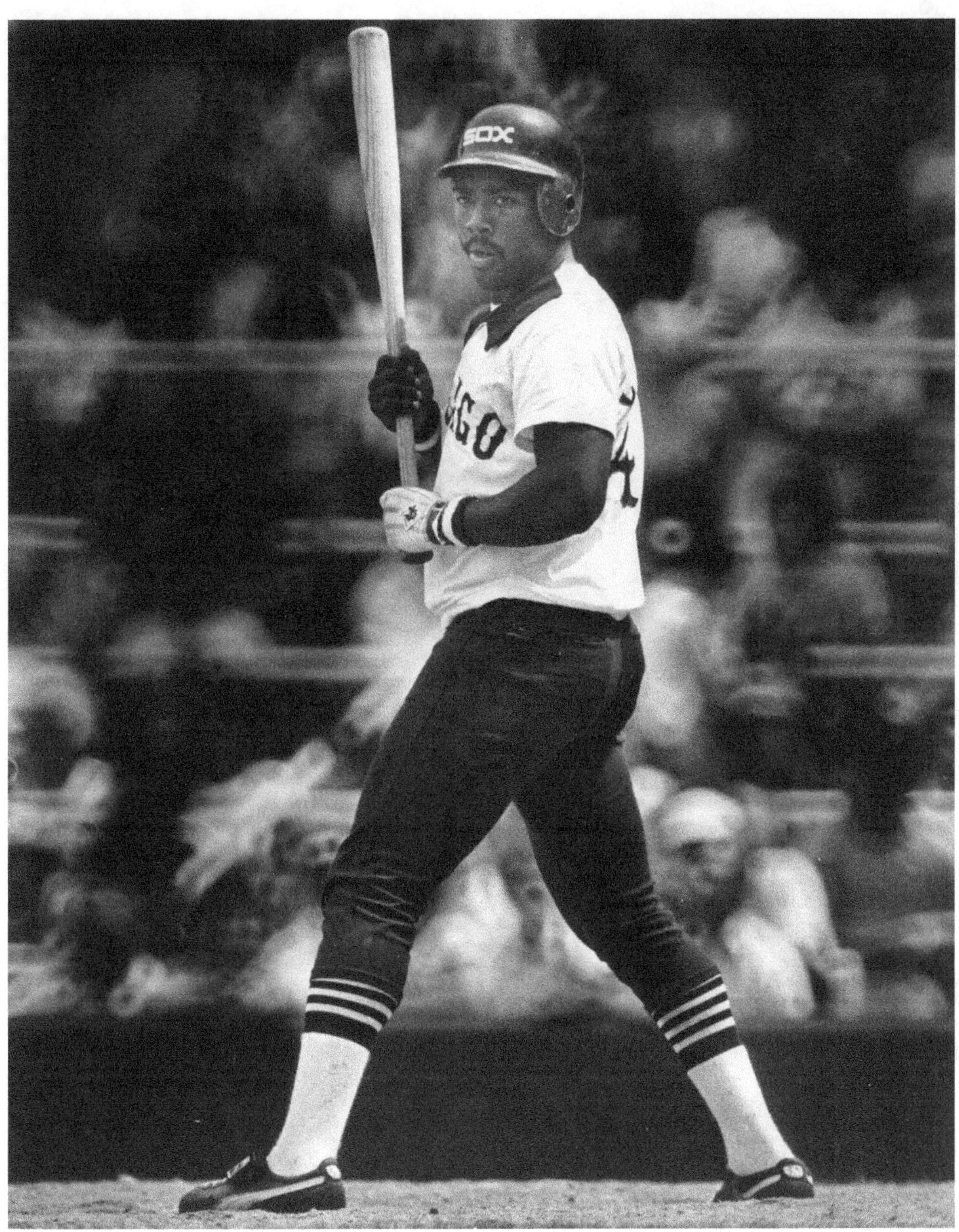

Chet Lemon had his best year with the Sox in 1979, hitting .318, walloping 17 homers and knocking in 86. Too bad most of the remainder of the team had a bad year. (Leo Bauby collection.)

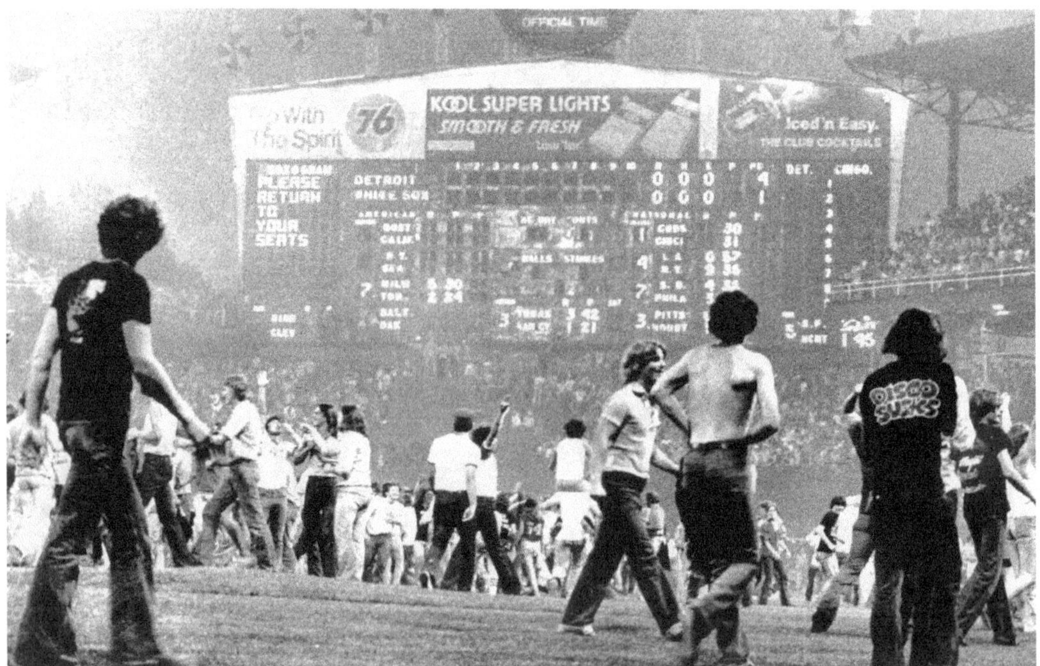

Would this be a White Sox book without a picture of Disco Demolition? The franchise has not been able to run away from the legacy even though it happened a little over a quarter of a century ago. Worse yet, just think if one of these fine gentlemen showed up at your door asking for your daughter's hand in marriage? (Leo Bauby collection.)

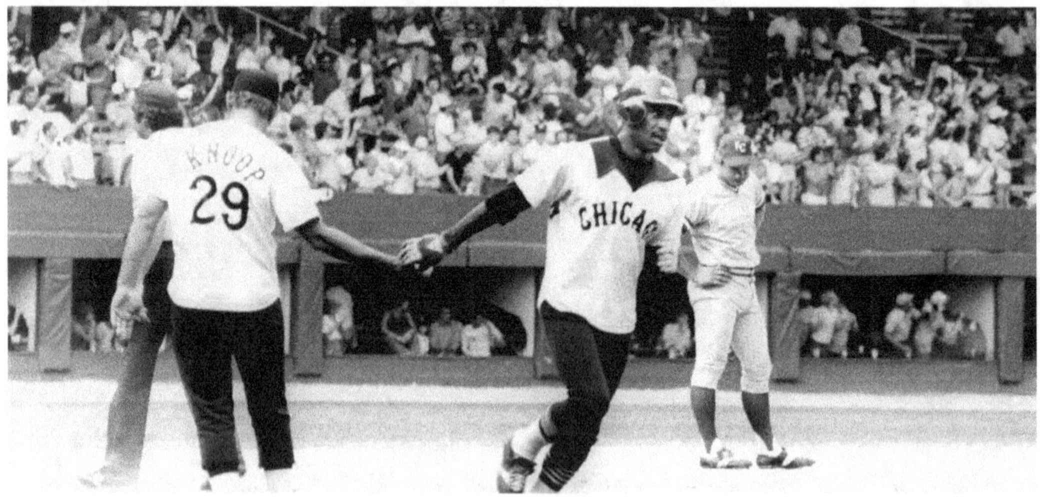

Claudell Washington makes his way for home. Washington was picked up in a trade for Bobby Bonds in May of 1978. He hit three homers in a game just a few days after Disco Demolition. Most fans agreed that Washington had talent, but also figured he went right back to sleep after slugging the three homers. (Leo Bauby collection.)

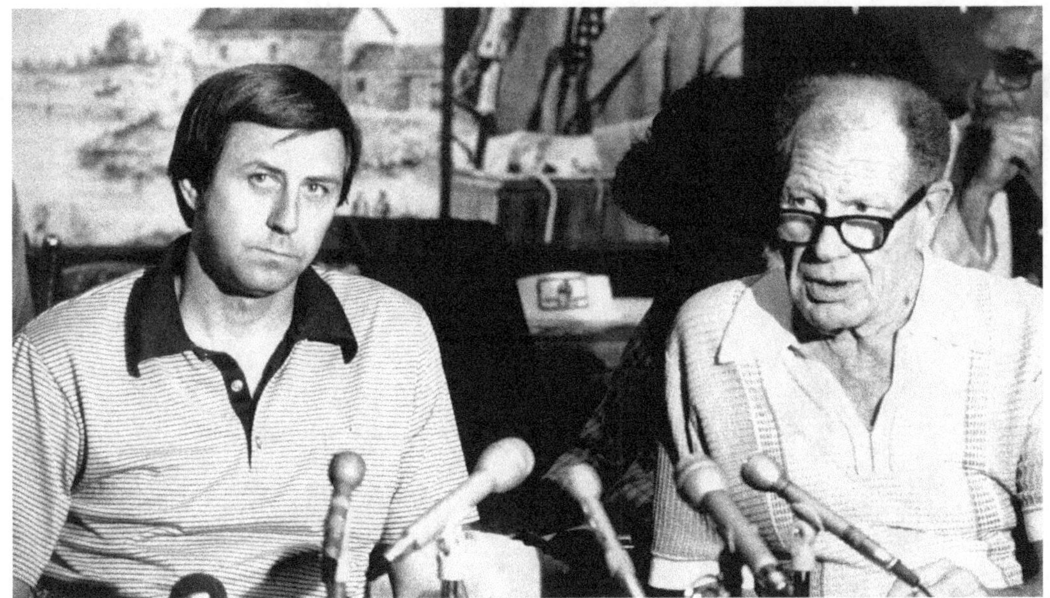

Don Kessinger (left) appears with Bill Veeck to announce his resignation as Sox manager in August of 1979. He is pretty somber looking, but the failure of the team that year couldn't be hung on his shoulders. Even Veeck admitted that Kessinger was not armed with enough talented players. Kessinger was one of the classiest players to put on a Chicago baseball uniform, and he deserved better. (Leo Bauby collection.)

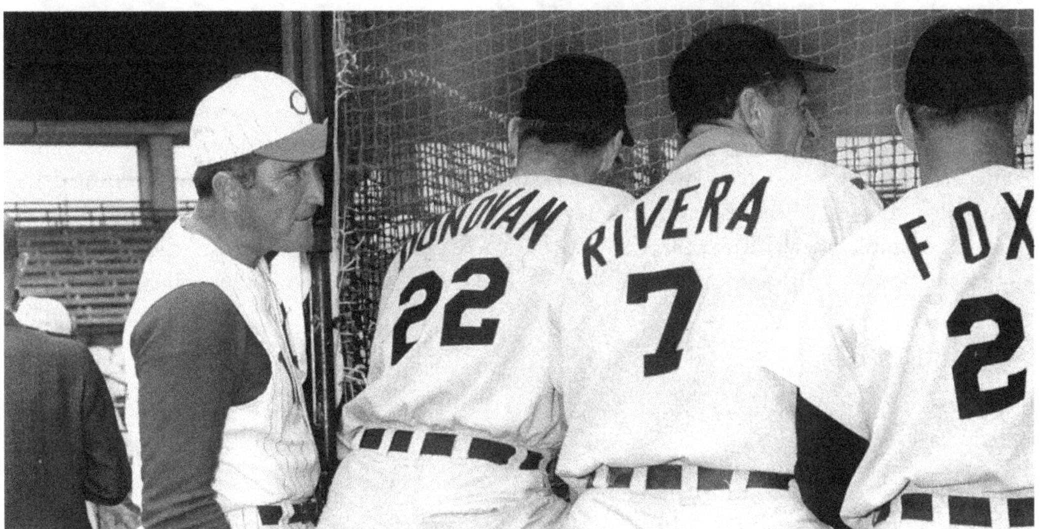

What was the big deal about names on the backs of uniforms? Bill Veeck took a great deal of heat when introducing the concept in 1960. With all the expansion during the last 40 plus years, it is probably a very good thing that names are on the backs of uniforms. (Leo Bauby collection.)

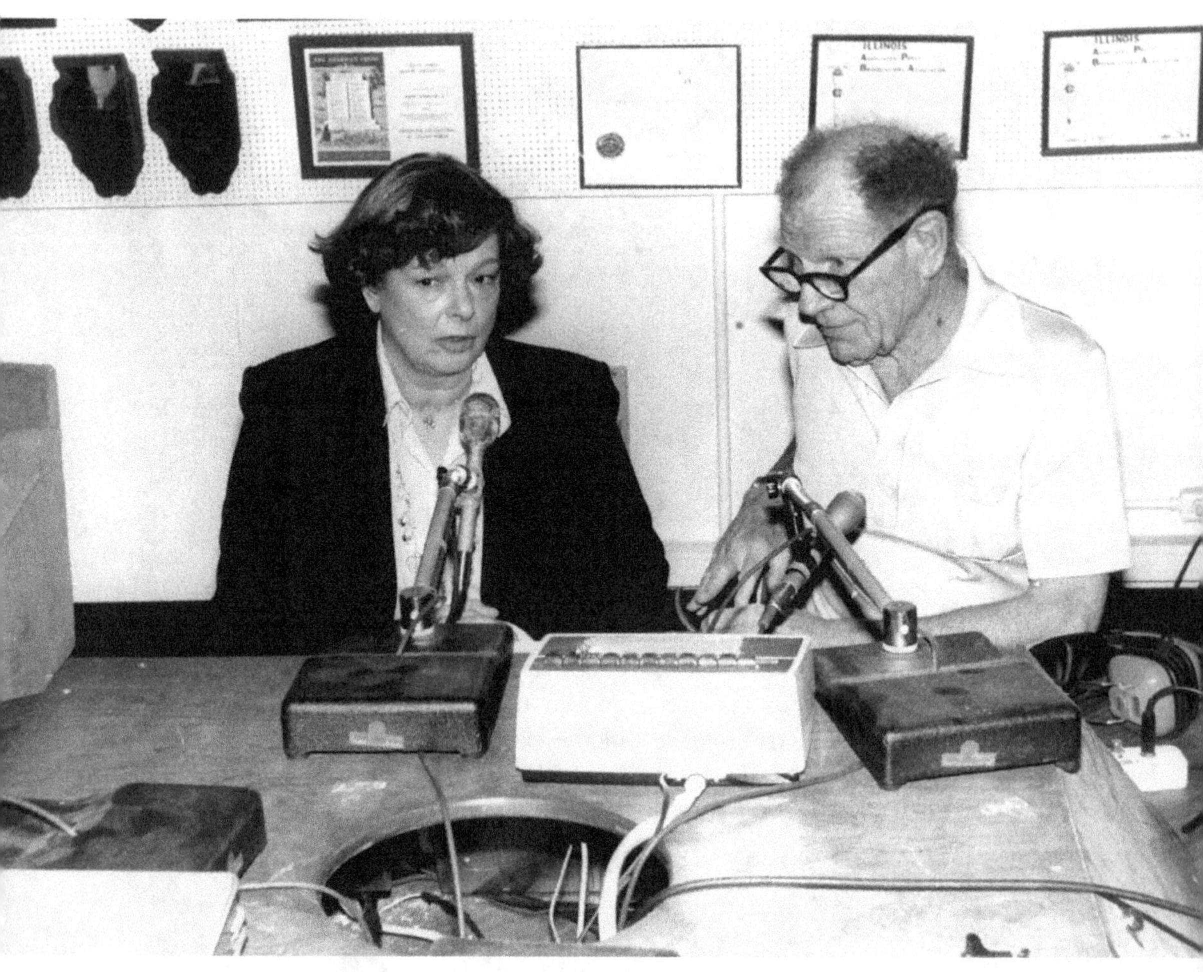

Sometimes people wondered why Bill Veeck was so popular even when his teams weren't so good. The simple answer was that Veeck was a charismatic man who was accessible to the fans. This included a Sunday morning radio show where he and his wife, Mary Frances, took calls. By 1980, some of those calls were getting hostile. (Leo Bauby collection.)

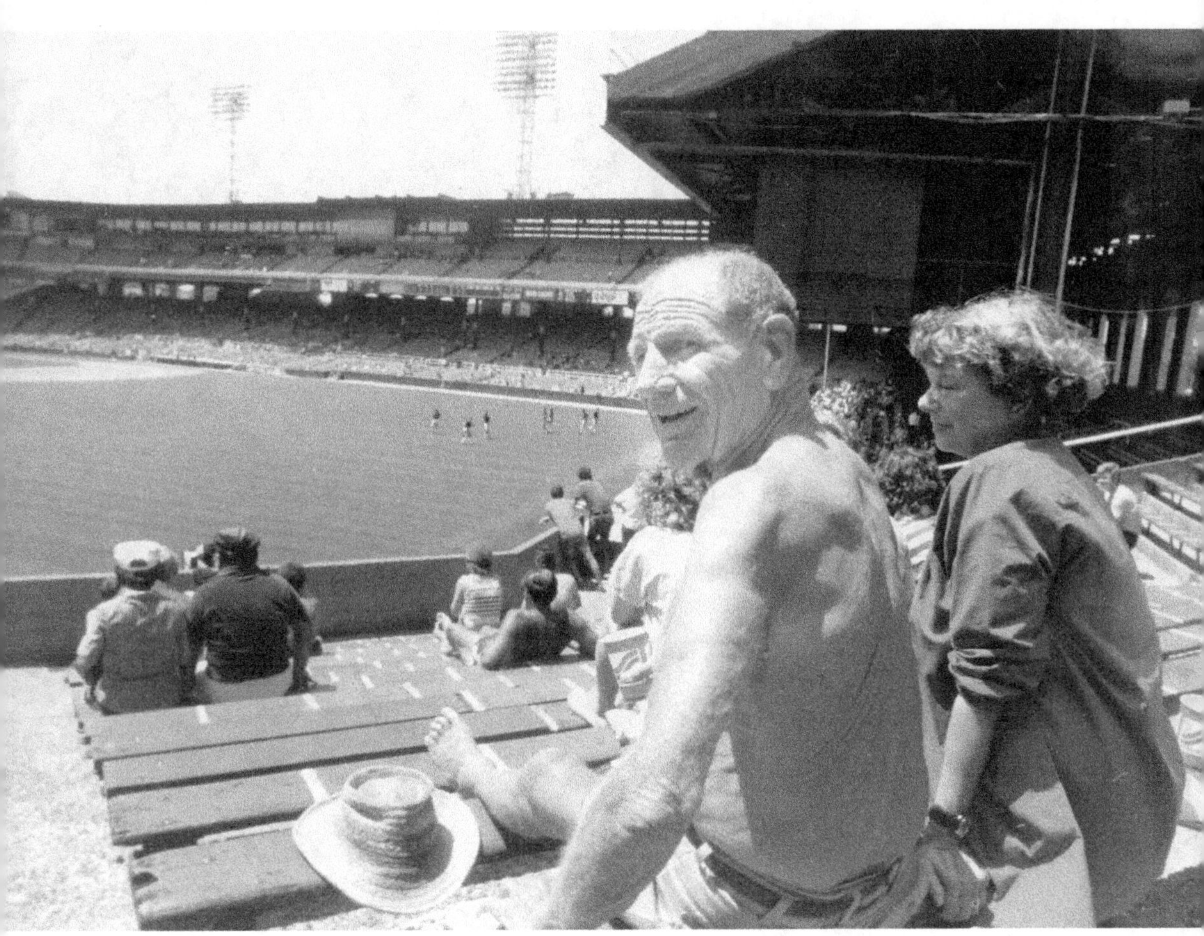

The shirtless Bill Veeck is seen sunning himself during his last game at Comiskey. He is sitting in the center field bleachers. Veeck had spent more time during the last years of his life at Wrigley than Comiskey. (Leo Bauby collection.)

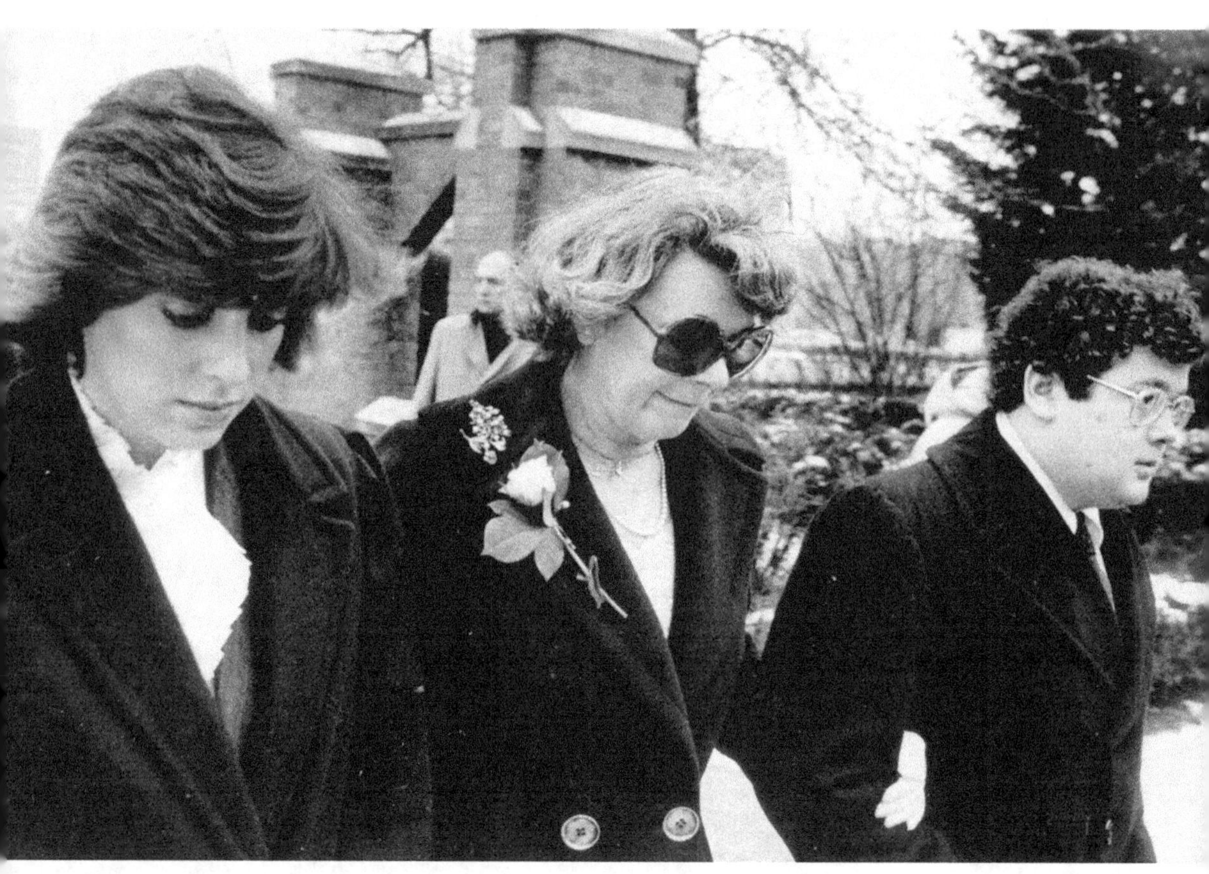

Bill Veeck died on January 2, 1986. His baseball legacy is still being debated. That legacy is considerable. Here, mourners remember a man who had lived a full life. (Leo Bauby collection.)

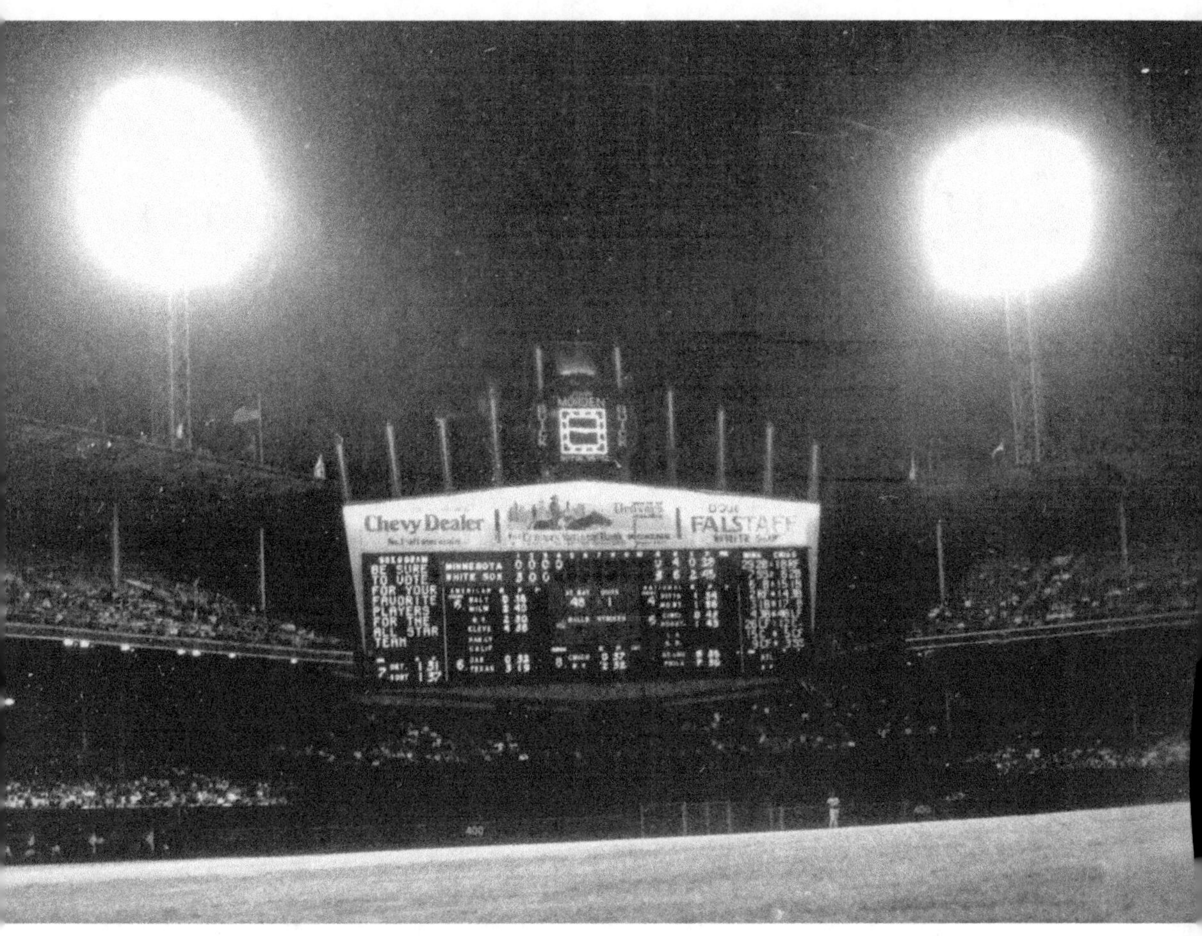

One of Bill Veek's most endearing gifts to the Chicago White Sox fans was the Monster in center field. (Leo Bauby collection.)

How the 1977 South Side Hitmen Were Dismantled

- Ralph Garr was sold to California Angels on September 20, 1979.
- Chet Lemon was traded to the Detroit Tigers for outfielder Steve Kemp on November 27, 1981.
- Richie Zisk was signed as a free agent by the Texas Rangers on November 9, 1977.
- Oscar Gamble was signed as a free agent by the San Diego Padres on November 29, 1977.
- Jim Spencer was traded to the New York Yankees with pitcher Bob Polinsky and outfielder Tommy Cruz for pitchers Stan Thomas and Ed Ricks on December 12, 1977.
- Eric Soderholm was traded to the Texas Rangers for pitcher Ed Farmer and infielder Gary Holle on June 15, 1979.
- Alan Bannister was traded to the Cleveland Indians for outfielder Ron Pruit on June 14, 1980.
- Jorge Orta was signed by the Cleveland Indians as a free agent on December 19, 1979.
- Jim Essian was traded to the Oakland A's with pitcher Steve Renko for pitcher Pablo Rorrealba on March 30, 1978.
- Brian Downing was traded to the California Angels along with pitchers Chris Knapp and Dave Frost for outfielders Bobby Bonds and Thad Bosley and pitcher Richard Dotson on December 5, 1977.
- Ken Kravec was traded to the Chicago Cubs for pitcher Dennis Lamp on March 28, 1981.
- Lerrin LaGrow was sold to the Los Angeles Dodgers on May 11, 1979.
- Lamar Johnson was signed by the Texas Rangers as a free agent on January 15, 1982.
- Wilbur Wood was granted free agency on November 2, 1978.
- Francisco Barrios was released by the White Sox on September 1, 1981.
- Steve Stone was signed as a free agent by the Baltimore Orioles on November 29, 1978.

www.ingramcontent.com/pod-product-compliance
Lightning Source LLC
LaVergne TN
LVHW081556100826
845153LV00004B/394

* 9 7 8 1 5 3 1 6 2 3 8 4 5 *